CONTINUITY AND CHANGE IN
EUROPEAN SOCIETY

Continuity and Change In European Society

Germany, France and Italy since 1870

MARTIN KOLINSKY

SAINT MARTIN'S PRESS

AFFILIATED PUBLISHERS: Macmillan Limited, London
also at Bombay, Calcutta, Madras and Melbourne

Contents

Acknowledgements

In the course of writing this book, I have had the opportunity of discussing sections of it with a number of people and I wish to express my indebtedness to them. I owe a great deal to Professor Michalina Vaughan, University of Lancaster, Professor T.B. Bottomore, University of Sussex and Professors Joseph Ben-David and S.N. Eisenstadt, the Hebrew University of Jerusalem, for their encouragement and support. I have enjoyed many discussions with students at the Universities of Birmingham, Jerusalem (1971-72) and the Negev (Beersheva, 1971-72). A special word of thanks is due to Ya'akov Barr for a series of intense debates, and to Shlomit Shagam for her careful scrutiny of the text. My wife Eva shared her knowledge of German affairs with me, and has been a constant source of encouragement and unstinting help. I have benefitted from the astute comments of William Paterson, University of Warwick and R.E.M. Irving, University of Edinburgh. To David Croom, my thanks for being such a friendly and helpful editor and publisher. Although all have helped to shape my understanding of the social and political processes which are discussed in these pages, I am alone responsible for the general line of interpretation, as well as for any errors or omissions.

I dedicate this book to my Mother, my brother Allan and to the memory of my Father. I also dedicate it to Esther and Betty, and to the memory of their parents who were lost in the Holocaust of the Second World War.

Chapter 1 Introduction

The political concept of 'Western Europe' emerged in the Cold War as a contrast to the Communist-dominated states of Eastern Europe. Its explicit reference was to democratic, liberal, free, open and self-determining societies. Confronting the 'Iron Curtain' countries, the contrast seemed self-evident and provided little motivation for looking more closely at the problems of democracy within Western Europe. The tensions and polarisation of the Cold War pushed into the background and somewhat obscured the fact that previous experiences of democracy in the larger nations of Western Europe had ended in disaster. The Weimar Republic of Germany was destroyed by the establishment of one of the most murderous dictatorships in history. A decade earlier the liberal system in Italy had crumbled under the impact of extremism and intransigence and had given way to Fascism. In France the decline of Republican democracy was marked in the 1930s, particularly after the defeat of the Popular Front government. The restructuring of institutions in the post-war period, stimulated at first by a high level of idealism and then carried forward by the Marshall Plan and other American initiatives, brought new conditions of prosperity, growth, and transnational co-operation. But the initial impact of the Resistance movements in France and Italy was dissipated within a relatively short time by internal social and political conflicts which became increasingly entangled in the larger confrontation of the Cold War.

In France this resulted in the weakening of parliamentary processes, which was then deeply aggravated in the 1950s by colonial problems. The ensuing paralysis was transformed into the Gaullist Fifth Republic, which raised executive authority to a heigh of virtually unchecked predominance. The conflicts in Italy were not as compact in their intensity as in France, but the cramped wrestling of traditionalist and modernising tendencies has persisted intractably for three decades. The political framework did not break down, but the search for means of consolidating the democratic centre has been fraught with difficulties, and the initiation of effective programmes of social reform has always been frustrated. In Western Germany, the new institutions of the Federal Republic were not lubricated by living democratic experiences and traditions. Hence the stiffness of the Adenauer period, dominated

by the unbending Chancellor, was followed by erratic behaviour in the
1960s. In particular, the resolution of the difficulties experienced by
the two major parties in a Grand Coalition government (1966 to 1969)
meant the virtual abandonment of the principle of parliamentary
opposition.

A basic question arises from these situations: to what extent are
democratically constituted political systems able to operate in
socio-cultural environments where non-democratic traditions are
strongly developed?

The answers depend on the strength of those traditions in relation to
other tendencies. In France the style of authority was modified after
the events of May and June 1968 and the subsequent retirement of
President de Gaulle. The powerful libertarian traditions of France may
prove significant in future developments within the Fifth Republic, or
beyond. In Italy, the Catholic Church exercises a massive influence on
political relations. But as the brief reign of Pope John XXIII
demonstrated, the Church is not monolithic and is sometimes capable
of contributing to the quest for democratic stability. These are
problems which are explored in some detail later in the book. It is
sufficient to state here that the possibilities for change are latent in
these situations. This has been underlined in Western Germany since
1969. The Grand Coalition, which confined inter-party dialogue to the
closed bargaining of *Bundestag* committees and contributed to the
growth of extremism outside the *Bundestag,* was replaced by a new
coalition government headed by the Social Democrats. The principle of
parliamentary opposition was restored, extremist groups lost the
ground they had gained, and a new era of relations with East Germany
and Eastern Europe was opened.

These developments occurred in a unique setting. The military,
technological and political aspects of the Second World War
transformed the framework of international relations. The global
heights of power reached by the United States of America and the
Soviet Union reduced the status of the European nations, and turned
the problem of Germany into a focal point of Cold-War tenstions. The
radical alteration of international structures fundamentally
differentiates the post-war and inter-war periods. Particularly as the
changes have become institutionalised in transnational frameworks of
co-operation: NATO, the Council of Europe, the Common Market, the
European Atomic Energy Community and a number of other
organisations. These new contours of organisation and power are

unique to the post-war situation and make any attempt to draw simple and direct parallels between tendencies in the 1960s and 1970s and those in the inter-war period very misleading. In this respect, Bonn is not in the same country as Weimar.

But it is doubtful whether the impact of transnational institutions, including the Common Market, have deeply affected the internal socio-political dynamics of member countries. It would be very difficult to determine the influence on these arrangements on the social structures of the larger European nations and on the orientations of their political cultures. The impact may not be negligible in the long run, but at the time of the enlargement of the Common Market there were no outstanding modifications. What had been accomplished was the organisation of areas of overt common interest, so that economic growth, mutual trade and military security were enhanced. But there was no significant transfer of power from the nation-state to transnational authorities, and a new impetus for democratic innovation and renovation was most conspicuously not provided. Yet the new relatedness of the various European nations has great importance: the small countries havè gained in status; frameworks were provided for the recognition and absorption of West German recovery; and a measure of practical idealism was realised which will undoubtedly promote further efforts.

But the object of this book is to underline the point that these changes have not eclipsed the profound continuity with the past which is at the core of each country. The perspective of continuity traces *(a)* the adaptation of older socio-political structures and tendencies to new situations, and *(b)* emphasises the existence of unresolved problems concerning the nature of social modernity in the three larger nations of Western Europe.

Part 1 PRIOR TO THE FIRST WORLD WAR

The chapters in this section are concerned with the formation, in the nineteenth century and up to the First World War, of the modern structures and political cultures of Italy, Germany and France. National unification provided a territorial, administrative, and political framework for industrial developments in Italy and Germany. But unification was the outcome of profoundly different struggles – in Italy the *Risorgimento* led to the creation of a liberal state, whereas the creation of the German Reich was the artefact of Prussian domination. The extremely rapid, condensed process of industrialisation, which enabled Germany to rival the power of Britain by the turn of the century, occurred within an authoritarian context. But the political structure was flexible enough to be able to absorb some of the social demands and to incorporate in a distorted manner some of the democratic consequences of modernisation. In contrast, the Italian political framework proved to be increasingly inflexible and unable to cope with the consequences of social change, even though the process of industrialisation was relatively much slower. The enveloping crisis was suspended by the advent of the First World War, and was then intensified in its bitter aftermath. In France, where national identity had been long established, the question of the social and political nature of modernisation was fought out in a series of skirmishs in the Third Republic, culminating in the Dreyfus Affair. The moderate Republicans, by winning over a substantial proportion of the peasantry and by carrying out a programme of educational reforms and secularisation, were able to strengthen parliamentary institutions.

The role of the peasantry in France was unique: its attachment to the Republic enabled the secular middle class to dominate conservative opponents and to establish a considerable basis of social modernity. The very opposite occurred in Italy and in Germany. The struggles of the peasantry during the *Risorgimento* were not utilised by the modernising forces as a means of building and consolidating the Italian national structure. Instead, the isolation of the peasantry enabled the Church to attempt to channel the resentments and frustrations of the countryside against the emergent secular State. In Prussia, the potential antagonism between peasant and landlord did not become manifest, so that until after the First World War there were no determinative efforts on the part of the peasantry to dissociate themselves from the leadership of the Junker aristocracy. Correspondingly nineteenth-century aristocracies differed enormously in the extent of their socio-political influence and in their relations with the state. At one extreme, the Prussian Junkers were in unchallenged control of political, administrative and military institutions. Whereas in contrast to their relatively cohesive, homogeneous and semi-closed power constellation was to be found the fragmented Italian aristocracy: clerical and traditionalist in Rome, secular in Piedmont and Tuscany, indolent and corrupt in the South where it controlled local government but was as indifferent to its problems as to those beyond. There were no shared political or military traditions which could help to weld the diversity into a shared caste outlook. Italian aristocratic families were too provincialised and too dispersed, in a socio-political sense, to seek common action. The fundamental conflict between the liberal State and the Catholic Church, which polarised the tensions between modernisation and traditionalism, found them on opposing sides. In contrast, the French aristocracy was neither as cohesive nor as fragmented. It was involved in a turbulent dialectic of revolution and counter-revolution. Between 1815 and 1870 it was able partially to reassert is values and traditions, but in an institutional context which had been decisively moulded by the reforms of the Napoleonic era. The struggles in the first decades of the Third Republic, which came to their climax in the Dreyfus Affair at the turn of the century, represent the efforts of the aristocracy — in its positions of influence in the Army, upper hierarchy of the Church and higher civil service — to wrestle control from the secular *bourgeoisie.*

In the following chapters, Italy is discussed first because it attained national unification before Germany, and later became the first Fascist state. Moreover, certain features of the Italian situation are very pronounced: the struggle of the modern state against the traditionalism embodied in the Catholic Church; the fragmentation of society with the isolation of the middle classes from the peasantry and the workers; and the consequent failure to cope with social demands and to create an atmosphere of compromise and broadly defined common purpose. Germany is discussed next because its developments both parallel and contrast with those of Italy. In addition to the above-mentioned points about national unification and industrialisation, there was the failure of political parties to develop responsible participation in the political process. In Germany this was due to the dependence of the middle class on the dominant power structure, and to the subordination and partial incorporation of the organised labour movement.

We turn to France for experiences which contrast significantly. The Third Republic was not dominated by an authoritarian ethos nor dependent on a social elite, nor was it cut off from peasant and labour support. However these were relative tendencies, not absolute, and much remained tense and problematic in French political culture.

Chapter 2 Italy: Nationhood and Church

The *Risorgimento* (resurgence) was a movement for national independence and unity which had its roots in the eighteenth century and received strong impetus from the changes arising from Napoleon's campaigns in Italy. In the following decades there was a broad struggle against Austrian domination and for unity, in face of historic regional diversity and the opposition of the Papal States. The complex movement culminated in the expansion of the state of Piedmont under the leadership of Count Cavour and led to the proclamation in 1861 of the constitutional Kingdom of Italy before the national parliament at Turin. It was another decade before Rome was established as the capital.

The ideology of the *Risorgimento* was profoundly influenced by the ideas of the French enlightenment and the French Revolution, and at a later stage by the British reform movement. These ideas were adapted to Italian circumstances by a variety of groups, who had in common a stress on nationalism, liberalism and secularism. After the failure of the 1848-9 revolutions, the two major formations were the Party of Action, which originated in Mazzini's Young Italy movement, and advocated a republican and democratic programme; and Cavour's constitutional monarchism which gained the support of the former liberal-moderate groups. The two formations had in common hostility towards foreign domination, opposition to the temporal power and immunities of the Church and a desire to sweep away the barriers to economic, cultural and political unity. These ideological currents were pronounced within the middle and lower middle classes and among sections of the aristocracy. The aristocracy was not a caste of landowners such as the Prussian Junkers, whose unity was focused around highly developed military, legal and political institutions and common traditions.

In the Italian peninsula, there were no unifying institutions and shared living traditions. In the Papal States the aristocracy was clerical in orientation and in fundamental opposition to the modernising tendencies of the *Risorgimento*. In the South, in the kingdoms of Naples and Sicily, the aristocracy was feudal in origin and largely indifferent to the trends of the time. Its main interest was to be left unmolested in control of local government, so that it could subsidise itself without effort from taxes on the peasantry. An exception was

Naples itself where there was a current of liberalism among a section of the aristocracy. In other regions, the aristocracy descended from the ruling groups of the historic city-states of the late Middle Ages and Renaissance. Inheriting a powerful cultural legacy, it was a diversified social group involved with administrative, financial and business affairs, as well as land ownership, and was able to assimilate rising middle-class elements. In regions such as Tuscany, the secular outlook and enlightenment of the upper stratum enabled it to accommodate the direction of change which the Piedmontese initiated.

In contrast to the fundamental divisions within the aristocracy, the rising middle class was united in its desire for national unification and central government. These were essential if the conditions for free economic activity and development were to be created: the removal of internal tariff barriers and restrictive practices of guilds and trade monopolies, the building of roads and railways and the protection of the interests of Lombard merchants from Austrian discrimination. A notable part in the struggles of the *Risorgimento* was played by professional men, especially lawyers, and by students. For both these groups, there was small hope of profitable employment in a society dominated by hereditary considerations and seriously lagging in economic development. But such development proved to be relatively slow in coming after unification, partly because of the growth of a new landed gentry – people who invested their wealth in land rather than in commerce or industry.

Throughout the struggle for national unification, the peasantry remained in the background. Its own demands for land and for relief from taxation were not endorsed by other groups and did not become a major issue. There was little basis for an alliance with the liberal middle class which was either indifferent to the plight of the peasantry or considered the satisfaction of its aims as involving an extreme and unacceptable reorganisation of society. In this they saw eye to eye with the aristocracy which, faced with peasant unrest, was willing to accommodate the emergent national structure as a means of maintaining its social position.[1] Moreover, sections of the middle class believed more firmly in the virtues of land ownership than industrial investment and were interested in obtaining the vast tracts held by the Church and held in common by the peasantry. The only ally of the peasantry, which engaged in periodic but fruitless revolts, turned out to be the Church which responded to its loss of temporal power by condemning the new State as the negation of God.

Church-State Relations

Up to 1860, the Papal States were a physical as well as political barrier to Italian unification. Situated in the centre of the country, and occupying one-seventh of the territory, they cut off North from South. Moreover the religious influence of the Vatican over an essentially illiterate population had important political and social implications. These became apparent in the Church's response to emerging modern conditions, which was a forceful restatement of a mediaeval world-view.

The Church's reaction to the loss of temporal power was to encourage the revoltist attitude (unorganised and spontaneous protest) widespread in the countryside. In the 1870s and 1880s, the intransigent Catholic press campaigned violently against the State. Utilising popular grievances, such as heavy taxation, unemployment and land hunger the press attempted to enlist the peasant masses against Italian liberalism. The Church's 70,000 priests urged the illiterate faithful to boycott national politics and to hate the new state. The State's reaction was to punish priests who were actively inciting disorder. This led to a further deterioration of Church/State relations.

The former Papal territories of the Marches and Umbria were absorbed into the new Italy in 1860. Ten years later, Rome itself was lost. It was only the presence of French troops in Rome which had prevented the government from taking the city earlier. In 1870, with the outbreak of the Franco-Prussian war, the troops were withdrawn, and the Italian government lost little time in securing its future capital. For the next two decades, Vatican diplomacy was obsessed with the idea of persuading the Catholic states of Austria and France to intervene in Italian affairs in order to restore Rome to its control. But it was an unrealistic policy: it failed to appreciate the balance of forces within France and Austria, it failed to grasp the significance of the emergence of Prussia as the leading continental power, and above all it failed to appreciate the temper of the times.

The Syllabus of Eighty Errors,[2] issued by Pope Pius IX in 1864, was an item-by-item rejection of the Piedmontese government's liberal ideas. It was a protest against the closure of convents and monasteries; against the confiscation and sale of Church properties; against secular education; against civil marriage and divorce. In short, it protested against legislation designed to limit the influence of the Church. The *Syllabus* was a plea for the broad exercise of church authority, especially for the restoration of ecclesiastical courts, and for the return of clerical control in educational matters. The *Syllabus* was widely regarded as a condemnation of basic liberal rights, such as religious tolerance of minorities in Catholic countries, and even as a denial of the freedom of speech. European alarm was re-awakened in July 1870 by the decree of Papal Infallibility (*ex cathedra* on doctrinal matters) and the decree of Papal Absolutism by the Council of the Vatican. These were crushing blows to liberal Catholicism which sought adjustment to modern conditions.

The Italian government tried to placate the Papacy, and to normalise the situation by passing the Law of Guarantees in May 1871. But the Pope rejected the terms of settlement and declared that it made him a prisoner in the Vatican. Since he could not dominate the State, which offered partial compensation, he withdrew from all relations with it. A few years earlier, in 1868, it had been declared inexpedient *(non expedit)* for Catholics to vote in parliamentary elections in Italy. The *non expedit* was repeatedly confirmed and strengthened in the following decades. In 1895, Pope Leo XIII, imagining that the Italian state would collapse if all Catholics refused to participate in political life, transformed it into a compulsory prohibition.

By the turn of the century, however, the simple withdrawal position had become untenable. Many Catholics, while adhering to the Church, nevertheless wanted to participate in the affaris of the country. Beside the intransigent forces of Italian Catholicism, there were also conciliatorist tendencies. The position of the bishops, for example, was such that they were far less intransigent than were parish priests. Bishops had to be acceptable to the government before they were allowed to take possession of their sees. Moreover, with the growth of Socialist influence in the urban areas and among farm workers, many Catholics felt compelled to find a political means of countering it. In 1891 this was recognised officially with the publication of *Rerum Novarum,* which took up the social question of the condition of the Catholic masses.[3] It permitted the development of farm organisations and trade unions on the basis of an ideology of class reconciliation and charity in socio-economic relationships. It was followed by the publication of a document entitled "Programme of Catholics confronted by Socialism" by Toniolo, a leading Christian Democratic thinker of the time.

With the emergence of these problems, the old, bitter conflict was modified. In 1904, the Vatican for the first time permitted avowed Catholics to stand for parliamentary elections. Catholic trade unions began to develop. In industry they were only one tenth the size of Socialist unions, but they were somewhat more influential in

agriculture. Tacit agreement between Church and State developed on
some issues. In a sense, then, time moderated the problem which
various Italian statesmen had tried to solve. Cavour's solution was
expressed in the formula, "a free Church in a free State", and later
Giolitti stated that "the best thing for Church and State is to be like
two parallel lines which never cross each other, never diverge and never
meet". In fact, the Church would never be "free" in the sense it desired
because that would have meant the destruction of the State. Nor could
there be two parallel lines because of interaction of many important
issues. But no real settlement was reached. An important beginning was
made in the post-First World War period when an autonomous political
party of Catholics was organised. It might have provided an effective
base from which Catholics, as such, could have participated in the
political life of the country, but within a short time the Vatican found
it necessary to repudiate the party. It proved to be an embarassment in
the situation of Mussolini's rise to power and consolidation of regime.
These problems will be discussed in the next section; here it is
appropriate to consider Italy's economic development, because the
social changes connected with it gave rise to new conflicts. These
became superimposed on the older pattern of conflict, and in a chain of
explosive events led ultimately to the fusion of the nationalist cause
with Fascism.

Economic Development

Several factors account for the relative slowness of economic
development. One was the absence of natural resources so that coal and
industrial raw materials had to be imported. Another was the lack of
capital for investment. Foreign capital was not attracted to an area
where natural resources were so limited; nor was Italian private
investment, which tended to be diverted from industry into government
stocks and land purchase. It was left to the State to take the initiative,
which it did through its control of the banking system. After 1861 the
foundations for future growth were laid: railroads, iron and steel,
ship-building, merchant marine and a textile industry which could
compete internationally. But from the beginning, industrialisation was
marked by a geographical imbalance: the basic industries were
concentrated in the North and the South remained stagnant.

The scale of industrialisation in the North progressively expanded to
include chemicals, building materials, rubber and the production of
electricity, which was a valuable source of energy. But in comparison
with Britain and Germany, Italy's growth was small. Agriculture

remained the most important sector of the economy for a long time. It was not until the 1930s that industry and mining contributed more to national income than did agriculture.[4] And it was not until after the Second World War that there was a larger proportion of the active population in industry than in agriculture. In the overall costs of production the abundance and cheapness of labour was not sufficient compensation for very high import costs of raw materials. Under these conditions, Italy could not become a real industrial leader nor a major international power — despite its extremely high expenditure on maintaining a large army and its efforts to build a front-ranking navy.

Nevertheless by the turn of the century the scale of industrialisation continued to increase, and Italy enjoyed a period of prosperity which lasted until 1914. Italy's intervention in the First World War, in the spring of 1915, resulted in a great expansion of war industries. But it also had negative effects: industries producing for civilian consumption were severely retarded; foreign trade was disrupted and Italy was subjected to a submarine blockade; and, requiring loans and credits from her allies, Italy became greatly indebted to the United States and to Great Britain. In all, the enormous costs of the war created immense inflationary pressures, with widespread distress. Peasants were discontented because of government controls on agricultural prices, while workers were hit by food shortages and the rising cost of living. The purchasing power of wages declined more than one third by 1918, and did not show an improvement over the 1913 level until after 1920.

The war gave certain industries a big push. In 1899 Agnelli created Fiat *(Fabbrica Italiana Automobili Torino)*, and the war turned it into the largest group of factories in Italy, producing seventy per cent of all vehicles. The expansion of the motor industry carried other industries with it, particularly rubber. Impetus was also given to textiles and chemicals, and the petroleum industry began to develop as well. But the transition to the post-war situation was not easy. The iron and steel industries were not very efficient during the war, and they collapsed in the slump after 1919. Other sections of the economy experienced serious difficulties, and between 1919 and 1921, the number of bankruptcies trebled. The labour market was flooded with the release of men from the army, and there was massive unemployment and strike movements. Hunger too was widespread, and food riots erupted in July 1919 despite government action to keep bread prices low. And in the same month, unemployed war veterans of peasant background began a movement of violent land seizure. The government was obliged to tolerate expropriation until as late as May 1922; but the landowners resisted strenuously, creating the basis for agrarian Fascism. Before examining the impact of these events on the political system, it is necessary to analyse the development of the Italian labour movement.

The Labour Movement

Socialism was rapidly spreading by the 1890s. The Socialist Party was founded in 1892, and exerted a growing influence in the major centres of industry and also in the rural areas. In the latter, especially in Sicily, radical societies of day labourers, called *fasci*, were formed. Most of the *fasci* became affiliated with the Socialist party, although they were much more revolutionary than the party itself which was under the moderate leadership of Filippo Turati. After 1890 there were violent and bloody agrarian strikes, culminating in the autumn of 1893 with severe unrest in Sicily. It was crushed by the proclamation of martial law and the dispatch of 50,000 troops. Repressive measures against the Socialists followed. The party was dissolved and its leaders prosecuted, although in fact they were not connected with the Sicilian events. The measures only temporarily stifled the unrest, which became more diversified between 1896 and 1898, with more peasant uprisings, urban riots in Rome, Florence and Milan, anarchist actions and student disturbances. An attempt was made to introduce an authoritarian style government with a "Cabinet of Generals", but this gave way to a "Cabinet of Conciliation" and eventually to the liberal prime minister Giolitti.

A period of liberal reform ensued. Giolitti was tolerant of labour organisation and industrial strife because he believed that it would be possible to meet the Socialist party half-way. He believed that it could eventually be incorporated into the democratic parliamentary process. In 1895 the Socialist party had set out a minimum programme of immediate social reforms and a maximum programme of long-term revolutionary aims. It was similar to the programme which the German Social Democrats had adopted a few years earlier. As far as Giolitti was concerned, the minimum demands — factory legislation, the right to strike, progressive income tax, government neutrality in industrial disputes and universal suffrage — were acceptable, and he hoped that eventually some of the moderate Socialists would accept cabinet positions under his leadership. These hopes were no doubt strengthened when the General Confederation of Labour (CGL) was established in 1906 under reformist leadership. The central trade union body was led in the direction of collective bargaining and moderate social reform.

Opposing the moderate reformist orientation was the "cyclone unionism" of the Revolutionary Syndicalists.[5] They advocated the use of a mass general strike to win control of the means of production, and saw the trade unions as a revolutionary force which could organise the industrial process on a co-operative basis. They were contemptuous of Giolitti's "bourgeois" democracy, and advocated a total boycott of parliament. But the Revolutionary Syndicalist minority was strong only outside the principal industrial centres, and so did not represent a great threat to the organisational predominance of the CGL moderates. In the political wing of the labour movement, the revolutionary Maximalists were an active minority. But in the first decade of the century, the heyday of Giolitti's liberalism, attention was concentrated on building the electoral machine, with management of municipal affairs and parliamentary representation given priority. At the same time, the co-operative movement developed, and Giolitti helped by granting public works contracts to the producer co-operatives.

Giolitti's hopes, however, were not fulfilled. The structure of the General Confederation of Labour was such that the national unions or federations had to compete against the Chambers of Labour for predominance. The Chambers of Labour were "horizontal" organisations which brought together the various local trade unions on a communal or provincial level.[6] They served as both an employment office for the locality and as a political centre. Although the national unions were able to assert their dominance, the Chambers continued to play an influential role because of their concern with problems in their localities. In this way, Revolutionary Syndicalists and Maximalists had the opportunity of exerting an influence which checked the reformist aspirations of the CGL leadership. After 1912, several Chambers came under revolutionary control, the most important being those of Milan and Bologna. In 1912 the revolutionary wing of the Socialist party emerged so strongly that it was able to expel the reformist leaders. The result was that the moderate CGL leaders found themselves isolated from a large body of radicalised opinion within the labour movement as a whole. This was intensified by a mounting wave of strikes which culminated in the Red Week of June 1914. Extremists like Mussolini, then editor of the leading Socialist paper *Avanti*, accused the CGL of treason because it attempted to call off the strikes. In the turbulent era which was to follow the war, the moderate leadership of the CGL increasingly lost its initiative and control over events.

The Political System

The Italian parliamentary system worked reasonably well before the

First World War when the political stage was narrow and occupied by small groups. But with the advent of mass parties and the intensification of social conflicts the old liberal machinery broke down. It was not able to adapt to the new conditions because of the peculiarities of previous developments.

Count Cavour, as Victor Emmanuel's Prime Minister, played a crucial role in consolidating the unification of Italy, in moulding its institutions, and in raising Piedmont to a position of great influence in the new state. His role parallels that of Bismarck in exerting Prussian domination in Germany. Both of these leaders carried out vital reforms and were astute diplomats. Cavour secured the active aid of France and the sympathy of England in Italy's struggle against Austria. But there were crucial differences between the two statesmen. Unlike Bismarck who had the support of the monarch in riding roughshod over liberalism, Cavour recognised parliament as his main check against the king, and wanted to develop its independence. But Cavour died suddenly in June 1861, only a few months after the Kingdom was proclaimed; whereas Bismarck's career as Chancellor extended from 1871 to 1890, thus exerting a far deeper and more lasting influence over his country.

The Italian Parliament was bi-cameral, with a Chamber of Deputies and a Senate. The constitution provided for a formal equality between the two houses, but the only real power the Senate had was that of delaying legislation already passed in the lower house. The franchise was originally restricted by property qualifications, so that in 1870 not more than half a million people were eligible to vote. However, the franchise laws were progressively liberalised in 1882, 1912 and 1919, when Italy achieved universal manhood suffrage. The ministers were appointed by the king, with the consent of Parliament, and were usually chosen from the Chamber of Deputies. As parliamentary practice developed, the cabinet was generally responsible to the Chamber of Deputies. But the real power of the king is not to be underestimated. He was influential in foreign affairs, and he retained a special relationship with the Army. The oath of personal allegiance to the king was meaningful to the officer corps. Moreover, the king, by appointing ministers could influence, if not always control, the personnel and tenure of the cabinets. For example, it was the formal action of King Victor Emmanuel III, and not the wishes of his ministers or of Parliament, which brought Mussolini to power in 1922.

This system of government was based on a written constitution which was granted in March 1848 by Charles-Albert, King of

Piedmont-Sardinia, as a concession to the revolutionary times. It continued to operate as Italy's basic law for a hundred years, surviving the Fascist regime and the immediate aftermath of the Second World War. It was replaced by a republican constitution on 1st January 1948.

Certain aspects of the system are worth noting in connection with the rise of Fascism. The development of democratic local government was inhibited by the adoption of the prefectoral system of provincial administration. Following the French model, the prefects of the seventy-five provinces were appointed by the Minister of the Interior and were directly accountable to him. The prefect had a dual role: to supervise the communal and provincial governments on behalf of the central government and to act as chief law enforcement officer. He played another role in Italy, unofficial but crucial. He became notorious as the agency through which ministers and deputies attempted to control the voting in national elections. In this way, electoral procedure was frequently abused, with bribery and compulsion on a vast scale. A second peculiarity, which became a dominant practice after 1876, was called transformism. This was the practice by which cabinets were set up without regard for the party affiliations and political principles of its members. It meant that for the sake of a cabinet position, a parliamentary deputy was prepared to abandon his party label, his political principles and his electoral mandate. Political credibility was reduced to vanishing point, and in Parliament the parties were split into minor personal factions, relying on patronage and questionable favours to gain support. Corruption became so extensive that the parliamentary system itself was widely regarded as meaningless.

Transformism arose from the multiplicity of parties, which necessitated some form of permanent coalition government. There were thirty-three different coalition cabinets between 1861 and 1896 — almost one a year. Transformism was workable in skilled hands, such as those of dominant politicians like Depretis, Crispi and Giolitti. The last-named was especially gifted in the art of breaking down parties into small factions and separate selfish interests and then weaving his coalitions out of these shifting fragments. But in face of severe dislocation and deep crisis which Italy experienced after the First World War, transformism became an expression of parliamentary incompetence, corruption and sham.

It is not surprising that there were many critics of parliamentary decadence. The liberal thinker Mosca considered that the system of representation was inadequate and that the State was controlled by a narrow political class. And more generally the belief was widespread that liberal democracy would have to be replaced by open despotism. If the prosperous conditions in the first decade of the century postponed it for a while, there were already signs of what might happen in Crispi's reaction to social unrest in the 1890s. His repressive measures against the Socialists were reminiscent of Bismarck's laws against the German Social Democrats. Although these laws were rescinded when Crispi fell from power, the same tactics were again resorted to in the spring of 1898 when labour disturbances in Milan reached insurrectionary proportions. A state of siege was proclaimed in the northern centres, which resulted in severe persecution of Socialist and Radical groups. But there was widespread revulsion against the severity of the measures, which included the threatened curtailment of the basic public freedoms of press, public meeting and association. The revulsion ushered in the Giolittian liberal period, which coincided with the growing prosperity at the turn of the century.[7]

However, labour agitation and the drive for more extensive welfare and social legislation continued. The reaction against it was significant. The various small groups of extreme nationalists began to combine. They were joined by romantic literary men like d'Annunzio who were attracted by doctrines of violence. The first Nationalist party congress was held in 1910, and it gave Italy the beginnings of an active party of the extreme right.[8] It was supported by funds from many industrialists who favoured its policy of colonial expansion and its authoritarianism.[9]

When Italy intervened in the war against Austria in the spring of 1915, the decay of Parliament was sealed. The majority in Parliament and in the country was against intervention, but secret negotiations were carried out in London without its knowledge. The Italians were promised territory from Austria and elsewhere after victory. May 1915 was the dress rehearsal for October 1922 in the sense that the legislative assembly was exposed as an empty debating hall without real powers. War was delcared without its knowledge or consent. During the war itself the Chamber of Deputies remained passive, as government by decree was extensively adopted.

NOTES

1. See Denis Mack Smith's analysis of the 1860 revolt in southern Italy and the role played by Garibaldi in suppressing it. *Italy*, University of Michigan Press 1959, pp41-2.
2. See Ernest Helmreich, *A Free Church in a Free State?* Boston, Heath 1964.

3. Richard Webster, *Christian Democracy in Italy*, London, Hollis and Carter 1961, p7.

4. Shepard B. Clough, *The Economic History of Modern Italy*, Columbia UP 1964, p99.

5. Daniel Horowitz, *The Italian Labor Movement*, Harvard UP 1963, pp78-9.

6. John Clarke Adams, 'Italy' in Walter Galenson (ed.) *Comparative Labor Movements*, Prentice-Hall 1952, pp424-5.

7. Benedetto Croce, *A History of Italy 1981-1915*, Oxford UP 1929 transl., pp190-220.

8. *Ibid.*, pp264-6.

9. Mack Smith, *Italy*, p271.

Chapter 3 Germany: The Emergence of State Power

Like Italy, but in contrast to France and England, Germany was very slow in establishing itself as a nation. Before 1815, there was no central political authority in Germany; instead, there were over three hundred principalities, the majority of which were ruled by princes and counts, while the rest came under ecclesiastical authority or were free cities. This extreme fragmentation and particularism was an enormous obstacle to German unity and economic development as it produced a variety of legal codes, custom barriers, currencies and entrenched separate interests. In 1815, after the defeat of Napoleon, the Congress of Vienna reorganised Germany, following through the rationalisation process which the French emperor had begun. The number of states was reduced to a more manageable thirty nine, including four free cities, and were organised into a Confederation. Although the Confederation endured for over fifty years, it was not an effective instrument for promoting German unification. It remained a loose association of separate states, rather than developing a federal union like the United States of America. The federal Diet had no means of enforcing its decisions if the particular state governments did not accept and apply them, the states rarely if ever paid federal dues, and no federal army was organised.

But if the states were not influenced by the federal principle, the exercise of their sovereignty was nevertheless closely limited by the power of the largest states in the Confederation. Austria dominated the Confederation for quite some time, but was increasingly rivalled and challenged by the rising power of Prussia. Under the guidance of Bismarck, who became Prime Minister of Prussia in 1862, Austria was manoeuvred into a military conflict in July 1866. The Prussians emerged victorious in a short, decisive war. Following this, a North German Confederation was created under Prussian control. Moreover, the *Zollverein* (customs union created in 1834) was enlarged into a Customs Parliament which included not only the North German Confederation but also the southern states. This provided a basis for economic exchanges and developments on a national scale.

The next step was to consolidate this structure, from which Austria had been excluded, on a political level. The opportunity to do so was not long in coming. The Prussian war with France in 1870 cemented the bonds of German national unity. Following Prussia's decisive victory over France, the south German states entered into the North German Confederation. They accepted the proposal, made by the Bavarian King, that the Prussian Monarch should assume the Imperial title as head of the Second Reich. The only opposition to this was in Bavaria itself where Catholic opposition to a Prussian-dominated Reich was strong. But the hegemony of the Prussian giant, stretching all the way from Poland to the Rhine, was by now unshakeable.

The most significant aspect of these developments was that they were initiated from above and did not coincide with a revolutionary struggle to create a sovereign parliamentary system, as in the Italian *Risorgimento*. The achievement of German nationhood was belated, and came about in such a way that the liberal, democratic cause was buried under the national cause. The two were in conflict and did not merge. The possibility of large-scale democratic innovations arose with revolutionary actions in Vienna and Berlin in March 1848, following the February Revolution in Paris which overthrew Louis-Philippe. A Pre-Parliament was created in Frankfurt but the impetus of the liberal and radical elements in the middle class was unable to sustain itself for long. They did not develop a social programme which could articulate the aspirations of the peasantry and urban workers,[1] and indeed were afraid of the more radical demands arising from those sources.

In the meantime the power of the ruling princes remained intact as they retained their military forces. Coinciding with these social conflicts were a number of clashes on the frontiers which roused the nationalism of the middle class.[2] There was a Polish revolt against Prussia, a revolt in Schleswig-Holstein against Denmark, and a movement of Czech nationalism in Bohemia. The German liberals supported the Prussian and Austrian armies, which were under the control of the established rulers. When radical riots broke out in many western German towns, reaching Frankfurt itself at the end of September 1848, the Frankfurt Assembly appealed to the Prussian king to use his troops to quell the disorders. In short, far from being able to establish itself as an independent force, liberalism in Germany turned to the Prussian state for protection against other social forces at home and abroad. But the Prussian state was in no sense an agent of liberalism, and once order was restored, it was not long before the Prussian army dispersed the liberal Pre-Parliament itself. There was to be no democratic constitution in Germany until the Weimar Republic was established in 1919.

Army and State

The core elements of the Prusso-German state were the Army and the Civil Service. Both had developed long before the industrialisation of the country, and their dominant position remained undisturbed by it. To some extent this was due to the political abdication of the rising middle class, which was famous for its quietism and lack of response to liberal ideas in the eighteenth century, frightened by the revolutionary temper of the urban workers in 1848 (and later in 1918) and disciplined by the national cause. Still, an important question remains unanswered. The fact that the aristocracy was not seriously challenged is not sufficient to explain how it was able to perpetuate its socio-political power and ideology unchanged through such a fundamental social transformation as industrialisation and urban development in Germany. The fact that it was able to do so marks the great difference in political outlook which developed in the nineteenth century between Germany and the democratic societies of the West. Industrialism in Germany did not lead to liberal attitudes and basic changes in the political hierarchy; on the contrary, authoritarian attitudes and military-aristocratic status consideration were perpetuated. How this came about may be seen from the ideological, social and organisational basis of the Prussian power-state.

Talcott Parsons, in his essay on "Democracy and Social Structure in Pre-Nazi Germany", has suggested that the Prussian outlook was a combination of "a patriarchal type of authoritarianism with a highly developed formal legalism".[3] There are two distinguishing features of this type of authoritarianism: first, it involved no sense of responsibility to the governed population, they were simply objects of control; secondly, those in authority could not do what they pleased in the sense of promoting their own self-interest. On the contrary, they were not expected to have any other interest but that of the collectivity which they served. They were bound by a strict concept of duty to the state. In return for wholehearted service, the civil official and the military officer received special rights and privileges, and a special position of dignity and honour in society. Since this patriarchal type of authoritarianism was based on a strict concept of duty to the state, it was bound up with a highly developed formal legalism. The Hohenzollern rulers, from the time of Frederick William I (1713-40), aimed at creating a super-disciplined, super-efficient administration, and therefore elaborated a meticulously detailed service code of legal regulations and moral canons, which was to be followed to the letter.

Duty and discipline, then, meant obedience and unquestioning submission to higher levels of authority; and it excluded all sense of responsibility to the governed population.

The social basis of the Prussian state was the class of rural landowners, known as the Junkers, in the region east of the Elbe. There was a sharp contrast in rural society between the large-scale extensive farming in the north and the east and the intensive small-holding in the south and the west of Germany. The great landlords in the east did not indulge in absentee ownership but where directly engaged in agricultural activities. They were interested in acquiring more land and in exploiting the peasants as serfs or, after emancipation, as farm-labour. In fact, the way that the emancipation of the peasantry was actually carried out in Prussia enabled the great landowners to take possesion of about two-and-a-half million acres of farmland after 1811. They took possession of abandoned farms, and acquired land from the peasants as indemnity for their freedom. The result was that although the peasants were legally freed, the great landowners were the first to benefit. But peasant freedom was further limited because the Junkers were anxious to keep a very close control over their labour-force. To this effect an ordinance was enacted in 1810 which remained the basis of the Prussian law of master and servant throughout the nineteenth century.[4] It greatly restricted the labourer's freedom of movement and punished striking with imprisonment. This legal buttressing of traditional personal dominance was only one aspect of Junker power in their home districts. They were directly in charge of local police and judicial functions until as late as 1872, and until 1918 their political privileges went unchallenged. The Prussian House of Lords was reserved exclusively for them; and the three-class election law to the lower House of Parliament in Prussia ensured that they retained a determining position.

Therefore, in spite of the fact that the feudal system of hereditary social estates was abolished in the reform movement which Prussia undertook after suffering a crushing military defeat at the hands of Napoleon, Junker power remained intact. The reforms instituted by Stein and Hardenberg broadened the social composition of the Junker class, and at the same time strengthened its organisational power in the civil service and in the officers corps. Entry into these institutions was made less exclusive, but barriers were erected to ensure that candidates of non-noble origin were completely assimilated.[5] In addition to stringent professional qualifications (competitive examinations and long in-service training which presupposed a wealthy background), the political views and social outlook of the candidates were carefully scrutinised. Before examining this process in the Army more closely, the role of militarism in Prussian society should be considered.

The powerful army which Frederick William I created had to be supported by an economically underdeveloped society. So much so that the weight of the army resulted in the militarisation of the society itself. Military concepts of authority and discipline were established as models for peace-time civil government and for civil life in general. Relations between officers and men in the army were very harsh, paralleling the harsh relations which existed between landlords and peasants. This was further developed by Frederick the Great (1740-86) who reconciled the Junkers to the growth of his autocratic power by reserving for them exclusively the honour of a military aristocracy. At the same time Frederick desired that the common soldiers (peasant serfs) should be more afraid of their commanding officers than of any potential enemy.[6]

After its defeat by Napoleon, the Prussian military machine was reconstructed under the guidance of Scharnhorst and Gneisenau. The aims of the military reforms of 1808 were twofold. First to create a thoroughly professional General Staff as the elite of the officers corps. For this purpose the Prussian War Academy was founded by Clausewitz in 1810. Secondly, to break down the exclusively aristocratic and caste-like character of the officer corps in order to attract the best of the available talent without regard to social background. Although the social basis of recruitment was broadened, the officers corps did not lose its privileged caste qualities. In fact, these were strengthened by two innovations. One gave the corps itself the power to elect its members, whereas previously they were nominated by the king. the other was the setting up of a military Court of Honour with the power of jurisdiction independent of the civilian courts of justice. Thus the nobility remained the dominant group of officers. It had the power to keep undesirables out, and the instruments to preserve its particular standards of conduct and mentality. The innovations strengthened, rather than weakened, the sense of a closed, privileged caste, immune from all civilian control.[7] Over the course of the century many officers of non-noble background were admitted, but they were thoroughly assimilated. Even after the First World War, the close-knit social identity and enormous prestige were perpetuated, and were major factors in the political struggles of the Weimar Republic and the Nazi regime.

Industrial Revolution

Although German industrial development lagged far behind that of Britain in the middle decades of the nineteenth century, the movements towards political unification carried with them expanding economic opportunities. The Zollverein of 1834 was, under Prussian initiative and control, enlarged into a Customs Parliament in 1867 to include both the North German states and the southern (with the exception of Austria). By that time, the Ruhr, which was included in the territory of Prussia, was emerging as an important centre of industrial activity. Around the nucleus of coal and iron industries, there arose a complex of metalworks and engineering trades, as well as textile factories and chemical trades. The stage was set for extremely rapid industrial growth after the unification of the German Empire in 1871.

The connection between political unification and subsequent economic development was of fundamental importance; in it lies the roots of the relationship which later developed between the German industrialists and the Nazi regime. In marked contrast with the experience of Great Britain and the USA, there was in Germany a long-standing tradition of government intervention in the economic system. It was primarily based on an appreciation of the relationship between economic strength and military power. Nowhere was this better understood than in the militarised society of Prussia, where the army absorbed a disproportionate amount of available resources. The Prussian government was most alive to the strategic implications of certain developments and consequently promoted railway construction and road improvements. It was active in seeking the skills of foreign engineers and technicians, and it ran iron, lead and coal mines.[8] The very lateness of the industrial revolution brought a deeper awareness of its significance for national development and national assertiveness. England, the workshop of the world, was a clear enough model, and the lesson for Germany was plain: unless industry was promoted on a sufficiently large scale, the emerging nation could not assert a claim for leadership. Further, there was a realisation that economic development would not come by itself; it was well understood that the industrial revolution consisted essentially in the application of scientific knowledge to productive processes. Consequently both scientific knowledge and technical and engineering skills were highly appreciated, and great attention was paid to the supply and development of trained man-power.

Economic development then was actively promoted within a

well-defined political framework. The government did not "plan" the
economy in the Soviet sense, nor did it establish guide-lines in the style
of French indicative planning; but it was far from being a passive,
extraneous factor which might occasionally 'intervene' from the
outside in the British and American tradition. The role of government
in Germany was one of active encouragement in providing the
framework for economic development: the educational institutions, the
communications networks, the legal regulations and the overall policies.
Thus the pre-industrial Prussian mentality remained dominant in the
rapidly changing society. This indicates one of the main reasons for the
weakness of liberalism in Germany — the entrepreneurial middle class
learned to rely on the established rulers to look after their
politico-economic interests. Their expectations were fulfilled in the
Second Empire under Bismarck and his successors. And after the short
interlude of the Weimar Republic, with its tremendous economic
problems, they were glad to return to the haven of the "strong" state
under Hitler.

The unification of Germany in 1871 under victorious Prussia led to a
period of phenomenal economic growth. By the 1880s, the economy
expanded at a rate which was even greater than that of the spectacular
post-war recovery of the 1950s. From about 1875 to about 1895 total
real national income more than doubled, and then increased by a
further seventy per cent up to the outbreak of the First World War. In
the production of iron and steel Germany was able first to challenge,
then to surpass Britain. The same was true of other vital fields such as
chemicals and the electrical industry where German achievements were
outstanding.

In trying to explain the reasons for German success in competition
with Britain up to 1914, it is interesting to note that David Landes, as
an economic historian, found no crucial economic differences between
the two countries.[9] He suggested that there was nothing decisive about
relative differences in such economic factors as industrial resources,
population growth and supply of labour, availability of markets, supply
of capital and so on. What were important, in his view, were certain
social and institutional factors: the diffusion of primary education in
the population at large, the quality of apprenticeship training and
technical training and the high level of scientific knowledge, both
theoretical and applied. As already stressed, these developments did not
come about by chance, they were actively fostered by the realisation
that the industrial revolution must be harnessed to the political tasks of
German nation-building. Landes brings this out clearly in emphasising

the contrast between

> 'the late and stunted growth of technical and scientific education in Britain as against the vigorous, precociously developed German system .... where Britain left technical training, like primary education, to private enterprise, which led to a most uneven and inadequate provision of facilities, the German states generously financed a whole gamut of institutions ....'[10]

The political importance of elementary education, which underlies apprentice and technical training, was appreciated in Prussia long before the period of rapid industrialisation. After Prussia's defeat by Napoleon in 1806, the development of modern elementary education was among the reforms undertaken. In the words of Frederick William III, "We have indeed lost territory, and it is true that the state has declined in outward splendour and power, and therefore it is my solemn desire that the greatest attention be paid to the education of the people".[11]

The educational system was not only effective in terms of the training it provided, it was also a means of inculcating conservative and reactionary social values. With the growth of the labour movement, the school room was used for purposes of anti-Socialist indoctrination. More generally the *völkisch* ideology (illiberal, anti-Semitic and intensely chauvinistic) deeply penetrated into the educational system after 1873 and was actively promoted by a large number of teachers. It became so pronounced a feature of the whole educational system, including the universities, that even in the Weimar Republic little could be done effectively to check it.[12] The rise of the Nazi movement exercised a magnetic attraction on the teaching profession; according to the Nazi party census of 1935, thirty per cent of its political officials were elementary-school teachers. This was remarked upon in Germany at the time by the witticism that the Nazi state was created in the image of the elementary-school teacher. The situation contrasts sharply with that of France, where the elementary-school teachers played an important role in the struggle for a democratic, secular Republic. The difference in ideology stems from the nature of the political culture which permeated the middle range of the social structure in each country. The teachers were not simply passive recipients of the political culture, automatically passing it on; they actively contributed to its formation and dissemination. In Germany they sought to define a particular national cultural quality of "Germanness" which was viciously negative: anti-Semitic, anti-Slav, anti-French, anti-democratic, anti-socialist, anti-liberal.

The Political System

The main features of Bismarck's constitution reveal its authoritarianism unmistakably:

a) The Kaiser appointed the Imperial Chancellor as his agent. In contrast with the rest of western Europe, the Chancellor was not in any way responsible to the elected legislative assembly *(Reichstag)*. He had the power to dissolve the *Reichstag*, which did not possess the power to force him to resign, even if a clear majority wanted this.

b) Although the legislative assembly was elected by universal manhood suffrage, it was not a sovereign institution. It had only a limited influence on policy. Its consent was required for the expenditure of public money, including military credits. But this was routine and did not amount to control. Moreover the *Reichstag* could not initiate laws, but could only reject or delay laws proposed by the Chancellor. It was a very slim basis on which to build a viable parliamentary system. By the nature of the set-up, opposition consisted mainly in delaying tactics and the free unfolding of responsible, public participation through the medium of political parties was greatly inhibited.

c) The upper house, the *Bundesrat* or Federal Council, was composed of members appointed by the princes of the states. The states were not equally represented, and Prussia retained a decisive position. Far from functioning as a federal institution, the Council could be more accurately described as an instrument for carrying Prussia's initiative to various parts of the country.

The predominance of Prussia is not surprising when it is considered that by 1871, Prussia had expanded to comprise two thirds of Germany's total area and population, stretching all the way from Russia to the Rhine. The government of Germany, then, was fundamentally a dictatorship in the hands of the king of Prussia, who delegated his powers in military matters to the General Staff, in civil affairs to the Chancellor.

For this autocratic system to maintain itself in a rapidly changing society, a whole series of reforms and compromises had to be worked out. Bismarck saw this very clearly, and was active in promoting far-reaching changes. Between 1867 and 1879, he carried through a vast programme of reforms: legal and administrative procedures were standardised throughout the country; all restrictions on freedom of enterprise and freedom of movement were removed; and in general the country was provided with a modern commercial and industrial legal framework. To do this, Bismarck had to rely on National-Liberal votes, both in the *Reichstag* and in Prussian *Landtag*. The modern administration, which the conservative traditionalists opposed, was rapidly achieved for the National-Liberals by Bismarck. He thereby strengthened the autocratic governmental institutions by absorbing their fundamental demands, leaving them without power. What was accomplished was done for them not by them. The modern administration, serving as a framework for economic development, was given to them; the question of democracy, which they were somewhat interested in, could therefore be shelved.

But Bismarck's "liberal" phase brought him into direct conflict with the Roman Catholics on the issue of secular education. In March 1872 the Prussian *Landtag* passed a law placing the supervision of all schools in the hands of the State, and in June of that year members of religious orders were forbidden to teach in schools. The climax of the *Kulturkampf* was reached the following year when the independence of the Roman Church was attacked in the "May Laws" which gave the State the power to regulate all Church life. Catholic resistance began to develop, provoking further repressive legislation in the Prussian *Landtag*. Nevertheless the resistance, with Papal backing, continued. Out of this was created the Centre political party whose primary aim was to protect the rights of the Church. It therefore had an appeal, within the large Catholic minority, which transcended social class boundaries and differences in political outlook.

The *Kulturkampf* served a number of Bismarck's purposes, among other things giving him the opportunity to attack anti-Prussian forces inside the Reich (*e.g.* the pro-Austrians of western Germany and the Roman Catholic Poles in the eastern provinces). But as it progressed, he found himself relying too much on the National-Liberals for support, especially as they saw an opportunity to raise the demand for parliamentary government in Prussia. He considered, on the other hand, that if the rights of the Church were secured, the Centre party would not press for political change. It proved to be the case. Moreover, certain economic trends were developing in the late 1870s which cut across previous alliances. A campaign was mounted by industrialists and big grain producers for an end to trade liberalisation and a return to high protective tariffs. The manufacturers formed the Central Association of German Industrialists and made a powerful alliance with the agrarian-based Prussian Junkers, who were sensitive to American, French and Russian competition. Bismarck moved with the times. When Conservatives (representing agrarian interests), the centre and some National-Liberals (representing big business) formed a majority in the *Reichstag* in the winter of 1877-8. Bismarck took the opportunity to end the *Kulturkampf,* endorse the protectionists and split the National-Liberals.

Another issue arose which further strengthened Bismarck's bond with the Conservatives and reinforced the divisions among the Liberals: attempts to assassinate the Kaiser were blamed on the Social Democratic party. As a result, anti-Socialist laws were passed which made the party illegal, banned its press and sought to prohibit the trade union activity which the Social Democrats carried out. These laws, passed in 1878, were periodically renewed until 1890. They were applied in a very lax manner, at least compared with later standards: although several hundred people were imprisoned or forced into exile, individual Social Democratic candidates still stood at elections and were allowed to sit in the *Reichstag.* The laws were not at all effective in stemming the growth of the party; on the contrary, both membership and the share of the total vote increased steadily. The main consequence of the laws, also unintended, was to preserve the party's revolutionary ideology.

But Bismarck went further: he established a system of social security between 1883 and 1889. It was the first of its kind in the world, providing workers with a comprehensive scheme of compulsory insurance against sickness, accident and old age. Organised by the State, though not state subsidised, the scheme provided a remarkable degree of protection for the workers in a very convenient way. The employers made some contribution, while the workers themselves were obliged to pay for the greater part. The political benefits for the Bismarckian system of authoritarian government were significant: a major demand of the working-class movement had been granted before it could become a burning political issue. By grasping the direction of social trends, the authoritarian state had once more been able to introduce the necessary changes from above, without granting any political concessions whatsoever. Social security was provided at the expense of democracy rather than as part of its extension.

Although the labour movement in Germany was far too colossal and dynamic a social force to be bought off in a simple way, there was an undeniable calming effect. Reinforcing this was the enormous industrial expansion of the 1880s which created steadily rising standards of living. The combination of factors worked to bring out and strengthen reformist tendencies within the labour movement. Their influence was steadily to expand, eventually binding the major portion of the working-class movement into the authoritarian political system, a process which the advent of the First World War brought to a climax.

But the resistance to this tendency should not be underestimated, since it became a powerful force in German political life at certain critical periods, as will be shown later.

Labour in the post-Bismarck Era

In the years from the fall of Bismarck in 1890 to the outbreak of the First World War, the rapidity and scope of industrialisation and urbanisation drastically altered both the internal social structure of Germany and its international position.

The industrial working class became increasingly organised in the Social Democratic party and the trade unions. At the Erfurt Congress of 1891, the first held after the repeal of the anti-Socialist laws, Marxism was enshrined as the official doctrine of the party. It was in the light of the official long-term revolutionary objectives, that the more immediate demands for reform were stated: the eight-hour day, progressive income tax, factory legislation, the introduction of proportional representation, etc. In effect the Erfurt programme represented a synthesis of revolutionary aspirations, which were created by the radicalisation of the movement under Bismarck's repressive laws and a reformist orientation. The original balance was not easily maintained because in the following years, up to the First World War, the reformist orientation was powerfully reinforced by huge electoral successes with the SPD share of the total vote increasing to thirty per cent. The party, on its way to attaining a membership of one million, was the largest mass party in the world, with a seemingly unlimited capacity for further expansion. Moreover, the trade unions, which were fostered by the Social Democrats, expanded even more rapidly. From a total membership of a quarter of a million in 1890, the numbers reached over two million by 1914.

Whereas in England the trade unions, in the course of their development, sponsored the Labour party as the political wing of the labour movement, the situation was reversed in Germany. The Socialist parties established the Free Trade Unions in the 1860s and regarded them as recruiting grounds for the political movement. But in the period of rapid expansion from 1890 to 1905, the unions were able to assert their independence and concentrate exclusively on immediate bread-and-butter problems. This attitude, in which they formally dissociated themselves from the revolutionary ideology of the SPD, made recruitment easier, and the unions grew more rapidly than the party itself. The obvious consequence was that the SPD had increasingly to take trade union demands into account.

In the course of a major dispute in 1905-6 over the question of a mass general strike as the appropriate instrument for social revolution, the trade-union leaders supported the reformist wing in opposing such ideas, and came to assert a dominant influence over the formulation of major issues of party policy. In the years leading to the outbreak of war, the trade unions followed their own policy in such controversial matters as support for the arms race and colonial questions, and the party executive sooner or later supported it. In the war crisis of August 1914, the union leaders acted without reference to the party in issuing a resolution which committed the trade unions to the war effort. The resolution was issued two days before a meeting of the Social Democratic parliamentary deputies to decide whether or not to vote for war credits. The move was decisive in influencing them to vote for the war credits and to agree to a domestic political truce *(Burgfrieden)*, because to have done otherwise would have split the movement. But in the years before this *dénouement*, the working-class movement appeared to be a vast and growing political and social force operating against established interests. As major strikes erupted in 1904 and 1905, employer resistance increased. Two organisations were established to fight against trade union power and against strikes. By 1913 these amalgamated into the League of German Employers Associations.

The changes in the internal social structure of Germany, consequent upon rapid industrialisation, related closely to changes in its international position. Bismarck's caution in foreign affairs was replaced by the uncontrolled aggressiveness of Wilhelm II, and Germany became increasingly isolated. It became deeply involved in the problems of the Austrian-Hungarian empire in south-eastern Europe, its previously good relations with Russia deteriorated drastically, and it positively alarmed Britain with its crash programme of naval contruction. Moreover the tone of German policy was set by various propaganda leagues — the Pan-German league, the Navy league, the Colonial league — which succeeded in rousing intense chauvinistic feelings. Increasingly, the feeling of German superiority was instilled and people were convinced that a quick military victory would be theirs for the asking. It was not only the officers corps and the nationalist circles who thought in these terms, the feeling emerged strongly at every social and political level. It is revealed in the confession of a onetime left-wing Social Democrat, who describes the struggle between internationalist socialist principles and the rising tide of nationalism as the war was about to break out:

'.... not for everything in the world would I like to live through those days of inner struggle again! [On the one hand] this driving, burning desire to throw oneself into the powerful current of the general national tide, and, on the other, the terrible spiritual fear of following that desire fully, of surrendering oneself to the mood which roared about one and which, if one looked deep into one's heart, had long since taken possession of the soul. This fear: will you not also betray yourself and your cause? Can you not feel as your heart feels? [Thus it was] until suddenly — I shall never forget the day and hour — the terrible tension was resolved; until one dared to be what one was; until — despite all principles and wooden theories — one could, for the first time in almost a quarter century, join with a full heart, a clean conscience and without a sense of treason in the sweeping, stormy song: *Deutschland, Deutschland über alles.*'[13]

But a swift victory was not forthcoming — instead a long, exhausting war ensued which placed an unbearable strain on the material and political resources of the country, and brought to the surface all the internal conflicts which had been developing. The prolonged war led to the final disintegration of the Bismarckian state: neither the Emperor, the Army, the civil service nor the *Reichstag* proved capable of doing more than leading the nation to the brink of disaster and then abdicating responsibility for it. At first overwhelming feelings of patriotism led the political parties and interest groups to terminate their mutual struggles and agree on a "political truce" *(Burgfrieden)* for the duration of the war. Unheard of co-operation prevailed for a while, but the basic consequence of the political truce was much less the establishment of harmony among conflicting interests than the transfer of civilian authority to the Army. The Army would not tolerate any interference from the outside, particularly from the *Reichstag,* in military matters. Since the expected rapid victory did not materialise, Germany found itself unprepared for a prolonged total war on both fronts. To cope with the munitions crisis, the transport crisis, the coal crisis, the food crisis, the manpower crisis and the administrative crisis, the military increasingly expanded its sphere of authority. Eventually the Army came to manage the entire war-time economy, controlling the food supply and raw materials, and intervening in labour/management relations. Its excursion into this last area was to have crucial consequences in the immediate post-war period.

As shown in Gerald Feldman's well-documented study, *Army, Industry and Labor in Germany, 1914-1918,*[14] the Army's interest in industrial relations started in 1914 in an attempt to solve the conflicting demands on skilled labour as between industry and service in the armed forces. They were also drawn into this problem because of the need to regulate the multiple conflicts between employers and unions. The Army attempted to satisfy both sides where possible. Although there was a community of feeling and outlook between industrial leaders and certain elements in the Army (Colonels Bauer and Nicolai who were Ludendorff's advisors), nevertheless there was a consistent effort to see the unions' point of view on the part of other circles, led by General Groener as head of the War Office. The reason for Groener's solicitude was his clear understanding that the unions were needed to control the workers. As early in the war as January 1915, it was necessary for union leaders "to enlighten" their followers about the food situation; and when the number of strikes began to increase in 1916 and 1917, this necessity became more urgent. A policy of outright suppression of strikes in those circumstances would have had a drastically demoralising effect and could have led to revolutionary upheaval. Groener, in particular, was aware of the necessity of granting concessions to labour as his realisation grew that the war was lost. He wanted to perpetuate authoritarian political and military traditions across the abyss of defeat. His desire to carry on the Prussian tradition of reform from above, in order to prevent revolution from below, was cut short by his dismissal as head of the War Office in August 1917. But after the interlude of the Ludendorff dictatorship and the German surrender, Groener was presented with a second chance, which to a considerable extent, influenced the fate of the Weimar Republic.

The War Ministry (and later the War Office under Groener) did not regard the industrialists' desire to maximise their war profits, to keep their skilled workers and to perpetuate a rigidly authoritarian factory system as sacred principles. Instead, they granted a number of concessions to the unions on wages, freedom of movement and consultations. These concessions were gratifying to the union leaders. Moreover, the labour leaders found themselves increasingly consulted and absorbed into the wartime administration. Union representatives sat on the draft and arbitration committees all over the country, and also participated in the work of the authorities on the food problem. In return the union leaders were prepared to act as semi-official agents of the government and were encouraged to present their views to the workers. Through this process there was a marked rise in the status of the trade union leaders and of the moderate Social Democratic leaders compared with their position prior to the war. They were achieving undeniable respectability. At the same time, membership in the Free Trade Union movement, which had fallen off drastically in the first two years of the war, began to recover and easily passed one-million by 1917.[15]

The dilemma of the union leaders was not to become so identified with officialdom as to lose their influence over the workers, nor so identified with the radicalisation of labour, towards the end of the war, as to lose their semi-official position and enhanced status. But there was little chance of the latter, because few of them would have disagreed with the blunt statement of the Social Democrat leader Friedrich Ebert that he hated revolution like sin.

NOTES

1. Theodore S. Hamerow, *Restoration, Revolution, Reaction*, Princeton 1958, Chapters 8 and 9.

2. A.J.P. Taylor, *The Course of German History*, Methuen pp80-86

3. *Essays in Sociological Theory*, Free Press 1954 rev. ed., p109.

4. J.H. Clapham, *Economic Development of France and Germany, 1815-1914*, Cambridge 4th ed. p205.

5. Hans Rosenberg, *Bureaucracy, Aristocracy and Autocracy*, Harvard 1958, pp211 *ff.*

6. *Ibid.*, p60; Reinhard Bendix, *Nation-Building and Citizenship*, Wiley 1964. pp194-5.

7. Rosenberg, p217.

8. W.A. Cole and Phyllis Deane, "The Growth of National Incomes", *The Cambridge Economic History*, Vol. VI part I, pp17-18.

9. "Technological Change and Industrial Development in Western Europe, 1750-1914", *Cambridge Economic History* Vol. VI, part I.

10. *Ibid.*, p571.

11. Quoted in R.H. Samuel and R. Hinton Thomas, *Education and Society in Modern Germany*, Routledge and Kegan Paul, 1949, p36.

12. George L. Mosse, *The Crisis of German Ideology* Grosset and Dunlop 1964, pp152-7, 267-70.

13. Quoted in Carl E. Schorske, *German Social Democracy 1905-1917*, Harvard 1955, p290.

14. Princeton 1966.

15. *Ibid.*, p321.

Chapter 4 France: Patterns of Conflict

The Franco-Prussian War of 1870 is a landmark in the development of the political culture of western European society. The decisive victory enabled Prussia to create a new, enlarged German power under its hegemony. The authoritarian system of Prussian government was welded into the political framework of German statehood. At the same time, the withdrawal of French troops from Rome, where they had been protecting Papal sovereignty, enabled the liberal-secular state of Italy to establish its capital in the mediaeval Christian seat of power. In France, the Second Empire of Napoleon Bonaparte III was destroyed and the struggle for a secular, democratic Republic commenced. The problem was not centred on the achievement of national unification, but sharply posed, following the military defeat, were the conflicting choices of authoritarianism *versus* liberal-democracy, of Church influence versus secular influence in public affairs. What distinguished France from her neighbours was that clear-cut, unequivocal solutions were not found.

The unresolved tensions and antagonisms of French society created its specific quality of unpredictability manifest in the series of crises which have punctuated the Third, Fourth and Fifth Republics. Given that each Republic was created against a violent background of war, and the menace of civil war, the frequency of crisis would suggest that it is an inherent feature of the socio-political system. One type of explanation is that crisis is the mechanism by which an overly-rigid society copes with social change.[1] This view, however, is too strictly functionalist in conception, and it is more pertinent to study the conflicts of values and interests which were the legacy of the French Revolution and the moderate pace of France's industrialisation and urbanisation.

The revolutionary traditions blazed during the Franco-Prussian War with the establishment of the Paris Commune. While the National Assembly, meeting in Bordeaux, made its peace with the Prussian invaders, the capital city refused to surrender. Fired by revolutionary patriotism and defiance, Paris was organised into a Commune, which lasted from March to May of 1871. The Commune was exalted by Marx, in the *Civil War in France,* as "the glorious harbinger of a new society". Its repercussions were felt in other urban areas — Lyons,

Marseilles, Toulouse. But it was crushed without mercy by the Thiers government. The National Assembly, elected in February 1871, was dominated by a two-thirds monarchist majority which intended eventually to establish a constitutionl monarchy. But the constitutional laws of 1875 in fact created the Third Republic. The reasons for this paradox are the profound social and political changes which will be discussed later. By the end of the decade the Republicans launched the first of a series of educational reforms, sparking off a major battle with the Church and the traditionalist sections of society. Free, compulsory and secular education was not fully secured in law until 1886. But the social divisions remained acute and, little more than a decade later, they appeared with renewed force in a new conflict area — the Army — when the Dreyfus Affair exploded in 1898.

The political culture of France, then, was heterogeneous and divisive. This was partly a consequence of the moderate pace of industrialisation and urbanisation, which allowed the persistence of a large agricultural sector characterised by small-scale peasant ownership. In this half-industrialised, half-traditional state of uneven development there existed a multitude of interests, beliefs and allegiances. The working class, for example, remained a minority of the population, with a specific sub-culture of its own which was regarded with apprehension by most middle-class Republicans. The Paris Commune was not purely a working-class affair, but its bloody repression enlarged the social gulf and the mistrust which existed between the classes. Confronting the working class, the secular Republic showed a conservative face: there was no significant social legislation and no concern to integrate the industrial proletariat in the political structure. Trade unions were not legalised until 1884, and then were not granted a legal existence within the factories.

Nevertheless it was the wish of the moderate Republicans to establish a deep social consensus in which their values would be central — and in some respects they did manage to achieve a measure of success, which stands in sharp contrast to the weakness of the liberal impulse in neighbouring Germany. But there was a motley assortment on the Right which did not accept the Republic — the Monarchists, the Bonapartists, the Church hierarchy and various groups within the traditional establishment. The Dreyfus Affair revived and enlarged the scope of the conflict by opposing the Army and the University. The League of French Patriots, entrenched in the Army, the Navy, the Church hierarchy and in key areas of public administration, were hostile to the Republican form of government and contemptuous of the democratic process. Out of their ranks emerged a new group of vociferous extremists, Action Française. Opposing them was the League for the Defence of the Rights of Man, consisting of intellectuals and academics, who wanted a Republic based on equal rights. For the League state-supported secular education was one of the chief weapons in the necessary moral rejuvenation of France, and was the only way the larger political framework of democracy could be guaranteed. The Republicans triumphed in the struggle, and some of their opponents eventually acquiesced in the situation but always with distrust and distaste. Their ultimate revenge came with the Fall of France in 1940 and the establishment of the Vichy regime under Marshal Pétain. On the Left the revolutionary tradition expressed itself in various forms of syndicalism, anarchism and Marxism. Never satisfied with the bourgeois republic, always hoping to transform it in a revolutionary direction, it nevertheless formed an essential part of the ultimate defence of parliamentary democracy in France.

The Third Republic was a compromise among these diverse elements. It was not a compromise in the sense of a negotiated agreement to which the various parties could give their consent. Rather it was a compromise of stalemate in which the weaker side accepted the authority of the stronger, without granting the Republic its full legitimacy. Therefore, although the Republic lasted seventy years, until 1940, and although some of its traditions reappeared in the Fourth and Fifth Republics, the elements of uncertainty, of exposure to sudden crisis and of the menace of civil war, were never far in the background. It would certainly be an oversimplification to see every crisis since 1870 as essentially the same. The complexities of French socio-political life would be grossly underestimated if the specific situation and meaning of each major crisis — 1877, 1898, 1936, 1940, 1958 and 1968 — were not given their due. Nevertheless it is possible to see a recurrent pattern of conflict — a conflict of values and interests — which periodically emerges with great force to divide the society. In summary form, it may be described as a confrontation between a democratic and an authoritarian orientation. It is present in all western societies, but its peculiarly French aspect is that the conflict has remained basically unresolved, ambiguous and in a state of high tension.

The Political and Administrative System

The conflict between democratic and authoritarian orientations was expressed on an institutional level in the sharp antagonism which existed, and still exists, between the legislative and executive branches of government.[2] The antagonism goes back to the French Revolution when the monarchy was swept away and an all-powerful revolutionary legislative assembly was established. Later it gave way to the extreme executive rule of Napoleon.

The sharpness of the contrast between executive will, exercised through a vast centralised bureaucracy, on the one hand and legislative authority on the other was never really mitigated until the establishment of the Third Republic. The constitutional laws of 1875 attempted to create a balance of powers, giving the Chamber of Deputies broad legislative powers, which were nevertheless checked and limited by the executive. While it meant that parliament would have an important role, it was very far from the full democracy of the 1792 assembly. On the other hand, executive powers were more like those of a limited constitutional monarchy than of a Bonapartist dictatorship. The similarity to a limited monarchy was not accidental. The Third Republic originated as a compromise between the royalist majority, who saw the office of the President of the Republic as a kind of substitute monarch until the real one (Legitimist or Orléanist) could be brought back, and the middle-class republicans, who wanted ministerial responsibility to parliament.

The President was given powers which are reminiscent of the conception of that office which General de Gaulle put into practice in the Fifth Republic, except that de Gaulle enlarged the scope of executive initiative. Moreover, the Senate, although a branch of the legislature, was deliberately created as a conservative restraint on the potentially democratic impulses of the lower house. The Senate was set up as the stronghold of rural, traditional France. Each commune, regardless of size, was given equal representation in the Senate, with the result that urban populations were grossly under-represented, and the local, provincial outlook of the rural areas predominated. Later adjustments were made, but the basic imbalance remained.

The institutional safeguards — a strong President, not directly responsible to parliament, and a traditional-minded Senate — to keep parliamentary democracy within the limits considered tolerable by nineteenth-century royalists were certainly impressive. But the situation changed in unexpected ways, diminishing their effectiveness. In the years after 1871, the two thirds majority of monarchists in the national assembly drained away in subsequent by-elections. The elections of 1876 returned a republican majority of nearly two thirds. The victory was confirmed a year and a half later, after the MacMahon crisis, and was further strengthened in 1879 when the Republicans achieved a majority in the Senate. These major changes came about, as several historians have emphasised, through the conversion of the bulk of the peasantry to Republican ideals.[3]

The MacMahon crisis of 1877 arose out of the Republican electoral victory. Marshal MacMahon had been elected President by the monarchist dominated assembly. He then had to face a Republican Chamber which refused to accept the conservative ministers he appointed. In accordance with his constitutional powers, he therefore dissolved the Chamber on 16th May 1877. Before the new elections took place in October he purged the entire administration of prefects, municipal councillors and mayors who were suspected of Republican sympathies, and replaced them with officials who had run the Bonapartist regime of the Second Empire. Despite the support given to MacMahon by the Church and the notables of rural France, the peasantry was won over to the Republican point of view by the intensive campaign led by Gambetta, Thiers and Jules Grévy. As a result of the electoral defeat (326 Republican seats to 207 seats for the Right), the office of President was diminished, and the balance of power shifted decisively in favour of the legislative branch. The key point in the shift was the establishment of ministerial responsibility to parliament – a principle which Bismarck was always able to block in Germany. As a result of the practical application of this principle, the office of Prime Minister emerged. In the 1875 constitutional laws, there was no mention of it, but with the presidency now reduced to a symbol (and reserved for political nonentities), the Prime Minister came to assume most of the executive power, while being dependent on the support of the Chamber of Deputies.

The trend in which the legislative branch held predominance over the executive was thus set up in 1877, and continued up to 1914, despite the intention of the constitutional laws. Between the wars the trend was reversed as a result of increasing ministerial instability and parliamentary immobility. The average life of governments between 1870 and 1914 was a fairly respectable ten months, falling to eight months from 1914 to 1932 and to an absurd four-month average life between 1932 and 1940.[4] As the ministerial instability increased, recourse was made more and more to government by decree-laws. The effect was that parliament renounced its responsibility for enacting laws in particular spheres, especially economic, and the Prime Minister of the moment was given the power to handle the crisis or emergency by decree. Inevitably parliament was reduced to a hollow shell, and the executive was strengthened at its expense. Ultimately, it meant that the centralised administration ran the country because top civil servants were the only continuously present decision-makers.

Working behind the crisis-ridden atmosphere of the open political forum is the vast, centralised administrative machinery of the French state. Napoleon re-organised and strengthened the monarchial bureaucracy of the *ancient régime*. He deliberately created a highly trained, privileged, dedicated civil-service elite. So firmly did he build the administrative structure into the organisation of the nation that succeeding regimes of different political complexions have not fundamentally changed it, but only modified some aspects.

One important area of change was in the field of education, which was reconstructed and expanded in the Third Republic. Another change inaugurated in the Third Republic was the partial democratisation of local government. Mayors of communes and municipal councils were elected, and were given some independence from the control of appointed agents of the central government. This permitted some genuine life to be breathed into local government, at least on the level of the commune.

But the weight of the central bureaucracy was still overwhelming at the higher level of the *département* as under Napoleon, and to the present, the prefects of the *départements* were civil servants appointed by the government. The prime role of the prefect was and remains the exercise of a co-ordinating function over the whole field of government activity, including the police, at the *département* level. His responsibilities were predominantly upwards to the central government (directly to the Minister of the Interior) rather than in a democratic direction.

The prefects, in fact, were members of the *grands corps,* the very elite of the higher civil service. Other members of this decisive body, who are the generals of the civil service, are the members of the Council of State, the supreme administrative court and government advisory body; members of the Court of Accounts, who inspect the accounts of all government agencies, and who therefore exercise control over their activities; and the Inspectors of Finance, who are versatile financial and economic experts in charge of the Treasury.[5]

The account of the central administration is brief and incomplete, but it is enough to highlight some of its chief features. It exercises extensive control over the main areas of public life, down to and including the local levels. Marx was hardly joking when he complained that every mouse in France was under supervision. Secondly, the administration itself is rigidly hierarchised, and crucial decision-making rests with a small core of highly trained, mobile and versatile officials. Thirdly, the influence of the bureaucracy is not politically neutral. It forms the core of an administrative pattern of authority which is not easily compatible with parliamentary democracy. In the Third and Fourth Republics the central bureaucracy exercised considerable discretion in its application of reforms passed by the legislature.[6] It acted, time and again, as a selective filter through which urgent changes had to pass slowly. But under conditions of legislative impotence, the bureaucracy assumed a more active role. Under Vichy, and more recently, under General de Gaulle it acted as the auxiliary of the strong executive, serving as the medium through which he governed. The political 'intermediaries' (elected parliamentary deputies) were definitely subordinated to the executive-administrative arm of government.

Secular Education

Victorious in the MacMahon crisis of 1877, the Republicans sought to consolidate their new power by reconstructing and expanding the educational system. Whereas in Germany the *Kulturkampf* was declining in intensity at this time, the conflict between the Church and the Republican state became increasingly bitter over the issue of secular education.

The struggle for the control of education was a clash of cultural orientations between those who championed science, reason and social equality, and those who defended traditional authority. But the explosiveness of the issue in the Third Republic lay in its political dimension. The Church was largely identified with reaction against the revolutionary and modernising forces in French society. As such it had gained a privileged position in the period of monarchical restoration after the fall of Napoleon. It was looked upon as one of the pillars of stability and order, and its control of primary education was not challenged. After the revolutionary days of 1848, part of the reaction was to extend the Church's grip in this area — the Falloux law, 1850. Under the Second Empire, Napoleon III required Church support in order to legitimise his *coup d'état,* and so further concessions were made to the clergy. The long-standing identification of the Church with the active forces of political reaction was reinforced in the Third Republic when it openly supported the MacMahon side in the 1877 crisis. For the Republicans therefore, to remove as vital an area as education from the control of the church was a matter of political survival.

Another source of Republican motivation for school reform was the role attributed to education in nation-building. A large part of the blame for the defeat in the Franco-Prussian war was attributed to the primary school system. At the same time, great admiration was expressed for the virtues of the Prussian system. The secular school, organised and controlled by the State, was seen as a means of rebuilding national morale, and re-asserting national strength. It is not surprising, then, that some of the main leaders of educational reform, headed by Jules Ferry, were advocates of colonial conquest and colonial expansion. But this should be seen in the context of Franco-German relations: some of the Republican leaders advocated colonial expansion as an alternative to conflict with Germany over the territory of Alsace-Lorraine. Regardless of attitudes on external relations, the positive role of educational reforms in rebuilding the nation after the decisive military defeat was widely stressed.

In 1879, on the anniversary of the passing of the Falloux law, Ferry placed two proposed laws before the Chamber of Deputies. The first proposed to exclude all those who were not professional teachers from the Committee of Public Instruction — this was aimed at the bishops who formed a majority on the committee. The second proposal was that no one should be allowed to teach in state or religious schools if they belonged to a non-authorised religious order. Only five orders were state-authorised in France, and these did not include the main teaching orders of Jesuits, Dominicans and Marists. This blew open the school issue which was debated with great verbal violence in parliament and the press and at public meetings.

Ferry himself, as Minister of Education, was not as outspoken, but conducted the anti-clerical battle with firmness and a good sense of parliamentary strategy. Instead of wholesale legislation, he initiated a series of partial reforms, which were carried one by one. In 1881 a law was passed ensuring that public primary education would be free. It was a very popular measure because in the religious schools there was an ostentatious practice of social discrimination against children of the 'lower' classes which had offended many people. Ferry's reform brought about the association of the idea of "free education" with the idea of "equal educational opportunity".[7] The point was not forgotten in the civic textbooks, which replaced the manuals of religious instruction. A passage from one of them read in part:

"The real lack of equality, which must be deplored, is that all the children are not educated in the same manner . . . . Formerly it was thought to be perfectly natural that the middle-class child would learn latin and mathematics, while the working-class child would hardly know the alphabet. *But the Republic has changed all that.* Because it is based on the principles of equality. Thus the Republic is doing everything it can to educate the most impoverished."[8]

In 1882, Ferry put through two important laws: one made school attendance compulsory for all children between the ages of six and thirteen years, and the other secularised primary education by replacing religious instruction with civic instruction. At the same time, it abrogated the Falloux Law, withdrawing the right of ministers of religion to inspect primary schools. The independence of the secular teacher with respect to the *curé* was established, and in the folklore of the Republic the stage was set for an epic village drama with the two as antagonists. The further step of secularising the teaching personnel was delayed until 1886, when members of religious orders were forbidden to teach in state schools.

As a consequence of the Dreyfus affair, anti-clerical feeling was sharply revived, and the area of conflict was widened. The formal separation of Church and State was effected in 1905 and further anti-clerical measures included the closure of thousands of Catholic schools in the early years of the century. After that the issue faded into the background. But it is not without interest that after the fall of France in 1940, the Vichy regime blamed the military defeat on the secular schools and attempted to introduce religious instruction into the state schools. It was found impossible to do this, so the regime settled for a policy of state subsidies to the private Catholic schools. The provisional government immediately repealed them at the Liberation. Even then, the issue was not closed as the question of financial aid to Catholic schools raised controversy in both the Fourth and Fifth Republics.

Two of the topics which have been treated in the previous chapters on Italy and Germany — the labour movement and economic development — are more conveniently discussed in the case of France in the context of the inter-war period (see Chapter eight). These aspects of French development, together with the political and educational changes described in this chapter, contribute towards an explanation of why Fascism did not become a mass-based movement capable of taking power in France.

NOTES

1. Michel Crozier, *The Bureaucratic Phenomenon*, Tavistock 1964.
2. Nicholas Wahl, "French Political System" in Samuel H. Beer and Adam Ulam (eds.), *Patterns of Government*, Random House 2nd ed. 1962.
3. See for example David Thomson, *Democracy in France Since 1870*, Oxford, 4th ed., p40.
4. *Wahl*, p291.
5. After the Second World War, Inspectors of Finance have also served as heads of nationalised corporations and other public bodies. They are influential in many sections of the planning commission as well. See Jean Blondel and E. Drexel Godfrey, Jr., *The Government of France*, Methuen 1968, Chapter 7.
6. Thomson, p56; Wahl, p280.
7. Georges Duveau, *Les Instituteurs*, (Paris, Seuil, 1957), pp118-9.
8. Quoted in *ibid.*, p119.

Part 2 FROM WAR TO WAR

The first three chapters in this section discuss the rise of Fascism in Italy and Germany, and Fascist reorganisation and control of society. The chapter on France provides a contrasting situation where Fascism did not succeed in attaining power. The selection of topics suggests parallels and contrasts in the situations of the three countries — the post-war circumstances, the problem of nationalism, the social bases and various appeals of Fascism and the roles of labour, business, landowners, the judiciary and the Army. The analysis of the situation in France is followed by a theoretical discussion (Chapter nine) of the nature of the social process underlying the emergence of Fascist dictatorship.

Chapter 5 Italy: Fascism

The brittle structures of Italian society were severely shaken by the First World War. Though on the side of the victors, Italian hopes of gaining territory were only partially fulfilled. Compared with the promises made in 1915, and the exaggerated hopes of the nationalists, the results of the Versailles Peace Conference were disappointing. The South Tyrol and Trieste were given to Italy, but no former German colonial possessions were obtained, and the Allies supported Yugoslavian claims on Dalmatia. Italian nationalists therefore regarded the conclusion of the war as a 'mutilated victory'. As in Germany, right-wing extremists expressed feelings of national humiliation by branding as traitors those who supported the Wilsonian peace settlement. In defiance of the government, d'Annunzio, war hero and poet of the radical right, led an illegal occupation of Fiume (today Rijeka), a town in the disputed border area between Italy and Yugoslavia. Despite its illegality, many army officers were prepared to follow d'Annunzio and the *Arditi* shock-troops in the autumn of 1919. It was symptomatic of the disturbances created by the war in the institutional framework of the Italian state and society.

Magnifying these disturbances was the economic crisis in the aftermath of the war. Characterised by falling production and runaway inflation it had a drastic effect on the middle strata, the peasantry and the working class. For the tradesmen and artisans, small businessmen, small property owners, members of the liberal professions and those living on fixed incomes, the severe inflation meant a serious threat of economic ruin, if not actual poverty. These fears were intensified by grave social unrest among the peasantry and urban workers.

Peasant land seizures commenced in the summer of 1919, spearheaded by returning veterans who could not find employment. Land-hungry peasants occupied the wastelands and even some cultivated land around Rome belonging to absentee landlords. In the following months peasant occupations also occurred in the South and in the central regions of the North. In addition, peasants and farm workers in the central regions and the North were becoming increasingly organised, and were raising radical demands. There were two distinct socio-political tendencies among them. The "Reds" were the peasants and especially the farm labourers *(braccianti)* organised in

48

trade unions affiliated with the General Confederation of Labour and the Socialist party. They demanded regular work and an end to the large-scale unemployment. Quite distinct were the "Whites", Catholic groups who organised the small peasantry and share-croppers on a co-operative basis, and agitated for land redistribution.

These tendencies were anathema to the landowners. Land seizure and demands for land redistribution were direct threats, while the development of peasant co-operatives and the unionisation of farm labour implied far-reaching changes in the traditional pattern of dominance, which the landowners refused to accept. The strength of the landowners' position was that they controlled the limited employment chances which were desperately sought by crowds of landless *braccianti.* They had always reacted to peasant demands with violence, but in the aftermath of the First World War, sporadic local violence was not sufficient to suppress the extensive agitation and the spreading network of co-operation. Instead of searching for a bargaining relationship with the co-operatives and union organisations, the landowners' objectives were to eliminate them and to enforce the traditional relations of dominance and subordination. Towards the end of 1920, they turned to Fascism as a means of destroying the various organisations of the peasants and farm labourers. Fascist terror reigned throughout vast areas of the countryside.[1] By the middle of 1921, the Fascists were in occupation of most of the Po valley, and the greater part of Tuscany, Umbria and Apulia, as well as parts of Venetia and Piedmont.[2]

Meanwhile in the northern urban areas there were strikes and agitations, which culminated in the factory occupation movement. In the immediate post-war period, the General Confederation of Labour (CGL) experienced a dramatic increase in membership. From under a quarter of a million in 1918, membership approached one-and-a-half million by the end of 1919, and was over two million by the following September. Nearly 900,000 farm workers, 160,000 metalworkers, 200,000 building workers and 47,000 railway and transport workers were organised, and in a militant mood. Under their pressure, the eight-hour day was introduced in many industries, grievance committees were established, and collective agreements negotiated. But the severe inflation created continuous demands for wage increases. And more sweeping demands were raised: for the nationalisation of industry, and for the creation of factory councils which would enable workers to participate in, or even control, the running of the factories. These demands were not satisfied, but were perpetuated by a tidal wave of

strikes: in 1919 there were 1,663 strikes (over 200 in agriculture); in
1920 there were 1,881 (nearly 200 in agriculture); and in 1921 there
were over 1,000 (under 100 in agriculture).[3]

The response of the employers was to organise themselves for
combat. In March 1920, at the height of the strike movement, the first
national congress of Italian industrialists met at Milan to form
Confindustria, the General Confederation of Industry. It included both
the chief industries and three quarters of the smaller firms. The
conference drafted a detailed plan of counter-acting union demands. In
August, the General Confederation of Agriculture was formed for
similar purposes. It won wide membership among holders of diverse
kinds of agricultural property, including wealthy peasants. The creation
of these national organisations meant that industrialists and landlords
would no longer fight in stray units. To the intermittant and localised
efforts of the workers, they could now oppose strongly centralised
forces. They were immensely strengthened by the failure of the
workers' "factory occupation" movement of September 1920.

The factory occupations started in Milan in response to a lock-out
by the Alfa Romeo Company, and quickly spread throughout the
North. Giolitti, who had become Prime Minister once again in June
1920, adopted a neutral stance. His policy was to let the workers
remain in control of the factories until they became disillusioned about
their ability to pay themselves wages and to keep production going. The
labour leaders were divided. The Maximalists wanted to seize all
property and establish a Communist state. But the national council of
the CGL, which would have had to carry this out, wanted much less.
They wanted workers' control of the factories, by which they really
meant limited participation somewhat along the lines of the British
joint-production committees of the 1940s. By the middle of September
feelers were put out for settlement. Then representatives of workers
and employers met in Turin, and finally accepted Giolitti's conciliation
which included the proposal that workers be given the right to
participate in the management of the factories through plant
committees. Factories were evacuated by the end of the month, and
work resumed at the beginning of October.[4]

The factory occupation movement had lasted one month and, as was
soon apparent, the workers gained very little from it. They were
demoralised and disillusioned.[5] But the employers had been severely
shocked, and feared that Russian Bolshevism was stalking them. Their
deeply ingrained sense of property and authority was hard hit, their
fury and desire for revenge aroused. Workers' solidarity dissolved and

the enormous social force represented by the unions melted away. By 1921 membership in the CGL had dropped over thirty per cent, and by the following year it was under half a million and declining steadily. This demoralisation coincided with the steep rise of Fascist power.

As Giolitti had envisaged, the failure of the occupation movement broke the morale and solidarity of labour. But it had two other consequences which he had not foreseen. Employer resolve, organisation and combativeness were strengthened. They were now prepared to support Fascism both politically and financially. Moreover, the way the government handled the occupation movement did not appear to the threatened middle class as a clever waiting tactic. It seemed positive proof of the State's impotence. In their eyes, the State had abdicated its prime responsibility of restoring order and stability.[6]

It was only when the possibility of a Socialist revolution, or the firm grounding of democratic institutions on the basis of a centre-left coalition had collapsed, that Fascism was able to develop. The Fascist movement was powerless in the early months of 1920; but in the last three months of that year, after the failure of the factory occupations, it increasingly dominated the scene. Fascists attacked Socialist-administered municipalities, co-operatives and trade unions. In April 1921 they destroyed the labour organisations of Turin and showed Communist threats of reprisal to be hollow. The pattern was repeated throughout the country, with the result that all autonomous trade union and political activity was first paralysed and then eliminated. The government did nothing to stop the Fascist attacks; the police and the Army were given no instructions. Fascism was able to exploit and dominate the tide of reaction on the Right, and the sense of disarray and hopelessness on the Left.

The old political leaders thought that Fascism could be absorbed into the liberal institutional structure with which they were familiar.[7] They thought its sting could be removed, if a little "responsible" exercise of power was granted to it. As was to happen in Germany later, there was a failure to understand the nature of the changes which were taking place, a failure to appreciate the dynamic thrust of Fascism. For there was a movement which was not simply another minority group on the political scene, but a movement which operated on the basis of murderous ruthlessness — a movement dedicated to the attainment of power, and devoid of any ethical principles or scruples. Moreover, it had the political and financial backing of the most powerful agrarian and industrial and financial interests and it could operate with the connivance and sympathy of many local authorities and of the police and army officers.[8] Furthermore, the backbone of the movement consisted of young, exasperated and determined people. Ex-officers, university students, sons of landowners and industrialists and people from the lower middle class who saw no future for themselves under the existing conditions, except as unemployed or underemployed hangers-on. And their actions gained popular support from those sections of the middle class who were in the throes of an unprecedented economic and social crisis — teachers, office workers, civil servants, business and professional men.

Although the personality of the leader should not be overestimated, neither can it be ignored. Mussolini had a superb sense of strategy and tactics in the struggle for power. He knew how to build a movement, control it and inspire confidence. To appreciate the point, one has only to contrast his comprehension of the political situation, and his ability to act, with the failure of the leaders of the other political parties and movements to grasp the problems. .

Creation of The Fascist State

It is worth considering the possible alternatives to Fascism in Italy. It was theoretically possible for the mass democratic parties, the Socialists and the Popular Party, to assume power jointly on the basis of a centre-left coalition. But a number of factors prevented this: the attitude of the Popular party and the Vatican was negative, as will be discussed below; Socialist uncertainties were increased by the formation of the Communist party as a breakaway movement; and the reaction which fed the Fascist movement was much too strong to be held back by patchwork coalitions. In fact, given the breakdown of the liberal political system and the strength of conservative forces, a different alternative might have come into existence: the establishment of a traditionalist autocracy as was later to occur in Spain and Portugal. However this presupposes a degree of economic stagnation and social immobility which was not characteristic of Italy. In the North the process of modernisation, that is of industrialisation and urbanisation, was relatively slow but continuous. The active, modernising forces of liberalism had been strong enough to unify the country and to create a national state more than half a century earlier. They could not be superseded by a traditional, stagnant conservatism. A new and much more drastic political concept was required: a concept which was both deeply conservative, because based on a tide of reaction, and in a certain direction, radical. When Mussolini said, "I am a revolutionary and a reactionary" he hinted at the essential nature of Fascism as radicalised conservatism.[9]

In order to consolidate his power, Mussolini had to go far beyond the immobilism of a traditional autocracy. He created the Fascist state which attempted to exercise total control over all aspects of a society in a continuous process of modernisation. Of course this was not at once apparent, and the regime developed rather slowly. After the March on Rome at the end of October 1922, Mussolini governed with a coalition cabinet which included Nationalists, Catholics and Liberals. During 1923 he quietly consolidated his power, re-staffing the prefectures, the police offices and the state administration with Fascists. Then he absorbed the Nationalists into his own party and dislodged the non-Fascists from his cabinet. In the election of April 1924, the Fascists won sixty five per cent of the votes, with the help of a specially designed electoral method backed by wholesale violence and intimidation. In response to the outrage, the Socialist deputy Matteotti courageously denounced fascist methods in parliament. He was shortly afterwards murdered; but the revulsion in the press and in the country was so great that for a while it seemed that the regime might not survive.

Mussolini was shocked at the volume and duration of public criticism, and the steps he took to prevent it from happening again marked a new phase in the regime's development. At the beginning of January 1925, he plainly assumed responsibility for the murder and challenged the Chamber of Deputies to bring action in the High Court of Justice. With this speech, the true dictatorship began. The other political parties were dissolved; the powers of the prime minister were greatly expanded, and the role of parliament reduced; local government was more tightly regimented; control over mass communications was established; the civil service was purged; and terrorism was unleashed on a broader scale to crush all forms of dissent. A tribunal for the defence of the state was set up in November 1926 to try "political crimes". The Fascist party emerged as the central institution of political and social control. Provincial party secretaries were established alongside the provincial prefects. The Fascist militia grew alongside the regular army and would have liked to transform the officer corps into an instrument of the party. Education came under Fascist influence, children and youth were organised into quasi-military units, and cultural and leisure activities were politically structured. The Nazi leisure-time organisation for workers, with the curious name of "Strength through Joy", was modelled on the Italian *Dopolavoro*.

There was one significant area, however, where Mussolini was forced to move cautiously: in his relations with the Vatican. To appreciate the problems here, it is useful to look at the aftermath of the First World War from the Catholic point of view.

Church and Fascist State

Only a certain group of conservative Catholics, known as Clerico-Moderates, had favoured Italian intervention in the war. They were primarily motivated by fear of internal revolution in Italy, as exemplified by events during "Red Week" in June 1914. They saw the war as a means of consolidating internal order and the *status quo*. But in general Catholics were strong neutralists, and as the war dragged on, with its massive sacrifice of life, there was a tremendous growth of anti-war feeling in the country. It provided an important impetus to Socialism and to movements of reform – within Catholic organisations as well. The former conservative domination within these organisations was eroded and a new type of leader appeared, such as the Christian Democrats, Gronchi and Tupini, and above all Don Luigi Sturzo. Sturzo, a priest, became the liberal head of Catholic Action and organised the *Popolari,* the independent Popular party. With Vatican approval it was launched in January 1919. It was conceived as a party of Catholics with liberal inclinations; not as a Catholic party of a confessional nature. It was to act autonomously, independent of direct Vatican control.

In the November 1919 elections the Popular party gained twenty per cent of the votes, second only to the Socialists with thirty five per cent. If a centre-left coalition had been possible, democratic institutions would have been strengthened. But the Popular party, standing for class integration rather than social change, blocked the Socialists.[10] Between 1920 and 1922 they acted as auxiliaries of Giolitti in his efforts to stabilise a situation which was building up into a fearsome crisis. The Popular party could not play a more positive role because it was internally divided. It finally split in 1923 and 1924. Its right wing decided to support Fascism in order, it was said, to save constitutional legality. The rest of the party put up a last ineffectual resistance. One major handicap in resisting Fascism was that the Vatican had virtually abandoned the party. It had been losing favour with the Vatican for some time because it had deliberately shelved the whole Roman question. It was viewed as "no better than the Liberals"[11] who remained enemy number one. When Pius XI became Pope in the winter of 1922, the process was brought to its conclusion. He restored conservative domination of Catholic organisations, and worked against

Christian Democratic influence. Moreover, the possibility of an alliance between the Popular party and the Socialists in opposition to Fascism was openly condemned by the Church. The Jesuits campaigned against it, and in September 1924 at the height of the Matteoti crisis the Pope himself spoke against it.

In fact, a new game was being played between the State and the Vatican. Mussolini realised the value of religion as a means of securing his power. The crucifix was put back into the school rooms. Bishops were invited to bless Fascist party standards. The Church was generously compensated for its material losses of the past. In return, the Vatican was encouraged to abandon the Popular party and the Catholic trade unions. The Clerico-Fascists exercised strong pressures in support of Mussolini. Including the right-wing of the Popular party, they saw the liberal-democratic world as a Masonic conspiracy which the Fascist power-state was destined to sweep away. As long as the constitutionality of Fascism could be preserved, they felt that the rift between Church and State could be overcome. As for Fascist brutality, their consciences were soothed with the view that the Liberal State had been guilty of persecuting Catholicism. There followed three years, from 1926 to 1929, of difficult negotiation for a settlement of relations with the Fascist regime.

An agreement was formally reached in February 1929. The terms of the settlement are still in existence in Italy. The treaty declared Catholicism to be the sole religion of the State, and the sovereignity and independence of Vatican City was affirmed. For its own part, the Holy See declared the Roman question settled, and recognised the Kingdom of Italy under the dynasty of the House of Savoy, with Rome as its capital. The Concordat assured the Church of wide influence. Religious teaching was extended from primary education to the secondary schools, and the Church authorities had the right to approve teachers and textbooks. Graduates of church schools were guaranteed equal standing with state school graduates. The Church was given special tax exemptions and privileges. Religious marriage was given civil effects. Moreover, Catholic Action, a lay organisation under the direct control of the Church, was allowed to continue as long as its activities were confined strictly to religious purposes.

The Fascist regime in Italy, unlike the Nazi totalitarian structure, was not able to establish a complete ideological hegemony. It had to make concessions to the Church. But the Church was not a free agent. It placed its survival on caution, and carefully avoided becoming a rallying point for anti-Fascist opposition. In foreign affairs, the Church supported some of Mussolini's actions, notably the Ethiopian War and aid to Franco in his destruction of the Spanish Republic. But Mussolini's enchantment with Hitler was not welcomed, and in 1939 Pope Pius XII strongly urged Italy to stay out of the war because the survival of the Church itself might be placed in jeopardy.

The Corporate Structure

The regime did not immediately start to build a controlled economy. On the contrary, government expenditure was initially reduced, and private capitalism was given a freer rein in matters of wages and taxes. The policy coincided with the return of prosperity in Italy, and met with the approval of liberal economists. But in the summer of 1925 the policy changed in the direction of protection and government controls, and by the early 1930s, national self-sufficiency (autarchy) became the principal aim. In connection with these changes, the notion of the Corporate State, proclaimed in 1926, was gradually elaborated through a series of legislative enactments.

The idea was to regulate the conflicts between capital and labour by renovating the guild system. Syndicates of employers and workers were to collaborate to settle their problems, always bearing in mind that their mutual objective was to further the national interest. A complex structure of industrial and agricultural corporations was created, capped by a National Council of Corporations, and presided over by a special Ministry of Corporations. But the corporate super-structure was in reality little more than an elaborate ideological facade. The corporations did not formulate economic policy; this remained the prerogative of the dictator and his associates. The corporations were simply a means through which the business community could work in conjunction with the party and government bureaucracies.[12] In the process the workers' interests were largely ignored.

The outstanding characteristic of the twenty-year period of Fascist rule from the point of view of labour was that the unions were converted into controlled Fascist syndicates which functioned as part of the apparatus of party and government.[13] Since the power to strike was withdrawn, and other controls were imposed, the workers' representatives were in a decidedly subordinate position. As a result, real wages did not rise above pre-First World War levels. It is sometimes stated that living standards nevertheless improved because of elaborate social service provisions. But the services were of more value to the regime as good publicity than of real value to the population. Actual expenditures on social services absorbed a smaller proportion of national income than it did in most of the other European countries.[14]

Perhaps the most important innovation was the Institute for Industrial Reconstruction (IRI), which survived the downfall of the regime and played a very important role in post-war economic development, participating in three quarters of the investments made by the State in industry. The IRI was created in 1933 to subsidise private industry, which was badly shaken by the depression, and to save the three main commercial banks which had been over-generous in extending long-term loans to private companies. Within a few years, the IRI controlled many of the firms in the armament and mechanical industries, and had a wide variety of other manufacturing and banking interests. The IRI was the main agency through which the Fascist state could intervene and support private enterprise in a period of crisis without adopting the politically explosive method of nationalisation. Notwithstanding the few and minor unwelcome measures which the Fascist regime imposed on industrialists, the collaboration between the two was relatively successful. Although Fascist aims of achieving economic self-sufficiency and a high level war economy were not remotely realised, industrial production rose considerably between 1935 and 1939 and an enlarged basis was laid for post-war developments. Before it could be realised of course, the political and material rubble left behind in the destruction of Fascism had to be cleared.

The War and Resistance

Under Fascism the various sources of power were concentrated in a single ruling centre. In the spheres of politics, economics, administration, mass communications, education, leisure, the police and judiciary an effective domination was established. Access to positions of influence and prestige in all significant areas of public life were carefully controlled and restricted. For example, there were various decrees in the 1920s which dismissed politically suspect teachers from their jobs. The danger of dismissal forced the rest to conform, especially as a Fascist Teachers' Association was created to exercise constant surveillance and pressure. In 1931, every university professor had to swear an oath of allegiance to the regime; only eleven out of 1200 refused. In 1933 it was decreed that all new teachers must join the Fascist party; in 1937 membership of the Fascist Teachers' Association was made compulsory; and by the middle of the 1930s, pressure was building up to force teachers to take an active part as officers in the quasi-military youth organisations. The activities of these organisations, devoted to the inculcation of "Fascist culture" took up much of the pupils' time and cut heavily into regular school hours.[15] In the civil service, similar pressures were at work. From 1933 no one could get a civil service job unless he was a party member. In this respect, the Italians went further than the Nazis.

Although the Catholic Church was not brought under strict control, its room for manoeuvre was circumscribed and its influence was used in support of the regime. The officer corps was irritated by the party militia and was somewhat aloof from Fascism, but there were no Army plans for rebellion.

The replacement of independent organisations (trade unions, cultural and youth associations) by Fascist structures was an attempt to convert the naked coercive aspect of power into legitimate authority. It was quite successful. Participation in the various youth organisations was high during the 1930s, particularly in the urban areas. Up to February 1939, membership was voluntary, depending on the consent of parents or guardians. But there were many attractions, as well as pressures, which account for the vast enrolment which eventually topped the five-million mark. There were inexpensive summer camps and excursions, and a wide range of recreational facilities. Parents, especially in the middle class, wanted their children to be able to have party membership as it was essential for future career prospects. Similarly, *Dopolavoro* provided inexpensive vacations and excursions and educational facilities for hundreds of thousands of workers. Whereas membership in the Fascist syndicates was compulsory for workers, membership in the *Dopolavoro* was not. The situation differed from Germany, where all members of the Labour Front had to join "Strength through Joy". Even so, membership in *Dopolavoro* was large, growing in the 1930s to over four million. To a considerable extent, then, legitimation of the regime was achieved on certain levels. For a variety of reasons people were willing to accept or at least to acquiesce in the situation.

But the existence of a rigid power structure created opposition and resistance. Under normal democratic conditions, there is general consensus about the nature of the political system, so that conflicts are incorporated into a "civic" normative structure and the role of opposition is legitimate. Under Fascism, opposition in matters of ideology, interests, and socio-cultural values are necessarily opposition over ends, that is, anti-Fascist. So that as opposition developed, it became a major source of change in the social structure. However, there were differences in the German and Italian situations which must be emphasised. Brutal and vicious as was the Italian repressive apparatus, it paled in comparison with the grim atrocity of the Nazi dictatorship. The Nazis were effective in shattering the resistance potential and in cowing opposition. Resistance in Germany was fragmented, individualised; it never attained the public force of an open resistance movement as in Italy. The difference lies not only in the repressive methods; the regime was accepted in a more calculated and opportunistic way in Italy than it was in Germany. The Nazi movement struck a deeper Messianic chord in the German middle class; it was redemption, salvation and glory for the Germans in a way that many Italians, who went along with Fascism, found unrealistic. The significant point is that the development of an open resistance movement in Italy, during the war, contributed to the destruction of Fascism from the inside and opened the way for a return to a democratic system. The Italian resistance was a popular struggle for freedom. In Germany there was no comparable development of active resistance against Nazism.

The development of resistance in Italy therefore merits further attention. After 1925, the anti-Fascist tendencies were scattered. Inside Italy, there was an underground skeleton Communist organisation, and some anti-Fascists in the Vatican. But the latter, although they played a role in the resistance during the war, were kept in check. The alliance between the regime and the Church was consistently upheld by the upper-class group of Clerico-Fascists, who had broken away from the Popular party. They were the favoured intermediaries between Church and State, and were supported by a strong pro-Fascist tendency within the Vatican itself, which was especially prominent among the Jesuits. Overt resistance appeared useless after the reaction to the Matteotti murder had died down, and people accepted the regime if not through conviction, then through necessity and calculation. The Liberals, including Giolitti and Croce, admitted to the need for dictatorship, and confined themselves to a careful intellectual rather than political opposition.[16] Outside Italy, anti-Fascist groups led the hard life of exiles, chiefly in France. These included Anarchist, Republicans, Socialists and Communists, as well as influential individuals such as Carlo Rosselli, Don Luigi Sturzo, F.S. Nitti, G. Salvemini and Carlo Sforza.[17]

As the dictatorship became more firmly established, and basked in a certain amount of foreign approval, the dictator became increasingly impulsive in his behaviour. He adopted a belligerent foreign policy which was predicated on the disciplining of the Italian nation. The party was increasingly centralised, and its grip on the State tightened. Even though overt resistance was crushed, the political police and militia became more powerful. The demands for colonial conquest became imperative, and the drive for a self-sufficient war economy commenced. In October 1935 Ethiopa (Abyssinia) was attacked, and in the following year Mussolini intervened in the Spanish Civil War on Franco's side. In 1936 the Rome/Berlin Axis came into being; Mussolini was enchanted with the dazzling prospects of imperial glory.

Musssolini did not enter the Second World War until 10th June 1940 when he joined the attack on an already defeated France. At the time it seemed to be a bet on the winners. But given the bungling of the Italian military efforts (in Greece and Africa), a growing subordination to Germany developed, and with it discontent grew. Hundreds of thousands of Italian workers were drafted into labour service in Germany, and were treated as members of an inferior breed. The Gestapo arrived in Rome, and it was not long before Italy was treated as a colony of the Reich. The realisation grew that Italy had entered the war irresponsibly, and had no idea of what it could expect to gain. There were strikes, clandestine newspapers, widespread disaffection at all levels of society, plots against Mussolini, and from May 1942 onwards drastic purges inside the Fascist party.

The Allies landed in North Africa in the autumn of 1942, and in the following spring they landed in Sicily. In July the mainland was invaded. On the night of 24th and 25th July 1943, a fortnight after the invasion, the Fascist Grand Council adopted a resolution of no confidence in Mussolini. The next day the King signed the appointment of Marshal Badoglio as prime minister. The Fascist party was abolished and the leading Fascists were dismissed from their positions. The first of the transitional war-time governments was set up with a cabinet of "non-political" administrators, governing without parties or parliament. It was a timely palace revolution. When the Allies completed the occupation of southern Italy, they tried to foster a new Italian government. At first there was deadlock as the anti-Fascist parties refused to co-operate with the discredited King and his Marshal. But in March 1944 the Soviet Union recognised the Badoglio government and the Communist party broke the deadlock by agreeing to a coalition government.[18] The Christian Democrats promptly joined them.

The Communists were led by Palmiro Togliatti, who returned from exile in Russia in March 1944. The Communist record of active resistance during the war gave them tremendous influence at the grass-roots level. Luigi Longo, who assumed the leadership of the

Communist party on Togliatti's death in 1964, was at the time the most important commander of resistance forces in the German-occupied North. The Socialists were not as well organised as the Communists, and had to reconstruct their party in 1942 and 1943. Under the leadership of Pietro Nenni, who had inherited the old Maximalist tradition, they joined Togliatti in a united front of the Left. Later, in the municipal elections of April 1946, they demonstrated the strength of the Socialist tradition by defeating both the Communists and the Christian Democrats in Milan. Included in the 1944 coalition was Alcide de Gasperi, leader of the Christian Democrats, who were the successors of the Popular party. They had a solid basis in the Catholic action movement, which the Fascists had been able to handcuff but not destroy. By taking a position in the centre of the political spectrum, the Christian Democrats played a crucial role in the post-war reconstruction. De Gasperi was prime minister from December 1945 to August 1953.

From 1943 onwards the representatives of the Action Party, the Liberals and the other main parties had agreed to co-operate with each other, and to play down their differences until the war was over. They worked together in the various Committees of National Liberation (CNL) and with less harmony in the various coalition ministries.[19]

The three parts of Italy underwent different military and political experiences during the fighting.[20] There was no actual resistance movement in southern Italy,[21] which was occupied by the Allies. In September 1943 an armistice between Italy and the Anglo-American forces was announced, but the Germans continued to fight. The Gustav line was established to the north of Naples by late autumn 1943. Central Italy, from Rome to Florence, remained under German rule until the summer of 1944. The liberation of Rome itself in June 1944 was accomplished without a battle because the Vatican had successfully negotiated with the Germans for a peaceful withdrawal from the city as the Allied forces advanced northwards from Cassino and Anzio. But north of Rome the fighting was again difficult, and the Italian resistance was military engaged. A popular insurrection led by the CNL contributed to the liberation of Florence, which had been made possible by the advances of the Allied forces. The pattern repeated itself in northern Italy where the CNL had been fighting for over eighteen months.

It was not until April 1945, as the Russians approached Berlin, that the Allies liberated northern Italy. While all the political parties contributed to the resistance struggle, the role of the Communist party was outstanding. The attitude of the Allied authorities was that while they wished to co-operate with the resistance, it was not to become too important and in particular, the Allied authorities did not want a political revolution to occur.[22] At the end of December 1944, an agreement was signed between the Italian government in Rome and the North Italian Liberation Committee, whereby the latter was legally recognised by the Rome government as its delegate. In turn, the Liberation Committee recognised the Rome government as the sole legitimate authority. This was a means of controlling the potentially revolutionary impetus of the liberation movement spearheaded by the Communist party. By the end of the war, therefore, Italy was governed by a coalition of the anti-Fascist parties.

NOTES

1. A. Rossi, *The Rise of Italian Fascism 1918-1922*, Methuen 1938 transl., pp90 *ff.*
2. *Ibid.*, p119.
3. Horowitz, p141.
4. *Ibid.*, p152.
5. Rossi, pp75-82.
6. Herman Finer, *Mussolini's Italy*, Gollancz 1935, pp126-7.
7. Rossi, p333; Finer, p134.
8. Rossi, pp104-5; Mack Smith, p348.
9. John Weiss, *The Fascist Tradition*, Harper & Row 1967, p92.
10. Webster, p58.
11. Quoted in *ibid.*, p78.
12. H. Stuart Hughes, *The United States and Italy*, Harvard UP 1965, rev.ed., pp78-9; S. William Halperin, *Mussolini and Italian Fascism*, Van Nostrand 1964, pp58-9.
13. Towards the close of the Second World War, Mussolini sought to strengthen the position of his "Social Republic" (in the German-occupied North) by introducing leftist policies. He initiated a programme of "socialisation" of large industrial firms. But resistance leaders appealed to workers in these factories to avoid involvement in what they described as a "colossal fraud". The appeal was highly successful, and only a minute proportion of workers participated in the relevant elections. At the Fiat plant in Turin, for example, only 405 valid votes were cast of a possible 32,676. Charles F. Delzell, *Mussolini's Enemies,* Princeton UP 1961, pp473-4.
14. Mack Smith, pp405-7.
15. Finer, pp468 *ff.*
16. Mack Smith, p432.
17. Rosselli founded the *Giustizia e Libertà* group, a spiritual predecessor of the Party of Action, which played an important role in

the Armed Resistance 1943-5. Nitti was a former Liberal premier and early opponent of Fascism who went into exile in 1924. Both Sforza, a Republican Senator, and Salvemini, professor of history, were influential anti-Fascist writers. For details on these and other influential members of the anti-Fascist exile and resistance, see Delzell, especially Chapter II.

18. Delzell, pp337-9; Federico Chabod, *A History of Italian Fascism*, Weidenfeld and Nicholson, 1963 transl. p103.

19. For a discussion of difficulties, see Delzell, pp459-63.

20. Chabod, p101.

21. A spontaneous revolt in Naples at the end of September 1943 forced German troops to withdraw from the city. See Delzell, pp283-4.

22. *Ibid.*, pp453, 463-7, 493-4; Chabod, pp114-6.

Chapter 6 Germany: The Weimar Republic

The Weimar Republic was created in the aftermath of Germany's surrender, and so it was easy for propagandists to associate it with the stigma of defeat and national humiliation. The more so since the surrender came as a panic surprise to the German people, who had not been informed of the true military situation. They had been led to believe that the 1918 spring offensive in the west, following Bolshevik Russia's withdrawal from the war, was a sign of impending victory. They were not told about the successes of the Allied counter-offensive which began in August 1918 and built up into an invincible position by the end of September. They were not told that in face of the hopeless military situation the German High Command had asked for an armistice. As far as they could see the German Army was still intact, fighting in France and Belgium, and the homeland was not invaded. Then why was there a surrender? What had happened? Who was responsible?

The Weimar Republic was endowed with a constitution, which in 1919 was hailed as the most democratic constitution in the world; but the origins of the Republic were not democratic nor was the social environment in which it operated hospitable to democratic ideas and values. The basic fact was that responsible parliamentary government was instituted in Germany at the end of the war *on the decision of the High Command under Ludendorff, without any pressure from the political parties.*

A democratic coalition had been possible in the *Reichstag* since 1912, when the Social Democrats and the Centre returned from the election as the leading parties. If joined by the Left Liberals, a clear-cut majority coalition would have come into existence. But even as late as the winter and spring of 1917-18, these parties made no effort to gain effective control of the government, which in any case was completely subservient to the dictates of the High Command. What united the politicians of these parties was not their urge for political reform, but their patriotism as expressed in the political truce and the voting of war credits. The most dramatic piece of evidence illustrating this attitude was their acceptance of the Treaty of Brest-Litovsk. In July 1917 these parties passed a resolution in the *Reichstag* which desired "peace without annexations". But after the October Revolution in Russia when the Bolsheviks withdrew from the war (following their policy of "revolutionary defeatism" to its logical conclusion), it appeared that Germany had won a major victory in the east. The German High Command dictated unfavourable terms including the annexation of vast areas of Russian territory, which the new Russian government was obliged to accept. The *Reichstag* endorsed the Treaty, even though it flagrantly contradicted the previous resolution of "peace without annexations". The Social Democrats did not vote against it, but took the neutral position of abstaining. The attitude of the democratic parties revealed their full compliance and involvement with the existing autocratic political framework. In the last two years of the war, with Hindenburg as Supreme Commander and Ludendorff as his Quartermaster-General, the High Command completely dominated the successive Chancellors — Bethman-Hollweg, Michaelis and Hertling.

But at the end of the war the High Command relinquished its power. It was not forced to do so by democratic parties bent on initiating social and political changes; on the contrary, it transferred power to the reluctant parties in the *Reichstag* for purely strategic reasons. It seemed that only a new, democratic government in Germany would be able to negotiate an armistice in which the Army would be preserved, if nothing else of the Imperial apparatus. A further consideration, with ominous implications, was that Ludendorff held the *Reichstag* responsible for the hopeless military situation because of its "defeatist" peace resolutions, and it should therefore dishonour itself by negotiating for peace with the enemy, while the Army stayed aloof and nursed its honour. This was the beginning of the "stab-in-the-back" legend in which the democratic politicians, and particularly the Socialists, were blamed for the defeat. It was one of those 'Big Lies' which people are ready to believe when the truth is more painful to them.

In the chaos of the last few months of 1918 there were popular pressures for radical social change. But the agitation occurred within a context of defeat, hunger and collapse. In October and November 1918, there was a series of mutinies in the fleet; spontaneous strikes and demonstrations in Berlin; the formation of workers' and soldiers' councils, modelled on the Russian soviets; and the possibility of a socialist revolution led by the Spartacists and Independent Social Democrats. A knowledge of the origin and political outlook of these groups is basic to the comprehension of the sequence of events known as the November Revolution.

It was noted that the Social Democratic Party was divided between a radical left wing and a reformist wing which obtained increasing support from trade union leaders. Between reformists and radicals, there was a large centre group to which the bulk of the party leadership belonged. Essentially they supported the Erfurt programme of 1891 with its harmless synthesis of Marxist revolutionary objectives and moderate short-term aims. In the early years of the twentieth century, they attempted to hold the balance between the two extremist wings. But after the 1905 dispute over the question of a revolutionary political strike, they aligned themselves more consistently with the revisionists against the revolutionary group led by Rosa Luxemburg. As this occurred, the composition of the party executive gradually became dominated by the reformists, replacing the old leaders who had belonged to the centre. For example, when August Bebel died in 1913, he was replaced on the executive by the career official, Friedrich Ebert, who was to become the first President of the Weimar Republic. In short, reformist strength in the party increased as the labour movement grew in size and strength.

On the outbreak of war the radical wing had no hope of influencing the movement against joining the military camp. But as the war progressed and circumstances at home became more difficult, this domination could not go unchallenged. In the hungry "turnip winter" of 1916-17 there was growing public support for the anti-war stand of Karl Liebknecht and his followers. The party leadership reacted by tightening discipline, by seizing the newspaper *Vorwärts* (the central party organ) from the control of the leftists, and then by expelling all opposition members. The violence of the reaction was not surprising if it is recalled that the prestige and status of the labour leaders was enhanced by their participation in the administration of the war effort. But the reaction also reflected the great distance which had been created between them and the rank-and-file membership. By being unable to tolerate the anti-war dissension within their own ranks, they opened the way for the creation of a new party on their left flank.

The Independent Social Democratic Party (USPD), established at Easter 1917, was an anti-war party consisting of three main orientations: on the right, there was Eduard Bernstein and a few revisionist intellectuals, together with Karl Kautsky; in the centre and comprising the bulk of the new party, were those left centrists who, although not revolutionaries, opposed both the war and the suspension of opposition which was enshrined in the political truce; and on the left were the followers of Rosa Luxemburg and Liebknecht organised in the Spartacus League. At its inception, the party numbered between fifty and sixty thousand, and grew to about one hundred thousand members by 1918. However, its influence was broader than that, especially in the workers' and soldiers' councils, and in the giant metal workers' union as well as in several smaller unions. In fact, it gained so much support in this period that it had equal representation with the Majority Social Democrats in the Provisional Government (which came into being upon the abdication of the Kaiser in November 1918). Although its popularity and size continued to grow over the next few years, it was not a stable political entity and it disintegrated under the fierce pressures of the period.

At the national congress of workers' and soldiers' councils, held in mid-December 1918, a proposal was made by the Independent Socialists for the immediate establishment of a socialist regime. But it was not endorsed by the congress nor was the Sparticist slogan, borrowed from the Bolsheviks, of "All power to the Councils". Instead of following these proposals to become a revolutionary agency, the congress decisively upheld the Majority Social Democratic republic on a permanent basis. It was a clear victory for the Majority SPD and its leader, Ebert, who presided over the Provisional Government. As a result of the congress, the Independent SPD moved further to the left, and the Spartacists broke off to form the Communist party (KPD) on 30th December 1918. But the SPD, obsessed with the danger of Bolshevism, moved to the right and looked for support from the Army in the task of restoring order.

The Unexpected Alliance

The alliance between the defeated Army and the uncertain Provisional Government succeeded in saving both of them from Socialist revolution, but the means employed damaged the prospects for democracy in Germany.

On 9th November 1918 full powers were handed over to the Provisional Government. Ebert, as head of the new authority, was uncomfortably aware of the parallel between his new position and that of Kerensky in Russia before the Bolsheviks swept to power. But contact was very shortly established with General Groener, who had replaced Ludendorff as Hindenburg's Quartermaster-General a few weeks before. The alliance formed between them was based on the following policy: the High Command would bring the Army home peacefully, would treat the soldiers' and workers' councils in a friendly spirit to prevent their radicalisation, and would co-operate with the government in the suppression of Bolshevism. At the same time the civilian government would bear the responsibility of negotiating the armistice, and the officer corps would maintain its traditional position as ultimate guardian of the State.

The understanding between General Groener and Social Democrat Ebert was not a fortuitous development. It was made possible through the war-time collaboration between the Army's economic administration and the trade unions which Groener had done so much to foster. And it was able to work in the uncertain aftermath of the war because Groener's flexible conservatism enabled him to comprehend the dynamics of the situation.

The armed force necessary to implement the understanding was created in the first few days of 1919 in the form of auxiliary shocktroops, called the Free Corps. Recruited by army officers, with the full approval of Ebert and his Social Democratic Minister of War, Noske, the Free Corps consisted mainly of former officers, students and some white-collar employees. Frustrated by the dislocations and stresses of post-war society, haunted by memories of the soldiers' community of the trenches, above all embittered by defeat in a war they "naturally" expected to win, the Free Corps members of the "Generation of the Uprooted and Disinherited" became fanatically devoted to the destruction of the radical left. They murdered the Spartacist leaders Rosa Luxemburg and Karl Liebknecht, along with many of their working-class followers in Berlin between 10th and 17th January 1919. A month later in Bavaria, the Independent Socialist leader Kurt Eisner was shot dead, and in early May the Free Corps bloodily suppressed the Soviet Republic which was set up in Bavaria after the Eisner murder. During the first half of 1919, they were also employed in savagely crushing left movements in the north, centre and west. After the collapse of the right-wing Kapp *putsch* in March 1920, Free Corps units and the *Reichswehr* bloodily suppressed uprisings in the Ruhr towns and in central Germany. Several long-term consequences followed from this use of murder to settle political difficulties.

The division between the Social Democrats and the nascent Communist party was aggravated in Germany beyond redemption. Little more than a decade later, in face of the common danger of the Nazi movement, there was no chance of establishing a Popular Front alliance, which might have gone some way towards checking the Nazis. On the contrary, the Communist charge against the SPD that they were "Social Fascists", although manifestly ludicrous was nevertheless given presumptive support by the previous use of the Free Corps. A second consequence was that a very dangerous precedent for the National Socialist movement had been set in the use of quasi-legal, organised violence against labour. Among the many Free Corps-type organisations which came into existence in the following years was the Nazi SA, which eventually became a serious rival of the Army itself. Thirdly, the role of the judiciary in dealing with political crimes was notoriously biased, granting virtual immunity from punishment for what were considered to be "patriotic acts" of murder. With the judiciary in this frame of mind, the prospects for an experiment in democracy were much diminished.[1]

Furthermore, while the SPD leadership fought against revolutionary tendencies, they made little effort to initiate certain *essential* reforms.[2] The higher ranks of the civil service, as well as the judiciary, remained the preserve of the old Imperial bureaucracy. It may have been considered inexpedient to forgo their services and to curb their influence, but in the long run the weight of their anti-democratic convictions contributed to the downfall of the Republic. The tragedy of this failure lay in he fact that the means to introduce democratic practices in the administration were available in the soldiers' and workers' councils, which had gained practical experience in the chaos of 1918-19.[3] But their potential in this respect was feared and negated by the Groener/Ebert alliance which wanted to restore the traditional structure. Another key area where the impetus for reform was weak, precisely because of the dependence on the Imperial civil service, was the educational system which was largely able to resist the introduction of democratic ideas and values.

However, blame for this failure must be fairly apportioned. The German middle class, in its vast majority, did not understand or desire such far-reaching changes. At best they were apathetically neutral; at worst, openly hostile to the ideals of the new Republic. The current of liberalism in the middle class remained as weak as it had been under Bismarck. The Left Liberals, now called the German Democratic Party, and the Catholic Centre party were coalition partners of the Social Democrats in the first years of the Weimar Republic. But they did not promote the reforms essential for the support of a democratic political system. Therefore, although the Weimar Constitution of 1919 was a remarkable document with a modern bill of civil, social and economic rights, there were simply not enough people in influential positions who wanted to see it become a living reality. There were some technical flaws in the constitution, in the structure of powers which it elaborated, but these were not the cause of its ultimate breakdown. An even more perfectly conceived constitution would not have been more acceptable, and for that reason would not have been able to withstand the disturbances which lay ahead.

Nevertheless there were certain features of the new political system which contributed to instability. The multi-party system made it impossible for one party to win enough votes to command a majority. Instead, government had to be based on insecure coalititons of parties. In the fourteen years of the Weimar Republic, there were no less than fourteen chancellors and twenty one cabinets, which meant that there was on average a cabinet change every eight months. This had two important consequences: the old Imperial bureaucracy acquired more political influence than it would have had if the parties had been able to develop as more effective instruments of government; and secondly, cynicism and contempt for the "weakness" of the parliamentary system became widespread and a "strong state" was desired to put an end to political uncertainties.

A further problem was the old one of German unity. The thirty-nine states of the Second Reich were reduced to eighteen *Laender* under the new constitution, and there was a strong movement towards centralisation, which weakened the traditional particularism of the states. The federal government had the power to override state laws where conflicts arose. Since there were nationwide parties which transcended *Laender* lines, it looked, on one level, as if the Republic was a unitary state with some measure of regional decentralisation. Especially as Prussia was now under the influence of the most unitary party, the Social Democrats. Junker domination of the Prussian legislature, which was based on the three-class electoral system, was replaced by an SPD/Centre party coalition elected on equal suffrage. The SPD was the major party in the coalition which lasted from 1920 to 1932, and which made the republican government of Prussia one of the firmest pillars of the Weimar constitution. But state separatism was still alive in south Germany, particularly in Bavaria where it became a serious problem. It was partly because of this situation that the famous Article 48 was written into the Weimar Constitution, giving the President the right to govern by decree in emergencies.

After the Free Corps destroyed the Soviet Republic of Bavaria in the spring of 1919, Bavaria became the happy hunting grounds of extreme right-wing groups. Hitler's fledgling National Socialist movement competed with other combinations of anti-Republicans, anti-Socialists, anti-Semites and inflated nationalists. In the autumn of 1923, at the height of the post-war inflation, a rebellion of the Bavarian government against the Republic was brewing. Hoping to take advantage of the situation for his own purposes, Hitler precipitated matters by staging a Beerhall *putsch* on 8th-9th November 1923. Although easily crushed, Hitler was very lightly punished. The judiciary was notoriously lenient with extreme right-wing acts of "patriotism". Hitler used his short time in prison to dictate *Mein Kampf* and to reflect that since a frontal assault on the Republic was not possible, the cover of legality would have to be used, and could be used. The problem which the Bavarian situation illustrated is that the federal government did not interfere with *Laender* where the right wing controlled the state government, but illegally overthrew left-wing state governments in Saxony and Thuringia in 1923, and illegally destroyed the SPD/Centre coalition in Prussia in July 1932, opening the way for the destruction of the Republic.

A third problem was the ambiguous role of the Army. Constitutionally, the German Army was made responsible to the *Reichstag* through the Minister of Defence. Previously he was responsible to the Emperor. But parliamentary supervision of the Army, which could have diminished its independent status and inhibited the military chiefs from formulating their own domestic and foreign policies, was not in fact attained. The first two Ministers, Noske and Gessler, were politicians who complied with the policies of their military advisors, including those evasions of the Versailles Treaty which enabled the army illegally to rearm and train. The next two Ministers were not selected from parliament, but from the Army itself. Generals Groener and von Schleicher were not at all amenable to parliamentary control. The intention of the Army, in holding itself outside civilian "interference", was to maintain its organisation and traditional role despite the severe constraints which the Treaty of Versailles had placed upon it.

The objective of the Army was not the direct exercise of political power. Its fundamental aim was to maintain its autonomy in a powerful state. To achieve this, the army leaders saw the necessity of working within the constituted legal framework and not against it. It was the point of Groener's alliance with Ebert at the end of the war, and it was repeated insistently by General von Seeckt[4] over the years 1920 to 1926 when he stated that the Army was above politics.[5] That is, it must serve the State as a permanent institution, without dabbling in current political affairs. Von Seeckt's aims were two fold: to prevent the development of political factionalism within the Army; and to raise its prestige and influence. The Army strove to restore its former position in society, and to minimise outside interference as far as possible. Since it was drastically reduced in size after 1918, being limited to 100,000 men, it deliberately selected its officers and NCOs from the traditional sources of the aristocracy and military profession. So great was its nostalgia for the past that even the traditions of the disbanded Imperial regiments were continued. But so effective were its evasions of the Treaty of Versailles with regard to training and the handling of modern weapons that when Hitler wanted to rebuild the German war machine he had firm foundations on which to expand.

While the senior officers respected the legal framework of the Republic because they saw that there was no other workable alternative, as the years went by many of the junior officers began to lose patience with this approach. They were increasingly attracted by Nazi propaganda which was carefully designed to appeal to them. In 1930, at the trial of three lieutenants who were accused of spreading Nazi propaganda among their colleagues, Hitler utilised the opportunity to speak directly to the younger officers who were attentively following the trial. He promised to create a great army in which there would be many opportunities for professional advancement. In the circumstances it could not fail to have a profound effect. A short time later, with the deepening crisis of the Republic, General Schleicher abandoned the policy of neutrality and plunged the Army into the political arena,[6] thinking that he could divide and harness the Nazi mass movement. It was an illusion which was not only to cost him his life, but more immediately helped to prepare the way for the Nazis' seizure of power.

The Situation of Labour

The situation of labour in the Weimar Republic was conditioned by the inflation, which lasted until the end of 1923; the reconstruction and recovery of 1924 to 1929; and the world depression and political struggles of the last years of the Republic.

The problem of inflation was created to some extent by the German method of financing the war. Instead of paying for it from taxes, the government chose to grant vast loans and to increase the volume of paper money in circulation, on the assumption that Germany would win and therefore could collect sufficient tribute in a short time from the conquered territories.[7] When this failed to happen, and instead Germany was confronted with reparations plus the loss of a certain proportion of its industrial resources in the territorial re-arrangement of the Versailles Treaty, the financial result was a steep deterioration in the value of the mark. When Germany defaulted in the payment of reparations and the French retaliated by occupying the Ruhr (January

1923), the currency became worthless. By the autumn of 1923 one dollar could buy over four billion marks.

The spectacular inflation, whose origin was not explained but conveniently blamed on the Versailles Treaty, had a drastic effect on some sections of the lower middle class, particularly those people whose savings and fixed incomes were wiped out. The basis of their security and independence was destroyed, and they were forced to find some new means of existence. Whether they became wage-earners or not, most of them were faced with a sharp decline in status and had to adjust to bleak conditions of hardship or outright poverty. Their social resentments provided a receptive audience for extreme right-wing propaganda. Many of the small self-employed tradesmen, artisans and manufacturers also lost their capital in the inflation and were forced down into the manual working class. And scattered in the turbulence of mass downward mobility were some whose families had once been wealthy and whose fortunes were now lost. Even when the process of economic recovery began after 1924, it was not possible for many of these people to recover their former positions, as the recovery was accompanied by a series of industrial mergers and rationalisation measures which, by eliminating smaller and weaker firms, increased the amount of downward mobility. At the same time unemployment was higher than it had been before the war. The high unemployment figures of the first years were due to demobilisation. From the winter of 1923-24 to 1928 unemployment fluctuated between half a million and two million, caused by the enlargement of the scale of production and its increasing rationalisation. Moreover real wages rose slowly from very low levels in the post-war inflationary period, and reached the 1913 level by 1928; that is, not long before the depression knocked them far down again.

With the onset of the depression, unemployment reached astronomical proportions. Out of a total labour force of some thirty two millions, approximately one-and-a-quarter million were unemployed in the summer of 1929. The figures rose steadily from over three million in 1930, to approaching five million in 1931 and over six million in 1932. As this occurred severe wage reductions were introduced. In 1931, wage-rates for industrial workers were forty per cent less than in 1929, and in 1932 an emergency decree cut all wages by a further ten to fifteen per cent. Social welfare benefits were cut down at the same time.

But mass unemployment and drastically lowered living standards as such cannot explain the rise of Nazism. The same economic crisis

rocked Britain, the USA and, to a lesser extent, France without leading
to the destruction of democracy. The difference in Germany was the
way in which these social phenomena were experienced and the
meaning they were given. A comparison with the Italian situation may
be helpful. Italian Fascism did not become a potent force *until the
labour movement had exhausted itself*. That is, until workers'
experience was that neither the revolutionary alternative of creating
new institutions and new social values was possible nor was there a
realistic opportunity to achieve the reformist aims of integration
through a viable extension of social, economic and political rights. In
Germany, the revolutionary alternative failed in 1918 and 1919; and by
the early 1930s the reformist alternative of establishing a democratic
republic was collapsing. This had a terrible effect on morale. It was not
that the working class in its millions wanted Fascism; on the contrary.
But its resistance to the Nazis could not be sustained. In the face of the
increasingly furious Nazi thrust, the labour movement became more
hopeless and was unable to assert an effective political resistance.[8]
Because of widespread unemployment and defeatism among workers,
both the ADGB trade union leaders and SPD leaders decided not to call
for direct action against the illegal dismissal of Social Democratic
ministers from the Prussian government in July 1932. Hopes that
national elections at the end of the month would strengthen the
Social Democrats were disappointed; the Nazis were returned as the
largest party with 230 seats and 13,745,000 votes.

In the following months the union leaders became increasingly
passive, unable to work out an economic and political solution to the
depression conditions which could serve as an attractive alternative to
Nazi policies, and unwilling to mobilise for general-strike action for fear
of risking civil war and disastrous suppression. Their apathy in face of
the Nazi menace derived from an anxious desire to preserve their
organisations in the hope that conditions would eventually improve. To
this end, the ADGB leaders were willing to withdraw from politics, to
dissociate themselves from the SPD and to accommodate themselves to
Nazi power. In spite of persistent Nazi attacks on the persons, property
and press of the trade unions, the hope of organisational survival
through compromise and lack of resistance persisted.

After Hitler became Chancellor every means of reinforcing the
pressure and intensifying the atmosphere of terror was exploited.
Capitalising on the *Reichstag* fire of February 1933, the waves of
arrests and arbitrary actions of the SA and SS continued through the
March elections into April, and included the setting up of the first

concentration camps. These actions were facilitated by the passage of an Enabling Law on 23rd March, which allowed the Nazis to suspend the constitution. Under these conditions the ability of the SPD to resist was exhausted and the ADGB executive submitted to Nazi initiatives. In mid-April they accepted Goebbels' idea of a "National Labour Day", and on the 29th April, their newspaper, *Gewerkschaftszeitung,* welcomed it as a "victory" for the labour movement. On May Day itself, they paraded under Nazi banners. The next day, having served the Nazi purpose of helping the new regime through the delicate problem of the traditional workers' day, the leaders were arrested. A short time later all trade union property was confiscated, and its assets taken over by a new organisation, the Nazi Labour Front.

NOTES

1. For a close, detailed analysis of this destructive process, see Heinrich and Elisabeth Hannover, *Politische Justiz 1918-1933* Frankfurt am Main, Fischer 1966.

2. This is not to deny certain SPD accomplishments in the field of social policy, e.g. extension of social security provisions.

3. See Helga Grebing, *The History of the German Labour Movement,* Wolff 1969 transl. pp102 *ff.*

4. See Gordon A. Craig, *The Politics of the Prussian Army,* Oxford UP, 1955, pp377-86 and pp416-19, for comments on the ambiguities of Seeckt's behaviour during the *Kapp putsch* and during the crisis of 1923.

5. It was one of the main points which Hitler learned from his Beerhall *putsch* in 1923.

6. For an interesting analysis of the process, see John W. Wheeler-Bennett, *The Nemesis of Power,* MacMillan 1967, 2nd ed. part II, Chapter 2.

7. Taylor, *The Course of German History,* p227.

8. For details of the responses of organised labour to the events of 1932-33, see Gerard Braunthal, "The German Free Trade Unions during the Rise of Nazism", *Journal of Central European Affairs,* XV (January 1956), reprinted as "The Failure of Socialist Labour" in John L. Snell (ed.), *The Nazi Revolution, Lexington, Mass., Heath 1959.*

Chapter 7 Germany: The Nazi Regime

The problem of interpreting the Nazi phenomenon is facilitated, but not solved, by the massive collections of materials on the Third Reich — tons of official documents and papers, eye-witness accounts, newsreel films, the records of war crimes trials and subsequent trials and investigations. Skilful analyses of these materials, such as those of Helmut Krausnick, Hans Buchheim, Martin Broszat and Hans-Adolf Jacobsen in *Anatomy of the SS State*, reveal the organisations, the workings and the planning involved and lead back more deeply into the primary questions of causes and motivations. But attempts at causal explanation inevitably contain a subjective element in the selection and presentation of tendencies. Hence there is a wide variety of interpretations in the vast literature produced mainly by historians and political scientists.[1] The most salient sociological dimension of interpretation involves contrasting perspectives on the nature of social stratification and change. On the one side are theorists of mass society, such as William Kornhauser, *The Politics of Mass Society*, 1959; and on the other side are those who stress the primacy of class antagonisms in the emergence of Fascism. The classical study is Franz Neumann's wartime analysis of *Behemoth: the Structure and Practice of National Socialism*. The following interpretation of Nazism evaluates these contrasting views in relation to the questions: Who supported the Nazi movement? Who were the members and leaders of the movement? How did the Nazis control German society? In which ways did they change it? On the basis of these considerations a comparative analysis of the Fascist phenomenon in Germany and in Italy is undertaken in Chapter nine on "Fascism and Modernisation".

1. Who Supported the Nazis?

The first thing to examine is the voting behaviour of the German electorate in the second half of the Weimar Republic. In the *Reichstag* elections of September 1930 and July 1932, the Social Democratic percentage of the total votes declined whereas the Nazi percentage rose sharply. There is, however, no direct connection between these two facts, since they represent basically different trends.

The Social Democrats were losing votes to the Communists, not to the Nazis. This is connected with the so-called *Verbürgerlichung* or *embourgeoisement* of the SPD. That is, party and trade union leaders came to adopt a style of life and a general social outlook which was markedly distinct from that of their following and bore some similarity to middle-class ethos. The rise in status and respectability which resulted from their participation in the war effort continued under Weimar when the SPD became the party of order and the *status quo,* with its commitment to formal democratic institutions. Nevertheless they were in a very uneasy and ambiguous situation. They owed their enhanced status to their role as representatives and spokesmen of the labour movement, which meant that they were exposed to attacks from conservative and reactionary forces; and at the same time, since they were partially integrated into the dominant power structure, they were relatively isolated from the grass-root sources of workers' discontent and aspirations. The result was that there was considerable room for a party to the left of the SPD.

The Independent Social Democratic Party (USPD), which arose on the anti-war issue, was not able to sustain itself for long as a serious rival to the parent party. In 1920 it split, one section joined the Communist party, while the other eventually rejoined the Majority SPD. The Communist party proved to be a much more stable entity, capable of attracting many young workers. The SPD, aware of the growth of a while-collar stratum in the occupational structure, increasingly concentrated on recruiting among them. This reinforced the impression that the SPD was becoming a middle-class party. The impression, however, was misleading because three quarters of the membership, in 1930, were working-class, mostly skilled and semi-skilled. The composition of the Communist party, in this respect, was not significantly different. The crucial difference was age. The Communists were young; the Social Democrats were middle-aged and over. In the *Reichstag* of 1930, over eighty five per cent of the Social Democrats were over forty years of age, while more than seventy per cent of the Communist deputies were under forty.

If the percentage of the total vote gained by the SPD and the KPD in the national elections between 1924 and 1932 is combined, the results are remarkably constant: thirty five per cent (December 1924); forty per cent (1928); nearly thirty eight per cent (1930); thirty six per cent (July 1932); thirty seven per cent (November 1932). Even in March 1933, in the last election held under full-blown Nazi terror, the combined vote was nearly thirty one per cent. It has been estimated that out of every hundred votes the Nazis won between 1928 and July 1932, only three came from former SPD and KPD voters. It would suggest that while tens of thousands of workers did vote Nazi, perhaps between one third to half a million, the great bulk of the labour electorate remained firmly against them.

Nor did the Nazis gain much from the Catholic Centre party. Its vote fluctuated very narrowly in these elections between somewhat over fifteen per cent and somewhat under eighteen per cent. In the 1933 terror election, the share of the vote remained at fifteen per cent.[2]

To find the sources of Nazi votes it is therefore necessary to look at the parties of the Protestant middle and lower middle classes. The German People's Party (DVP), which was the continuation of the old right-wing National-Liberal party under a new name, and the Left Liberals (DDP), a continuation of the former Progressive party, as well as the small business and other splinter parties were virtually abandoned in those years. The conservative party (DNVP) was seriously weakened as it lost the backing of small property owners (both rural and urban), while retaining most of its upper-class support. The sudden mushrooming of Nazi electoral power can be almost entirely explained by the losses of these parties. In the elections of 1928, the Nazis won 2.6 per cent of the total votes, increasing it to 18.3 per cent in 1930, and reaching a peak of 37.3 in July 1932. In the same elections the combined losses of the DNVP, DDP, DVP and small parties totalled 30.7 per cent. In addition the Nazis benefited from the support of former non-voters and of new voters. In the case of the latter the Nazis reaped the benefit of the intensification of *völkisch* influences on youth during the Weimar Republic.

The pattern of voting changed somewhat in the November 1932 elections. The Nazis lost two million votes, dropping to 33.1 per cent of the total votes − still the largest single party and well ahead of the Social Democrats, but perhaps past the peak. Both the conservatives (DNVP) and the Communists registered gains of around 2.5 per cent of the total vote, and the DVP, long in decline, picked up 0.6 per cent. What would have happened if free elections continued is difficult to assess, but it is significant that although the Nazis raised their share of the total votes to forty four per cent in the terror election of March 1933 the basic tendencies held and are visible in the results.

Social Classes and Occupational Categories

The patterns of voting behaviour broadly indicate the social sources of support for the Nazi movement. It is worth examining in some detail the different degrees of participation and support among the various social classes and occupational groups.

The Working Class

In his book on *The Politics of Mass Society,* William Kornhauser presents the following view:

"Mass theory . . . . expects Fascist movements as well as Communist movements to gain a large following among workers, since according to this theory people do not support Fascists or Communists primarily to further their economic interests, but as an expression of their resentment and hostility against the established order and in response to the pseudo-authority and pseudo-community provided by the totalitarian movement."[3]

A way of testing the validity of this theory would be to ask whether the Nazis gained "a large following among workers" in Germany. Kornhauser used the following table on the occupational distribution of Nazi party members 1933 and 1935:

Table 1[4] – Percentage Occupational Distribution of Nazi Party Membership 1933 and 1935

	Party Membership		Total Gainfully Employed*	
Occupational Classification	1933 (1)	1935 (2)	1933 (3)	1933 (4)
Manual Workers	31.5	32.1	46.3	38.5
White-collar employees	21.1	20.6	12.5	12.5
Independents+	17.6	20.2	9.6	9.6
Officials	6.7	13.0	4.6	4.6
Peasants	12.6	10.7	21.1	28.9
Others++	10.5	3.4	5.9	5.9
TOTAL	100.0	100.0	100.0	100.0

*Column 4 is added as decisive evidence of the National Socialist failure to win the same following among the urban proletariat as they won among the middle classes. In column 4 the agricultural wage-workers who were included with "manual workers" in column 3 are classified with "peasants", leaving as manual workers only those employed in non-agricultural pursuits and therefore predominantly urban. Even if all those "manual workers" whom the Nazis had won as party members were entirely non-agricultural,

which was undoubtedly not the case, the non-agricultural proletariat would still be considerably under-represented in the Nazi party both in 1933 and in 1935 as compared with employers and independents. +Skilled artisans, professional persons, merchants, etc., excluding independent peasants.
++Domestic servants and non-agricultural family helpers."

The table, which comes from Nazi party statistics, shows that slightly under one third of party membership in 1933 and 1935 consisted of manual workers. However in relation to other occupational categories, manual workers were under-represented in the party composition. Comparing the proportion of an occupational category in the party with its proportion in the gainfully employed population, a notion of relative over-or under-representation may be obtained. The urban middle class (professional men; self-employed artisans and businessmen, and their family helpers; white-collar employees; and civil servants) were significantly over-represented. Manual workers and peasants were relatively under-represented. Moreover, workers were conspicuously absent from the leadership cadres of the NSDAP, both before and after the seizure of power. The significance of this fact may be underscored by recognition of the organisational and leadership skills of skilled and semi-skilled workers in trade union, labour political and co-operative activities. Their lack of involvement in the Nazi leadership structure is of major importance in determining the social character of the Fascist movement.

A consideration of the actual numbers involved is useful. When Hitler became Chancellor at the end of January 1933, the Nazi party had 849,000 members. Of these over a quarter of a million were manual workers. Not a great deal is known about them, but it seems reasonable to suggest that they were for the most part unskilled workers. The Nazis recruited some Storm Troopers from the ranks of the unemployed, paying them a small daily wage as well as welfare and maintenance allowances. Many undoubtedly joined the Nazi party *via* the SA. At the beginning of 1935, total party membership stood at nearly two-and-a-half million. Of these over three quarters of a million were manual workers. The influx of half a million workers may be explained, in addition to the above point, by the destruction of the labour movement, in its political and trade union dimensions, during the period of Nazi consolidation of power. In judging the relative proportions of workers' involvement in the Nazi movement before the seizure of power, the following considerations are relevant:

(a) In terms of total membership the SPD alone was larger than the Nazi party up to the seizure of power. The Communist party was approximately one third the size of the NSDAP. In the autumn of 1932 the combined membership of the SPD and KPD was considerably larger than that of the Nazi party, and the left-wing parties won nearly thirteen and a quarter million votes.

(b) The combined *manual worker* membership in the SPD and KPD in the last years of the Weimar Republic was between 850,000 and 950,000. Of these over two thirds were skilled and semi-skilled. By contrast the bulk of the workers — over a quarter of a million — in the Nazi party were probably unskilled.

(c) The membership of the Free Trade Unions (predominantly Social Democratic in orientation), though declining in the depression years, was over four million in 1931.

With regard to *industrial* workers specifically, there is a reliable indicator of their attitude towards National Socialism: the works council elections. Franz Neumann emphasised their relevance:

"They are perhaps even more important than the parliamentary elections, for in choosing the council the workers based their decision almost exclusively upon actual social experience. The composition of the works councils in 1930 and 1931 is striking — not a single National Socialist in 1930 and only 710 out of 138,000 as late as 1931."[5]

Neumann pointed out further that when the Nazis took power and changed the works councils to "councils of confidence", they abandoned the elective procedure because of the unsatisfactory results it produced. Instead they introduced the appointment of council members by the Nazi trustees of labour.[6]

Taking together the objective data on labour's response to the Nazi movement — the pattern of voting in *Reichstag* elections, and in works council elections, as well as membership of the political parties — it would seem that the bulk of workers, especially the skilled and semi-skilled strata, were not greatly attracted by the pseudo-community of the totalitarian movement. The absence of workers in the Nazi leadership-cadres is also indicative. These factors correlate with the fact that the Nazi vote was highest in the rural and small town areas, and lowest proportionately in the urban and industrial areas. Nevertheless it remains indisputable that about one quarter of a million manual workers joined the Nazi party and that perhaps as many as half a million voted for it. One explanation could be that throughout the period of the Weimar Republic, and not only with the onset of the 1929 depression, there was a considerable influx of resentful lower middle-class people into the unskilled sections of the working class.[7] Some part of the "manual worker" support for the Nazis may have come from the victims of this mass downward mobility.[8] A second reason is that some workers (typically former Communists and young workers) were undoubtedly attracted by the "revolutionary" anti-capitalist views of the Nazis.

Organised Business

Although the "left wing" of the Nazi movement expressed anti-capitalist sentiments, these did not influence Hitler's plans. On the contrary, he was most interested in establishing contact with the leaders of organised business. The economic crisis of 1929 and the subsequent political uncertainties provided the opportunity. Hitler instructed one of his advisors, Wilhelm Keppler, to organise a circle of businessmen who would not necessarily be members of the Nazi party but who were sufficiently sympathetic to provide a channel of communication between the organisations. One outcome was that plans were created to overcome unemployment by extensive public works – not with the aim of building houses and improving land but – for military purposes.[9] Such plans were of interest to organised big business because they suggested that re-armament was a means of solving economic and social problems and of creating a rapidly expanding economy. At the same time it was made clear that the "responsible" leadership of the Nazi party did not believe in the anti-capitalist aspects of its ideology, and that the Hitler movement could represent a powerful weapon against labour organisations – particular as conflicts over wages and social security were acute and demands for nationalisation of industries were rising. Eventually the Hitler movement came to be acknowledged by the National Association of German Industry as a means of creating a stable political system, a dictatorship, in which long-range economic calculation would be possible. Although big business did not create the Nazi party, and had little to do with its rise to prominence, its support for the Nazis in the seizure and consolidation of power was significant.

Interest in Hitler's movement increased significantly after the elections of September 1930 when the Nazis gained a resounding success, raising their number of deputies from twelve to 107. Contacts with the National Socialists multiplied, and the view gained ground that Hitler might have a key role to play. However this opinion did not become virtually unanimous until late in 1932. In the presidential and

Reichstag election campaigns of 1932 industrialists and bankers supported the conservative candidates against Hitler. Nazi debts ran higher and higher, until the party faced virtual bankruptcy, and the results of the November 1932 *Reichstag* elections showed a loss of two million votes compared with the previous July. Although the largest party in the *Reichstag*, and virtual masters of the streets with a party army of 400,000 SA men, victory was far from assured and the risks of demoralisation were considerable. But the situation changed drastically when von Papen was forced to resign at the beginning of December 1932, and General von Schleicher became Chancellor.

Von Schleicher's attempt to win the support of the trade unions and the left wing of the Nazis implied taking radical measures which would damage the interests of both Junkers and the hard core of German business, especially steel, coal, insurance and banking. At this crucial point Hitler was seen as the trump card which would insure economic protection, long-term political stability, and remilitarisation without the limitations the trade unionists and Socialists would try to impose. Thus the Nazi debts were taken care of, the SA men continued to be paid and armed and by early 1933 there was virtually no opposition left in the ranks of organised business to the idea that Hitler should come to power and establish a dictatorship.[10] Nor in the following years of consolidation of power, preparation for war and war itself was there evidence of opposition to the Nazi regime from these quarters.[11] They played a crucial role in mobilising the economy for the war effort. Their involvement in the Nazi regime was total and unequivocal.

In brief, organised business came to Hitler slowly, and offered it little support until the last, critical moment. But once committed to the Nazis, there was no looking back. Apart from ideological motivation, which may or may not have been of importance in individual cases, organised business as a whole found the Nazi Regime and the SS state which grew up within it a viable framework for the development of their activities.

For his part, Hitler fully appreciated the contribution that big business could make if it accepted his goals, and he therefore was concerned to reassure it. The small business anti-capitalist ideology characteristic of the early Nazi movement was not immediately checked because it was an important part of the appeal of "left" Nazism, which animated the Strasser wing of the party. But no practical measures of any importance were ever carried out in fulfilment of anti-capitalist demands, except in relation to "Jewish" capital, which was first differentiated from and then absorbed into "Aryan" capital.

The relationship between big business and the Nazi state therefore may be characterised as *a full partnership based on mutual need for each others' services*. It is clear that Fascism was not the creation of capitalism since the sources of support for the former were quite varied, as will be shown in some detail below. But it is equally clear that if Nazism originated and grew independently of big business, it could not have come to power without the latter's support nor could it have operated its new society against the fundamental interests of big business if it wished to achieve its aim of military conquest. Equally big business accepted the Nazi state with gratification because it serviced its needs. David Schoenbaum noted that I.G. Farben "made a home for itself in the Third Reich"[12] — but so did a host of other big firms which should be mentioned alongside it: Krupp, Siemens, Flick, Quandt, Wolff, Stinnes, Mannesmann. Against these major names the fact that Thyssen, who was one of the early financial backers of Hitler, fled means very little, although Schoenbaum saw it as a counter-trend. Before Thyssen fled from Germany he was defeated by his major competitors Flick and the Göring combine. The flight seems to have been motivated more by lack of success than by political ideas.[13]

Furthermore, in order to grasp the relationship between big business and the Nazi state, it is important to understand the mentality of the former. An insight is provided in Hitler's speech to the *Industrie-Klub* in Düsseldorf in January 1932, in which he insisted on the primacy of politics in national life:

> For it was not German business which conquered the world and then came the development of German power, but .... it was the power-State *(Machtstaat)* which created for the business world the general conditions for its subsequent prosperity. *(Very true!)* In my view it is to put the cart before the horse when today people believe that by business methods they can .... recover Germany's power-position instead of realising that the power-position is also the condition for the improvement of the economic situation .... there can be no flourishing economic life which has not before it and behind it the flourishing powerful State as its protection .... there can be no economic life unless behind this economic life there stands the determined political will of the nation absolutely ready to strike — and to strike hard.[14]

The distinguished audience's reaction to this statement was one of enthusiastic approval: *"Very true!"* Schoenbaum suggested that this reveals the "real limits of German capitalism".[15] But the history of economic development in Germany as discussed earlier, indicates that a very different interpretation is more likely: that big business approved of the primacy of politics, that is, accepted the necessity of the State creating the political conditions in which economic expansion could be achieved. As a consequence of Germany's belated industrialisation, as well as the fact that it occurred within the specific context of national unification under the hegemony of Prussian authoritarianism, the German industrialist had a very different outlook from that of the American or British. Unlike the latter, the German industrialist did not resent the "interference" of the State in economic affairs, but was accustomed to regarding State activity as an essential framework for economic development. So when Hitler told the industrial leaders gathered at Düsseldorf that they should realise that it was the power-state which would create the premises for future economic expansion, it fully accorded with their desires and expectations, as their immediate reaction and subsequent actions fully revealed. This was not the limit of German capitalism, but the very conditions for its future prosperity. And, as will be discussed in Chapter ten, its effects were important for the post-Second World War "economic miracle".

What was revealed at Düsseldorf was a fundamental reason for their interest in what Hitler had to offer, and why they eventually bought his services. In this light, Braunthal's comment that leading industrialists exhibited "extreme naiveté in deciding which political horse to bet on" is jejune, whereas his description of the Nazi era as an "alliance of government with industry" is to the point.[16] It is more accurate than Schoenbaum's overemphasis on the "pressure of the State" against big business.[17] Once in operation the alliance developed in accordance with the logic of the situation it created. Nazi state pressures in the form of high taxes, controls and regulation of the capital market were accepted without difficulty because of the overall boost to the economy and the provision of huge public contracts to industry. In this context, the pressure-group tactics of organised business changed because the political leadership did not deviate from the major goals of expansion, which was the basis of the alliance. The emphasis shifted from organised pressure-group tactics to individual firms' self-concern. This is often seen as a loss of control on the part of industry, but it may well have been otherwise. Its common interests in economic protection and development being secured through the existence of the Nazi state, the strategy would then be for each firm to concentrate on getting as much for itself as possible. It was a logical consequence of the notion of "primacy of politics",[18] on which the alliance was founded and operated.

The idea that industry lost control, and had to submit helplessly to Nazi directives, would be meaningful only if there was evidence that it tried to dissociate itself from the situation after 1936. There was in fact little sign of discomfort and none of revolt. On the contrary, there is sufficient evidence of implication in even the most bestial Nazi activities of enslavement and systematic murder.[19]

The Middle and Lower Middle Classes

The data on both voting behaviour and party membership demonstrate forcefully that the main social area of Nazi support was the middle and lower middle classes. Generally speaking it was their disturbed economic situation throughout the inter-war period, and the consequent threatened or real loss of social status that provided the mass support base for the Nazi movement. Their attraction to Nazism arose from a desire for protection in a threatened, uncertain position in society. They were anti-labour and anti-capitalist, desiring a curtailment of the power of both major social forces which surrounded and menaced them. In so far as big business was also interested in the destruction of organised labour, this part of the wish could be gratified.

But the very condition of Nazi consolidation of power was an understanding with big business, and therefore the anti-capitalist demands of the radicalised lower middle class could not be fulfilled. On the contrary, once the re-armament programme commenced, and with it the militarisation of the economy, the Nazis ceased to endorse the small business ideology (except in relation to "Jewish" capital) since they had no interest in deliberately limiting the opportunities for industrial growth and large-scale production. However, the Nazi party provided some compensation for its failure to carry through its "revolution" against big business by being itself an agent of social advancement. An ardent and energetic Nazi, whatever his social background, could rise in status and power through the machinery of the party and its multiple affiliated organisations. There were as will be indicated later, many opportunities for the politically qualified.

These generalisations apply with particular force to the occupational category of self-employed small businessmen, artisans and professional men. They also apply, with some qualification, to their rural equivalents — the small and medium farm owners. The qualification is that the peasants were proportionately the most under-represented category in the party composition and leadership. However, there is probably nothing more significant in this than the fact that farm populations generally have the lowest degree of direct participation in national movements because of their relative isolation and fewer social ties with the larger society. A related point is that while the small family farmer in the Protestant areas provided a major source of Nazi electoral support,[20] it was not true of the larger landowners who maintained their traditional allegiance with the conservative party (DNVP). In this respect the German situation differed considerably from the Italian, where the large landowners formed a hard, driving core of Fascist support.

Apart from the self-employed rural and urban categories, another strong source of Nazi support came from white-collar employees, civil servants and teachers. They were not subject to the same direct economic pressures of competition with larger firms, and of having to pay relatively high taxes. In the case of the salaried white-collar groups, with their semi-intellectual concerns, it would seem rather that ideological questions were of greater importance in attracting them to the radical right. For example, the teachers, particularly elementary school teachers, were the highest represented of all professional groups in the Nazi movement and leadership. According to the party census of May 1935, out of nearly half a million political leaders and officials, about one third were teachers. It is true that the National Socialist Teachers' League, founded in 1929, remained very small until 1933, but long before the advent of Hitler, the professional journals and the main teachers' organisations, on both the secondary and elementary school levels, were stridently nationalist, *völkisch* and racialist. The secondary teachers were particularly influenced by their training at the university where the intellectual atmosphere was increasingly dominated by these influences. A similar tendency was noticeable in the white-collar unions of salaried employees and civil servants. Although the socialist trade unions for white-collar workers gained some ground in the early years of the Weimar Republic, they were unable to rival right-wing unions such as the German Federation of Salaried Commercial Employees. As the years went by the socialist unions lost most of their members while the anti-democratic extremist organisations of white-collar employees and civil servants grew considerably.

Permeating the middle ranges of the German social structure were a complexity of attitudes and resentments on which the Nazis could build their propaganda and ideology.[21] The universities were not ivory towers standing apart from these influences, but on the contrary nourished and helped to disseminate them in the major institutional areas of the society. The atmosphere of the student fraternities, by the second half of the nineteenth century, was one of chauvinistic arrogance, authoritarian elitism and militaristic culture. What the students heard in the lecture rooms from many of their professors in no way clashed with their leisure-time values. By the 1890s, the ideological content of a lecture not infrequently bore more than a superficial resemblence to the ideals of the Pan-German League. Anti-Semitism, which was widespread in European society, here began to take on a political dimension as it was linked with the German *völkisch* ideology and with anti-democratic and anti-socialistic attitudes. It was propogated by such influential and respectable people as the historian Heinrich von Treitschke and the court preacher Adolf Stöcker. This socio-political outlook, which was intimately associated with academic training, exercised a broad influence on the professional life of the country. The creation of the Weimar Republic did not rupture the tradition in the least. Secondary-school teachers, who received their university education before the war, did not change their beliefs but continued to teach the new generation what they had learned from the old.

Moreover, this powerful ideological current was reinforced by various aspects of the post-war situation, apart from the prevailing sense of wounded nationalism. Opportunities in the Army, as well as in industry and commerce were restricted, bringing many middle-class youths to academic study. It has been estimated that nearly one third of German students, after 1926, went to university because of lack of opportunities in other fields. But career prospects upon graduation were not promising. Several thousands were unemployed, perhaps as many as 90,000 by 1934. Thousands of others found jobs which were well below their training and capacity, such as university trained engineers who were reduced to the status of technical employees of trade school level.[22] For all of these people, together with the demobilised junior army officers, normal career opportunities were blocked, creating a strong sense of "spiritual unemployment" and disaffection with prevailing social conditions. It was precisely this sense of frustration among the young generation of intellectual and professional leaders that Lenin saw as one of the necessary conditions for revolutionary change. But in Germany it provided the spearhead for the counter-revolution. Hence the youthfulness of the Nazi party and the high proportion of university-trained people in some sections of the Nazi elite, including the SS.

2. Who Were the Nazis?

In discussing the question of who supported the Nazis the related question of who were the Nazis is to some extent treated, but it may be useful briefly to summarise the material and to indicate the specific features of the various component groups of the Nazi elite.

Total party membership showed a remarkable rate of increase over the decade 1925 to 1935. It was 27,000 in 1925, and over the next four years increased to 178,000 despite its lack of electoral success. By 30th January 1933 it had attained 849,000 members — over forty per cent of whom were between eighteen to thirty years of age. Then by 1935 total membership stood at nearly two-and-a-half million. After the assumption of power, the role of youth declined somewhat, and there was a marked increase in the proportion of adherents in their forties and fifties. A number of them were civil servants, whose proportionate share of party membership rose steadily from under seven per cent in 1933 to thirteen per cent in 1935 and to twenty eight per cent by 1937. Apart from this change, and a moderate increase in the proportion of self-employed businessmen, artisans and professional men, the occupational distribution of membership remained fairly constant. The urban middle class was significantly over-represented.

The size of the party's bureaucracy appraoched half a million by 1935, and expanded to 700,000 after re-organisation in 1936 and 1937. The enormous size of Nazi officialdom shows that the movement itself was a significant agency of social mobility in which "talent" could be rewarded regardless of social background. The extent to which it occurred is indicated in Daniel Lerner's analysis of the Nazi elite in the years 1933 to 1935.[23] Lerner divided the elite into three basic components — the propagandists, the administrators and the coercers. The propagandists came from the upper middle class and had experienced a sharp decline in status in the post-war situation. The rewards they had expected were denied them. They were the alienated intellectuals who rejected the democratic ideals and values of the Weimar Republic, because these represented a loss of status and personal downgrading for them, and because these personal frustrations were associated with a deep sense of national humiliation. By adhering to the Nazi cause they could fight to regain their previous high social position in a new context.

The Nazi administrators contrasted sharply with the propagandists on a number of points. Their social background was characteristically lower middle class or "plebian": peasant and small tradesman, from the farms, villages and rural small towns of under 5,000 inhabitants. Their educational attainments were much lower than those of the propagandists, and even where they went to university the choice of studies differed markedly. The propagandists showed a preference for the arts, while the administrators preferred courses leading to professional degrees. Moreover, the average age of the administrators was about five years older than that of the propagandists, and this made a considerable difference in terms of military experience in the First World War. After the war, the administrator did not return to his rural environment, which in many cases he had already left before military service, but tried to engage in some sort of urban lower-middle-class job. Work was hard to get in those years of widespread unemployment, and most of them were unable to find responsible positions – only jobs of a transitory and menial nature. It is therefore not altogether surprising that one in four of them joined the Free Corps shock-troops, as compared with only one out of eleven propagandists and one out of seven of a random sample of names listed in the 1934 *Führerlexikon* (The Nazi *Who's Who*). From the Free Corps it was a short step to membership in the fledgling Nazi party. It is striking to note that one quarter of the administrators joined the party before 1923, and that two thirds of them had joined by 1930. Since high rank in the party correlated with early membership, the administrators, as a group, predominated in the higher and middle ranks of the party hierarchy and in its affiliated action organisations (SS, SA, Motor Corps, etc.). They outnumbered the propagandists by two-to-one proportionately in both the higher and middle ranks of the party. So in contrast to the propagandists, who regained an initial high social status through their participation in an extremist movement, the administrators started from a low status position in society and rose to leading positions in the party apparatus.

The coercers were specialists in violence and terror, which the Nazis used as a means both of attaining and of consolidating power. The two main groups of coercers were the solders and the police, and there are some rather striking contrasts between them. Although the professional soldiers came from the highest stratum of German society – the Junker aristocracy – while the police originated in the lower middle class, the police outnumbered the soldiers in the highest ranks of the party hierarchy by nearly three to one. The police, like the administrators, were much more seriously uprooted and disturbed by the post-war situation, and consequently came earlier to the Nazi movement and rose higher in it.

In spite of these differences in the elite groups, their common attribute as Nazi leaders was their *marginality* with respect to the society which they transformed. Some of the indicators Lerner used in determining marginality were place of birth, age, education, age at marriage and occupation. With regard to education, a strikingly high proportion of Nazi leaders attended university, but only a low percentage of them managed to complete their studies. Moreover the data shows that the core Nazis also experienced difficulties in the occupational sphere — excessive job-instability was characteristic of seventy per cent of the random sample. Taken together, these may be the most significant dimensions of their marginality because it shows that these men had no active commitment to the existing framework of society. They were uprooted, restless, frustrated and resentful. They were dominated by a feeling that they had nothing to lose and everything to gain by violent change. Hence their audacity and brutality went beyond anything that their opponents could comprehend, or defend themselves against.

3. Nazi Social Organisation

To understand the Nazi phenomenon more fully it is necessary to examine their use of power to reorganise, mobilise and control German society. The principles of social organisation which they practised have been brilliantly sketched by Franz Neumann.[24]

The first princple, which Neumann contrasts with democratic society, is that the diversification and autonomy of various social groups and organisations were submerged beneath totalitarian rule. All public activities were co-ordinated and controlled from the top by means of extreme centralisation and hierarchisation of power and authority. The Nazi term for it was *Gleichschaltung* — the subordination of the entire institutional complex of society to totalitarian controls. In contrast to Italian Fascism which had to cope with the traditional power of the Catholic Church, the full concentration of power was established within a very short space of time in Nazi Germany. Nevertheless, *Gleichschaltung* was a policy which in practice ran into certain obstacles, particularly in relation to the army. It is useful therefore to add the following considerations to Neumann's point.

In a sense the Nazis had it easier than the Italian Fascists because the Catholic Church was a potential competitor and opponent on an ideological level which was virtually impossible to attack directly. On the other hand, the German Army was a much more serious obstacle than its Italian counterpart, and the Nazis could not afford to risk its enmity. In the early stages of the Nazi regime, the army leaders avoided full commitment to the Third Reich. In the end it was among a group of Army officers that the most serious opposition to Hitler occurred — the July 1944 plot. Under the Nazis conscription was re-introduced, the military establishment expanded and re-armament proceeded vigorously. Nevertheless the Army was not beguiled into allowing Nazis to take over the highest command positions, and continued to resist outside interference. In particular there was serious concern about the size of the Nazi SA as a rival force, and about the aspirations of its leader Röhm to amalgamate with the Army and to bring his men into the officer corps. Minister of Defence, General von Blomberg, although pro-Nazi, and President Hindenburg warned Hitler that if the problem was not solved martial law would be declared and the Army would take over.[25] Hitler complied by murdering Röhm and other SA leaders at the end of June 1934. The Army leaders were satisfied,[26] although the instrument used for the killings — Himmler's SS — was to prove to be a far more dangerous challenge to the Army's independence.

By 1938, the relations between the conservative Army leaders and the Nazi regime changed. Hitler's power was established, and his desire for conquest was too intense to tolerate the caution and the hesitation which the Army command tried to impose on him. He forced von Blomberg and von Fritsch to resign in 1938, made himself head of the armed forces, and promoted Nazi-inspired officers to the highest positions. In the course of the war, Himmler's SS empire grew enormously. The Waffen SS expanded to over 900,000 men. After the July 1944 attempt on Hitler's life, it was placed on an equal footing with the Army. Moreover, Nazi political officers were attached to all military headquarters to enforce ideological conformity and reliability.

The second principle of Nazi social organisation was the destruction of normal social relations at work and at school, in youth groups and church. The free run of social intercourse was inhibited; individuals were detached and isolated from each other. The individual was made to relate, not to his neighbour or workmate, but to the abstract categories of Party, Nation, Race. Neumann called it the *"atomization of the individual"*. A prime example of the re-organisation of social networks was the Labour Front, with a membership of twenty-five million. It included almost the entire working population apart from the civil service. The Labour Front was subdivided into administrative units and specialised organisations, but the individual member did not belong to these; he belonged to the total body, the Labour Front itself.

That is, the Labour Front was not built from local, concrete organisations in which the individual participant entered into a network of intermediate social relations as is the case in British trade union branches and working mens' clubs. Rather he was simply one member of an impersonal mass-organisation of several millions, bureaucratically controlled and manipulated. As Neumann wrote: "not only the relations between the enterprise and the worker but even the relations among the workers themselves are now mediated by an autocratic bureaucracy."[27]

The Nazis therefore deliberately created a "mass" society, by atomising and massifying the subordinate classes. From this Neumann derived three further principles of social organisation. The atomised mass, in which each human particle is in a state of isolation, is controlled and manipulated by a bureaucratic elite. "Bureaucratic" in the sense that all spontaneity is denied, and that action is mechanically determined by orders from above. Authority, prestige and special privileges distinguish the elite leaders from the mass of followers. Hence the variety of elite formations: the SS, the leadership of the Labour Front, the Hitler Youth elites, women's organisation elites, university student elites, peasant elites and so on.

The fourth aspect is that this structure of relationships can be maintained and controlled only by unrelenting propaganda. The mass media, the educational system, cultural and sporting and other leisure activities were all used for propaganda purposes. Nor were the workshops, factories and offices, transport and streets left free. Public opinion was constantly moulded and manipulated to keep it in a ready state of service for the unfolding party objectives. Hitler's initial foreign policy and military successes worked to keep the level of credibility high enough, should the public's taste for mass meetings, military displays, book burnings and pogroms weary. The successful moulding of public opinion legitimated the authority of the elite bureaucracies, and made the entire structure of domination possible. The success of the propaganda can be measured by the fact that no widely based resistance movement was able to develop. Nazism was destroyed by outside military force, with no contribution from an internal resistance movement.

But underpinning the role of propaganda and ideology was the basic control mechanism of the Nazi regime: the selective and unpredictable use of violence and the threat of violence. Terror was the fifth principle of Nazi social organisation. It was the heart of the Nazi concept of law, and the purpose of the SS police-state. The law was not conceived as universal, general and impartial in its application, with all men treated as equals regardless of any social characteristic, whether class, religion, ethnic group, political affiliation or occupation. On the contrary, the Nazi concept of law was particularistic in the extreme: there were no rules and norms which applied equally to all, and the judiciary was an arm of the State instead of being independent of it. Normal legal practices and procedures were twisted and perverted, above all in the infamous people's courts. As the war progressed, Hitler denounced the "leniency" of the judiciary, and from 1942 onwards the Nazification of the law and of the legal profession intensified. It is therefore all the more disturbing that, in the post-war period, the de-Nazification of judges was not carried out. It was one of the professions most immune to de-Nazification.[28]

The SS State[29]

The concentration camp and the SS were the ultimate expressions of the Nazi system: an empire of murder and torture. The first concentration camp prisoners were Germans, members of political parties opposed to the Nazis. Using the pretext of the *Reichstag* fire, Hitler issued a decree on 28th February 1933 which aimed to destroy the Communist party and its various organs. The armed formations of SA and SS, together with the police, unleashed violent actions against Communists and certain Social Democrats for over two months. The prisons of Germany overflowed with the thousands arrested and held in protective custody, and on 20th March Himmler set up the first concentration camp at Dachau, near Munich. The last elections had been held on 5th March. Hitler had still failed to win a majority of the votes, but his position was strong enough to paralyse all opposition. On 23rd March an Enabling Law was passed by a two-thirds majority, with only the Social Democrats courageous enough to vote against it. The Centre party voted for it. In effect the law suspended the Weimar Constitution and enabled Hitler to destroy all political opposition. On 2nd May the Free Trade Unions were destroyed, on 22nd June the Social Democratic party was banned, and in the following weeks the other political parties were forced to dissolve themselves.

The SA, the SS and the police were extremely active in carrying out these measures, and by the end of July more than 25,000 people were held in protective custody. More than half of these were in Prussia which had six state-supported concentration camps, in addition to a number of SA torture centres and camps. After the summer of 1933 the scope and intensity of the terror subsided. But over a thousand people a month were being arrested on charges ranging from suspicion of high treason to "subversive remarks" such as insulting Nazi leaders or spreading atrocity stories. Between 1934 and 1937 there was a quiet consolidation of the concentration camp system, together with a signficant extension of the categories of prisoners. In addition to political prisoners (who wore a red triangular badge), there were now Jehovah's Witnesses persecuted for their pacifism (purple badge); so-called 'anti-social' prisoners including Gypsies (black badge); so-called habitual criminals (green badge); homosexuals (pink badge); emigrants (blue badge). There were also large numbers of Jews whose social and economic position was deteriorating steadily and remorselessly. The Jewish prisoners were identified by a yellow patch meant to mock the Star of David. The camps were therefore used as a means of political control through the exercise of unprecedented viciousness and murder; and they were used as centres of terror against groups of people with "negative" characteristics according to Nazi ideology. Before the war, then, the Nazis were engaged in political and ideologically motivated murders on a scale which was small only in comparison with later events.

During the war there were two additional functions which the camps served. They provided a secluded environment for *part* of the mass murder programmes of the Nazis; and they were, especially after March 1942, one of the sources of slave labour for war industries. In the camps, SS doctors carried out "medical" experiments on prisoners, selected invalids, emotionally disturbed people and others whom they regarded as "undesirable" for extermination. In the camps, Soviet officials and communists were murdered in their tens and hundreds of thousands. They were taken from prisoner-of-war camps, *with the pre-arranged agreement of the High Command of the German Armed Forces (OKW),* and shot in the nearest concentration camps. But murder was not confined to the camps: following on the heels of the German Army as they penetrated deeply into Russian territory were SS units whose targets were Jews, Gypsies and communist officials. There were four of these SS units, called *Einsatzgruppen,* in Russia. Each consisted of between 500 and 1,000 men, and units were further subdivided into mobile murder squads, called *Einsatzkommandos.* Some of the commanders of these units were university graduates: Dr Otto Ohlendorf, commander of *Einsatzgruppe D* which was attached to the German 11th Army[30] in Southern Ukraine, held degrees in law and economics. His unit murdered 90,000 people between June 1941 and June 1942. Dr Paul Blobel, a former architect, was a prominent member of *Einsatzgruppe C* in Northern Ukraine. Another commanding officer in that unit was Dr Ernst Biberstein, formerly a Protestant pastor. Up to November 1942, over one million Jewish children, women and men were murdered. The cold butchery of Babyi-Yar, known through Yevtushenko's poem and Kuznetsov's documentary novel, was one place in that landscape.

But for the Nazi leaders murder by shooting was not efficient enough — it was too slow and it left behind too much evidence, since it was difficult to get rid of so many dead bodies. Therefore, by the end of 1941 experiments were being made to adopt the methods of the "Euthanasia Operation", gas chambers and ovens, on a larger scale. Preparations were being made to turn the concentration camps into death factories. The discussions, preliminary plans, the physical arrangements, and the administrative structure are all visible in the following ministerial memorandum of 25th October 1941:

"From: The Reich Minister for the Occupied Eastern Territories
            Controller: *AGR* Dr Wetzel
Ref: The solution of the Jewish Question
To: The Reich Commissioner for Ostland
Ref: Your report of 4.10.41 concerning the solution of the
            Jewish Question

With reference to my letter of 18th October 1941, I have now to inform you that *Oberdienstleiter* Brack of the Führer's Chancellery has agreed to collaborate in the manufacture of the necessary buildings and gas apparatus. The latter is at present in short supply, and production must be stepped up. As Brack is of the opinion that the manufacture of the apparatus will lead to much greater difficulties in the Reich than on the spot, he considers that it would be most useful to send some of his people — in particular his analytical chemist, Dr Kallmeyer — to Riga immediately to assume responsibility for all further developments. *Oberdienstleiter* Brack points out that there will be a certain amount of danger attached to the future proceedings and that special safety precautions will be required. In these circumstances I would ask you to apply to *Oberdienstleiter* Brack at the Führer's Chancellery, through your *Höhere SS and Polizeiführer* for the secondment of Dr Kallmeyer and such other assistance as you may require. In this connection I have to inform you that *Sturmbannführer* Eichmann, who is in charge of the Jewish question at the *Reichsicherheitshauptampt* is in agreement with this procedure. He tells me that camps for Jews are to be established in Riga and in Minsk, to which Jews from the Altreich will eventually be sent. For the present, Jews from the Altreich will be evacuated to Litzmannstadt and other camps, and those who are 'fit for work' subsequently transferred further east for use as labour.

In our present position we cannot afford to have scruples about taking advantage of Brack's facilities for the elimination of Jews who are not fit for work, as these will provide a way of avoiding any possible recurrence of the events which occurred, according to a report I have in front of me, at the shooting of the Jews in Vilna. Incidentally, I see from the report that the shootings took place in public, which can hardly have been approved.

Jews fit for work, on the other hand, are to be transferred further east for use as labour. It goes without saying that the men are to be separated from the women.

Please forward a report on your latest measures."[31]

The final reference in the letter points up a further aspect of the Nazi system – the use of slave labour for the war economy. Shortage of labour, particularly of skilled labour, was a very serious problem for the German war economy in both world wars since there were tremendous demands on manpower for military purposes. The means the Nazis employed to solve it was typical of them. When sufficient numbers of French, Belgian and Dutch volunteers could not be enticed into the new "workers' paradise", an organisation for the forced conscription of foreign labour headed by Gauleiter Sauckel was created, early in 1942. It was only partly successful in the west; and proved to be one of the major sources of the French Resistance as the Communists were able to organise the workers' fight against deportation. In the east, the Jews represented an important pool of skilled labour. This was recognised toward the end of 1942, at the same time as genocide efforts were intensified. It meant that those Jewish people, who were considered "fit for work" would not be killed immediately, but would be placed in the hands of the SS Economic and Administrative Office (WVHA). This institution, under Himmler's direction, established a number of industries essential to the war effort. It had links with many of Germany's leading firms, such as Krupp and I.G. Farben, providing them with slave labour. Under the WVHA, formed early in 1942, concentration camp slave labour was used on a vast scale for the war economy.

The use of terror – from intimidation of political opponents to their execution, from the degradation of civilian populations to methodical mass murder — was the very foundation of the Third Reich which unfolded with relentless logic from the Nazi seizure of power. From street fighting and bullying in the 1920s and early 1930s, it was a short step to murdering political opponents; and from unleashing war to exterminating Polish intelligensia, Russian officials, the physically and mentally handicapped, Gypsies, Jews and Resistance fighters — it was all part of, and contained within the elementary Nazi concept of enslaving Europe. That was the simple core of all the slogans, speeches, marches and violence. The instrument which was most closely involved in putting into practice the political ideology was the SS. Unlike the Army, the SA and the police, the SS was wholly and without reservation the instrument of the Nazi party. It alone was utterly reliable. And under Himmler's direction, the SS grew to enormous size during the war years. In addition to its political police and murder activities, it played an essential part in the war economy through its enslavement of foreign labour, its plunder of other nations' economic resources, and even its exploitation of the dead bodies of its murdered victims. Moreover its role in military affairs expanded steadily — the strength of the Waffen/SS was 150,000 by the end of 1940, rising to over 900,000 men towards the end of the war. Its aim was to prolong the war, to refuse defeat, to fight for time until Germany's newest weapons, the rockets and jet aircraft, could salvage the lost war.

In the SS state one can see the ultimate meaning of Nazism: an empire of death-fascination, of humiliation and murder for the sake of having that final power over other people. It was the only means the Nazis found by which to measure their "superiority". But the act of terrorising and devouring whole communities, in thousands of places, involved more than the SS. As John Weiss stated, "it was an act of German society . . . ." It required "the active participation of bureaucrats, businessmen, lawyers, judges, accountants, physicians, foreign-office officials, ordinary politicians, and soldiers, as well as party officials, SS men, and the murdering *Einsatzkommandos*".[32]

NOTES

1. See the collections of essays and readings in *The Third Reich* International Council for Philosophy and Humanistic Studies, Weidenfeld and Nicolson, 1955; John Snell (ed), *The Nazi Revolution*, 1959; Ernst Nolte (ed), *Theorien über den Faschismus*, Köln 1967; and Gilbert Allardyce (ed), *The Place of Fascism in European History*, Prentice-Hall 1971.

For interesting discussions of interpretative tendencies, see Wolfgang Sauer, "National Socialism: Totalitarianism or Fascism?", *American Historical Review,* December 1967; Renzo de Felice, *Le Interpretazioni del Fascismo,* Laterza 1972, 4th ed.; Karl Dietrich Bracher, *The German Dictatorship,* 1970 transl. Chapter 1; and John Weiss, *The Fascist Tradition,* Harper & Row 1967, pp134-44.

2. It is to be noted that not all Catholics voted for the Centre party and its Bavarian wing (BVP). In his study, *The Catholic Church and Nazi Germany,* Guenter Levy indicated that of a Catholic electorate of nearly thirteen million less than half voted for the Catholic parties while more than two million voted Nazi in the 1932 election (p19). In the March 1933 election the Centre party was bolstered by votes from non-Catholics, presumably from middle-class liberals opposed to both Nazis and Nationalists.

3. Routledge and Kegan Paul 1960, p220.

4. Hans Gerth, *"The Nazi Party: Its Leadership and Composition",* in Robert Merton et al., *Reader in Bureaucracy,* p106.

5. *Behemoth* New York, Harper & Row, 1966, p423.

6. *Ibid.,* p424.

7. Peter N. Stearns, *European Society in Upheaval* Macmillan 1967, gives a figure of half a million downwardly mobile from the lower middle class during the 1920s (p338).

8. S.M. Lipset and Reinhard Bendix, *Social Mobility in Industrial Society,* Univ. of California Press, 1959, present evidence from five elections in European countries and the USA in support of the hypothesis that "downward mobile persons are less likely to identify with the political and economic organizations of the working class than manual workers who inherit their class status" (pp69-70).

9. Eberhard Czichon, *Wer Verhalf Hitler zur Macht?* Cologne 1967, p36.

10. Reference is sometimes made to Bosch, a German liberal, as an example of opposition. However Bosch was present at a meeting of the most prominent bankers and industrialists in Berlin on 20th February 1933, in which three million reichsmarks were donated to the Nazi election fund. Hitler had told the meeting that he intended to put an end to parliamentary democracy and to create a dictatorship. Bosch's acquiescence in the support the meeting gave to Hitler is a measure of his isolation and of the pro-Hitler consensus.

11. In a sample of elites, only one of forty seven big business leaders suffered "major" persecution, 1933-44, as compared with twenty of forty five SPD and trade union leaders. See Lewis J. Edinger, "Post-Totalitarian Leadership", *APSR,* LIV 1, March 1960, p74, table III.

12. *Hitler's Social Revolution* Weidenfeld and Nicolson 1967, p157.

13. Neumann, p291.

14. Norman H. Baynes (ed.), *The Speeches of Adolf Hitler, April 1922-August 1939* Oxford UP 1942, Vol. 1, pp804-5.

15. *Hitler's Social Revolution,* p294.

16. *The Federation of German Industry in Politics,* Cornell UP

1965, pp18 and 21.

17. Page 157.

18. For a stimulating discussion and evaluation, see T.W. Mason, "The primacy of politics — Politics and economics in National Socialist Germany", in Woolf (ed.) *The Nature of Fascism.*

19. Himmler transformed the Keppler circle into his *Freundeskreis.* They made "enormous contributions" to the SS (Henry Ashby Turner, Jr. "Big Business and the Rise of Hitler", *American Historical Review,* Vol. 75, 1969-70, p65). In return the SS provided industry with huge resources of forced labour.

20. See Charles Loomis and Allen J. Beagle, "The Spread of German Nazism in Rural Areas", *American Sociological Review,* 1946, pp724-34; R. Heberle, *From Democracy to Nazism,* Baton Rouge 1945; A. Gerschenkron, *Bread and Democracy in Germany,* New York, 1966 new edition; Jeremy Noakes, *The Nazi Party in Lower Saxony,* Oxford UP 1971, esp. Chapters VI and VII.

21. See Weiss, *The Fascist Tradition,* pp16-18 and 27-8.

22. Kornhauser, pp187-9. See also Stearns p339.

23. "The Nazi Elite", in *World Revolutionary Elites,* Harold D. Lasswell and Daniel Lerner (eds.), Cambridge, Mass. MIT Press 1965.

24. *Behmoth,* pp400-03.

25. Wheeler-Bennett, *The Nemesis of Power,* pp319-20; Craig, pp476-7; Bullock, *Hitler,* p300.

26. See Herbert Rosinski's penetrating evaluation of Reichswehr attitudes, *The German Army,* Pall Mall, 1966, Chapter VI. See also Robert J. O'Neill's detailed study of the period, *The German Army and the Nazi Party 1933-1939,* Cassell 1966.

27. Neumann, p419.

28. See David Childs, *From Schumacher to Brandt,* Pergamon Press, 1966, Chapter 4: "Bonn is not Weimar but . . . ." During the Second World War 159 death sentences were passed in British Courts, compared with 16,000 in Germany, plus a further 10,000 passed by German military courts. (p46).

29. The following section is based in part on Helmut Krausnick *et. al., Anatomy of the SS State,* transl. by Richard Barry *et. al.,* Collins 1968.

30. Ohlendorf testified that the wristwatches of the victims were given to the front-line troops at the request of the Army. Nuremberg trial testimony quoted by George St George, *The Road to Babi Yar,* Neville Spearman 1967, p148.

31. Nuremberg Document NO.365, quoted by Krausnick, pp97-8.

32. *The Fascist Tradition,* p107.

Chapter 8 France: Popular Front, Defeat, Resistance

The Third Republic faced a series of crises in the first three decades of its existence. Each time the Republican form of government emerged in a stronger position, with the anti-Republican elements in the Church, the Army and Civil service correspondingly weakened. The Republican victory in the 1877 elections was followed by the struggle over secular education. Then in 1888 and 1889 the Boulangist crisis flared up. Although it fizzled out in a melodramatic anti-climax, it nevertheless manifested a chauvinistic, authoritarian and anti-parliamentary temperament which was taken up again on a larger scale ten years later in the bitter struggles over the Dreyfus Affair. However, the Republican system drew its strength from the support of the peasantry, the teaching profession, the anti-clerical middle and lower classes and increasingly from the industrial workers. Its durability was such that the basic political institutions were not shaken or threatened even in the years of war from 1914 to 1918. On the contrary, the Republican form of government was awarded an invincible legitimacy because it provided the political framework within which the country withstood a long and terrible war fought on its own territory. The military victory was achieved by the Republic. No other form of government was then possible. The certainty on this level stands in marked contrast with the post-war situations of neighbouring Germany and Italy.

But through these crises, and particularly the Dreyfus Affair, a new right-wing ideology developed. Its chief exponent was the royalist Charles Maurras of the *Action Française,* who absorbed the whole stream of counter-revolutionary thought since 1789. Its connection with Fascism on the *ideological* level was striking. All its major themes were developed by *Action Française:* extreme nationalism, authoritarianism, anti-rationalism, anti-intellectualism, anti-Semitism.

Action Française, was anti-Republican and royalist in the tradition of conservative thought, but what was new and of significance for the future was that it expressed these ideas in nationalistic terms. Previously in France, patriotism was a revolutionary attribute. In the French Revolution, patriotism and Jacobinism merged. The Communards of 1871 had refused to surrender to the Prussians; it was the monarchist Right which wanted peace. Moreover, the moderate Republicans inculcated a strong sense of patriotism in their

secularisation of the educational system. The League for Education, a
major force in the struggle for secularisation, used the slogan: "For the
Motherland by *book* and *sword*." It was not until much later, after the
Dreyfus Affair, that the slogan was modified under the influence of
anti-militarism and pacifism.[1] But in the Boulangist crisis and more
decisively in the Dreyfus Affair, patriotism was transformed into
nationalism, and identified with authoritarianism. As such it became
the property of the Right. Those who defended Dreyfus were accused
of weakening France by questioning the authority of the Army leaders
and by undermining military values. They were un-French, probably
foreigners or influenced by foreigners, and Jews.

When the young Maurras joined *Action Française* he convinced its
leaders that the struggle against the Republic should have as its goal
the establishment of a powerful monarchy. Although the Dreyfus
Affair was regulated by Waldeck-Rousseau's government of Republican
Defence, which unleashed a counter-offensive against the Church,
Action Française did not disappear. It never became a political power,
but through the writings of its leading spokesmen Maurras, Jacques
Bainville, Léon Daudet and Louis Dimier, it exercised a strong influence
on intellectual and political life. In 1908 a daily newspaper was
produced, edited by Daudet, which expressed the position of the
extreme right for the next twenty years. But its royalism, which by
1918 was the deadest of issues, isolated it from the main stream of
political thought. After the war, new rightist organisations sprang up,
stimulated by the example of Italian Fascism. These leagues flourished
only very briefly in the mid 1920s, but, during the economic crisis of
the next decade, they revived again on a much larger scale.

The most successful was the *Croix de Feu* of Colonel de la Rocque,
which claimed several hundred thousands of members in 1935, and well
over one million in 1938. Though la Rocque is sometimes characterised
as a Fascist leader, there are grounds for discounting this. In the first
place, the ideology of *Croix de Feu* was conservative, basically
emphasising respect for established order, rather than demanding the
creation of a new political system. Secondly, its political practice was
comparatively mild. After the Popular Front government dissolved the
leagues in June 1936, la Rocque's organisation became a political party,
the French Social Party (PSF). It decided to operate strictly as an
electoral party, and to accept the existing political institutions. The
decision is revealing: elections had taken place already, in May, which
meant that for the time being it would be impossible to secure the
parliamentary representation befitting a party of its size. In other

words, the parliamentary tactic was chosen at a time when it was most ineffective. As a league it was both declared illegal and reduced to inactivity in 1936; as an electoral party it was largely irrelevant, despite its large membership.

There were other groups on the extreme right, most notably the French Popular Party (PPF) led by Doriot. Founded in 1936 with the purpose of destroying Communism, within a year it recruited a membership of over 100,000. If there was a real Fascist party in France, this was it. But in the context of the time it did not have much more importance than had Mosley's organisation in Britain. After the fall of France, it played a certain role under Nazi patronage when Doriot became one of the leaders of the collaboration.

Without doubt, then, home-bred French Fascism had no more than nuisance value during the thirties. The problem is to explain its failure in contrast with the success of Fascism in capturing state power in two of the neighbouring countries.

In the first place, there was in France a very marked social stability and institutional continuity. The aftermath of the war did not have the profound and disruptive consequences which were experienced in both Italy and Germany. The existing political institutions were not in the throes of breaking down as in Italy, nor were they transformed as in Germany. Moreover, the rapid expansion of French industry in the two decades preceding 1914 was interrupted by the war. Consequently there were only moderate changes in the distribution of the labour force: a constant but slow decline in the numbers of persons employed in agriculture and a fairly substantial increase in industrial employment from 1921 to 1931. There was nothing drastic about the pace of economic development, nor about the rate of urbanisation. France was still more rural than urban, and its relative underdevelopment enabled it to resist the immediate force of the world economic depression which created mass unemployment in Germany, Britain and the United States. In France there was unemployment, but in the hundreds of thousands not millions; and some of it was reduced by the expedient of obliging half a million immigrant workers to leave the country.[2] The relative sluggishness of France's industrial development shielded her from the worst consequences of the economic crisis.

Secondly, coupled with the underlying social stability, the main stream of political life remained moderately conservative within the Republican framework. As exemplified by the dominant position of the Radical party, Republican political attitudes were deeply implanted in the broad middle strata of French society, both rural and urban. These attitudes developed through many crises and gained renewed legitimacy by the victory in the First World War. The contrast with the illiberal outlook of the middle class in Germany was sharp. There was activity at the extremes in France, but the main stream of opinion – while it shifted from right to left and back again – nevertheless remained firmly attached to the *status quo* and refractory to authoritarian adventures. Even some of the leaders of the extreme right, when it came to the point, wanted no more than bourgeois order and bourgeois peace and quiet. This attitude was part of the underlying defensive mentality of the French after the war, symbolised by the construction of the Maginot Line. The contradictory elements of this mentality led to the absurd military posture which Hitler was able effectively to exploit. There was, on the one hand, the realisation that the country had to be defended against the huge German menace. But on the other hand the desire for peace, for an end to war, drastically inhibited the formulation of a mobile, flexible and aggressive military and diplomatic policy. The Maginot Line was a mammoth expression of French desires for security, peace and the old way of doing things.

A third reason was that the labour movement was not politically exhausted and defeated as it had been in both Italy and Germany before the rise of Fascism. On the contrary, the labour movement responded powerfully to right-wing agitation in 1934, and went on to find a basis of electoral agreement which permitted the establishment of the Popular Front government in 1936. The Popular Front did not last long, but it did demonstrate a broad unity of action at a critical point against the danger of the extreme Right.

These are the basic reasons which account for the failure of Fascism in France. As René Rémond has stated, the French right in this period consisted of a vast majority of conservatives, a small minority of old fashioned reactionnaires and only a handful of Fascists.[3] Nevertheless its failure was not total. Fascist ideas gradually spread through the dominant class of French society, which later facilitated large-scale collaboration with the Nazi occupiers. In particular, the activities of many big businessmen, top civil servants and political leaders of the Vichy regime reveal the extent to which this ideology penetrated. Rémond has described the process in the last years before the war:

"Important sectors of conservative opinion drifted from a moderate attachment to parliamentary institutions to a sympathy, at first discreet and qualified, but then more and more open, for the authoritarian regimes of neighbouring countries. The press, even that supposedly non-partisan in politics, at the same time reflected and accentuated this drift, the magazines and weeklies more than the dailies."[4]

The Labour Movement

In both Italy and Germany Fascism came to power after the labour movement had exhausted its political potentialities. In France, however, the labour movement responded powerfully to the Fascist threat. The Popular Front government carried through a number of reforms in the field of social legislation and industrial relations, showing the vitality of the movement. Even though Léon Blum's government was overwhelmed by internal and external pressures, the reforms lost in the last years of the Republic and the labour movement torn to shreds with the approach of war, it again recovered its strength to lead the Resistance against the occupying power and the Vichy regime. In short, it played a very active and central political role in these years, and never long remained a passive victim of events.

Before analysing the situation in more detail, it is first necessary to sketch in the background developments of the labour movement.

When the Paris Commune was destroyed in 1871, the working-class organisations which had been created during the Second Empire were suppressed. A law of 1872 defined strikes as a plot against the social order, and it became illegal to organise a trade union. It was not until 1884 that a law permitting freedom of association was passed, authorising the creation of workers' and employers' organisations. It gave legal recognition to the fact that the organisation of the labour movement had resumed soon after the repression of the Commune. The first national workers' congress was held in 1876, but on that occasion and in the next few years, political debates were avoided. However, modernation rapidly gave way to a more revolutionary approach, and in 1879 the first socialist workers' congress was held. It adopted the views of the Marxist, Jules Guesde. He was convinced of the necessity of creating a political party which, operating through the parliamentary arena, would transform society. And he saw the role of the trade union as a strictly defensive one of protecting the workers' standards of living. Guesde's approach, however, clashed with a different revolutionary conception which was held by a number of trade unionists. Theirs was the doctrine of anarcho-syndicalism, which rejected parliamentary political action because it involved trusting bourgeois intermediaries who would divert the class struggle from its aim of emancipation through the expropriation of the capitalist class. The only way emancipation could be achieved was through direct action on the part of the workers: the general strike. It would be organised by the trade unions, not by a political party. Moreover, the trade union was not only a fighting organisation; after the victory of the general strike it would organise production and distribution, and would be the basis of social re-organisation. These ideas which were also current in Italy, became dominant prior to 1914, and were officially adopted by the General Confederation of Labour in 1906 (The Charter of Amiens). But in the last years before the war, the notion of a revolutionary general strike lost its appeal and increasingly appeared to be impractical and utopian. The outbreak of war in 1914 led not to the revolutionary general strike but to trade-union participation in the war effort. The anarcho-syndicalist doctrine was effectively killed.

Socialist ideas, on the other hand, proved to be more durable. The six different socialist parties of the 1880s and 1890s were regrouped into two parties by the end of the century. Guesde and Vaillant led the revolutionary tendency, while Jean Jaurès led the reformist tendency. In 1905 they united in a party which was called the French Section of the Workers' International (SFIO). Electorally it made great progress, gathering one-and-a-half-million votes in 1914. But the tension between the two tendencies was never resolved, and under the impact of events – particularly the Bolshevik revolution in Russia, and strikes and agitation in France in 1919 and 1920 – the Socialist party split in 1920. The minority, headed by Blum and Longuet, remained Social Democrats, attached to the Second International; the majority, headed by Cachin and Frossard, formed the French Communist party, which affiliated to the Third International. A split in the trade-union ranks followed. The General Confederation of Labour had emerged from the war with a decided reformist majority, whose views were put forth in the "Minimum Programme" of 1918. The Minimum Programme advanced a number of demands designed to improve the living standards and working conditions of its membership, including the nationalisation of key industries. It was aimed at turning the trade unions away from pre-war syndicalism in the direction of respectable business unionism, concerned with collective agreements and the institutionalisation of industrial conflict. But the syndicalist opposition to this orientation found common ground with the Communist militants in their emphasis on class struggle and internationalism. They joined together to split off into a new confederation, called the United General Confederation of Labour, in the Winter of 1921-2.[5]

Membership in the General Confederation of Labour (CGT) reached an all-time high at the beginning of 1920, with a figure approaching the two-million mark. By the end of the year, however, with the defeat of the general strike, it fell off to less than three quarters of a million. When the split occurred, the United CGT won a majority of these members (half a million) but by 1935 it had lost the greater part of them. The reformist CGT, on the other hand, recovered some of its numerical strength by the adhesion of the 300,000-strong federation of civil service unions. These figures reveal more than the relative strengths of the two confederations; they show that for most of the inter-war period, the vast bulk of the French industrial working class was unorganised.

The situation changed dramatically from 1934 onwards when the fear of Fascism created a wide-spread desire for unity in the labour movement. On 6th February 1934 an extreme right-wing demonstration demanded the resignation of the Radical prime minister Daladier. The demonstration erupted into a vicious battle which raged for several hours, and in which twenty people were killed and hundreds wounded. Despite his comfortable majority, Daladier resigned and a government of "national unity" was formed. On 9th and 12th February there were strike movements in protest — on the latter date a twenty-four-hour general strike of four million workers. There were also massive demonstrations throughout France, as unity in action was being forged in the labour movement.

The foreign policy of the new government strengthened the movement for unity in an unexpected way. As a result of negotiations with the Soviet Union for a defence pact in 1935, the Communist party abandoned its anti-militarism, and looked for alliances with both the Socialists and with the Radicals. In the summer of 1935, the PCF reached a formal agreement with the Radicals, whom they were to support until Munich. The agreement was for a moderate and vague programme in which nationalisations were ruled out. Even the mild "structural reforms" of the CGT, an adaptation of the 1918 Minimum Programme to depression conditions, which the Socialist party supported, were rejected as too extreme.[6] It was a repudiation with a vengeance of the "social Fascist" theory which the German Communists had used against the German Social Democrats as their reason for not joining forces against the Nazi threat.

On the trade union level, reunification of the CGT was accomplished in 1935, on terms which were disadvantageous to the Communist confederation. They were in a minority of two against six on the executive board.

On the basis of reconciliation the Popular Front coalition of Socialists, Communists and Radicals won a major electoral victory in the national elections of May 1936. For the first time the Socialists became the largest party in the Chamber, and Blum became Prime Minister. But before the new government was installed in office, a gigantic wave of strikes swept through the country, involving nearly two million workers — that is twice the number who were organised members of trade unions. Most of the strikes were of an apparently revolutionary nature: factory occupations. Commencing in May the unforeseen explosion reached its peak in June and July, declined in August, but revived in September, before diminishing over the next three months. The movement affected a great variety of industries — aircraft, metals, cars, textiles, chemicals, as well as insurance, hotels and cafes. And the population in the neighbourhood of occupied works demonstrated its active sympathy and solidarity with the men.[7] It was a re-enactment of the 1920 Italian factory occupation movement, but on a much larger scale. Moreover since the political conditions were more favourable for the movement, it was a unique industrial experience, unparalleled elsewhere.

Blum attempted to resolve the unexpected social crisis by negotiation with the CGT and the representatives of the employers (General Confederation of French Production). The outcome, known as the Matignon Agreement, provided for collective bargaining, employer recognition of trade unions, differential wage increases favouring lower paid workers, and the election of shop stewards. The agreement was signed early in June, and social legislation was rushed through parliament. It also included the establishment of a forty-hour week and the right to paid holidays. The main features of the legislation had already been obtained in other countries for many years; but in France industrial relations were in a very primitive state, and previously there had been little social legislation.

For the first time, the employers were forced to concede that the paternalistic conception of industrial relations was inadequate. But their response was not one of accomodation to the new conditions. On the contrary, they felt humiliated and strongly resisted carrying out the new legislation. The president of the Confederation was removed for having signed the agreement, and was replaced by a more aggressive and militant one who wished to repudiate the concessions. Moreover, the entire structure of the employers' Confederation was changed. The old loose federative structure was abolished and a central office with full powers of decision created.[8] The new structure was in fact a streamlined instrument for effective action. The nature of the employers re-organisation contrasted with the re-organisation of the trade union movement some months earlier. At the unification congress, the federalist structure was adopted against the Communist proposals for strict central executive control. Clearly the desire for autonomy was stronger and the political differences sharper, even at the point of unification, than were those in the employers' organisation.

The workers did not reject the Matignon Agreement, as in the similar situation of May and June 1968, but tended to ignore it. The agreement did not bring strike action to an end because other aims were not satisfied. On one level, the strikes intensified and reinforced the anti-Fascist thrust of the new Popular Front government. On another they struck at the paternalistic quality of social class relations. These aims, which were in some part revolutionary, were implied in the gathering momentum of the labour movement as expressed on the electoral level, in the waves of occupations and in the vast increase of political consciousness which was directly measurable in the rapdily expanded membership of all the working-class organs.

Having concluded the Matignon Agreement, the Blum government exercised considerable restraint in employing direct force against the strikers, relying instead on persuasion. In this, the government was greatly aided by both trade union and political leaders, Socialist and Communist, who wanted to check the strike movement rather than develop it further. It is significant that the Communist party, led by Thorez, claimed that all the essential demands had been met, so that it was necessary to return to work.

At the same time, the Communist party worked hard to strengthen its position in the CGT. Communist union officials gradually replaced the unofficial leaders on factory strike committees. Campaigning for "unity", they stigmatised those individuals and committees who disagreed with their policies as "disrupters" and "undesirables".[9] This was successful in preventing the militant non-Communist left from exercising much influence. On the other hand, the right-wing trade-union reformists organised themselves into a faction for the purpose of fighting what they called Communist "colonisation" of the labour movement. Later this group collaborated actively with the Vichy regime, one of their leaders (Belin) becoming Minister of Labour for a period. Meanwhile, the centre group led by Léon Jouhaux fought to maintain its once predominant influence. Although the fraternal strife for the control of the CGT was very bitter, there was basic agreement among the leadership of all the groups that the strikes should be stopped.[10]

Meanwhile, the CGT grew to an enormous size, as previously unorganised workers were joining the trade unions in hundreds of thousands. At unification, the CGT had about one million members, a year later it was almost five-and-a-half times greater. Many unions increased by enormous proportions: the miners from 75,000 to well over a quarter of a million; metal workers from 50,000 to over three quarters of a million. At the same time, mebership in both the Socialist and Communist parties expanded rapidly; the Communists more than doubled their membership to approach the 400,000 mark. But this enormous social and political force which mushroomed into unexpected existence in 1936 was not able to consolidate itself, and was to disintegrate almost as rapidly as it had arisen.

Disintegration and Resistance

The Popular Front government was not able to withstand the pressures on it. The government had hoped that its social legislation would generate sufficient purchasing power to increase demand, and therefore to stimulate production. But the inflation kept prices well above wages, so that the wage increases granted in the Matignon Agreement were below nominal value. In addition there was an enormous flight of capital from the country, which the government tried in vain to stop. The devaluation of the franc in the Autumn of 1936 brought only temporary relief, and in the following months the financial situation continued to deteriorate. By a substantial majority the Chamber of Deputies voted full powers in financial matters to Blum. However, the Senate twice refused to endorse this. On the second occasion, June 1937, Blum resigned. He was succeeded by a Radical prime minister who fared no better until he had completely re-organised the government, excluding the Socialist ministers.

The Popular Front was politically defeated, and the parliamentary system itself was seriously damaged. By 1938 government by decree was increasingly replacing the legislative process. After the Munich crisis of September 1938, decree powers were granted to the executive which annulled the social legislation of the Popular Front. In the drive for increased war preparation and in the atmosphere of international crisis the response of the Chamber was increasingly to abdicate its responsibilities by transferring its powers to the executive.[11]

The factional fight in the unions was embittered by the political events leading to war. In the CGT, the Jouhaux centre group which still held control, was hostile to the appeasement of Hitler's demands on

Czechoslovakia. At a CGT congress held shortly after the Munich crisis, the Jouhaux group allied itself with the Communists. At the same time, the right-wing *Syndicats* group favoured the appeasement of Hitler at Munich, and so moved further in the direction which enabled them to participate actively in the Vichy regime. The factional fight was further intensified when the congress was followed by the failure of a one-day general strike called for 30th November 1938.

Worker unrest had continued sporadically after the great explosion of sit-down strikes in 1936, spurred on by the continuously rising cost of living. The general strike was called in protest against government decrees which were to "liberalise" the forty-hour week, one of the most prized gains of 1936. Overtime at low rates was made semi-compulsory in some industries, particularly in armament plants and related war industries. No provision was made for consultation with the trade unions. The general strike was ruthlessly crushed by Daladier; and many employers, including the government itself, turned the failure of the strike into a revenge for June 1936. The extent of victimisation may be gauged from the fact that one group of moderate employers pleaded for it to stop.[12] The CGT was gravely weakened. Its membership had been falling steadily from its peak of nearly five and a half million in 1936. Between the failure of the general strike and the outburst of war, it was reduced to about two million members.

Communist influence in the CGT was fairly extensive though by no means total. They controlled twelve out of thirty industrial federations by 1939, including metals, engineering, building, chemicals and electricity. They had an important influence, though not control, among railwaymen and miners. The influence of the *Syndicats* group was primarily among the white-collar unions, though even here it was not too extensive as this was the stronghold of the centre group.

Political events rapidly changed the balance of forces within the CGT in 1939. The Nazi-Soviet pact of August 1939 caught the centre group, as well as the Communists by surprise. The Communists accomplished the change-over in political attitude with ease. But the centre group was extremely hostile to it, and later condemned the Russian invasion of eastern Poland. They joined with the *Syndicats* group to expel from the CGT those who would not condemn the Hitler-Stalin pact. In some cases it was necessary to dissolve entire unions; the most notable example was the important Paris regional federation. A week later, towards the end of September 1939, the government banned the Communist party and its publications. Not content with arresting leading Communists, the government also sent several thousands of "suspects" to detention camps without trial. Many non-Communist trade unionists were included. Other civil liberties were abused to the detriment of Socialists and trade unionists, while appeasers, defeatists and pro-Fascists did not suffer and Fascist propaganda was untouched.[13]

All this contributed to the confusion and demoralisation of the CGT, which was immensely affected by mobilisation for war. By 1940 membership had fallen to well under a million, almost half of whom were civil servants. The illegal position of the Communists was not altogether without advantages in the period of the phoney war. New government decrees were very unfavourable to the working class, and they could not be entirely justified by war conditions because military action was in a state of uneasy suspension for months. While prices rose sharply, wages were frozen and subject to special taxes. The authority of the employers was enhanced to semi-military status, while the trade unions were impotent. The Communist CGT weekly, *La Vie Ouvrière* appeared illegally and stressed that the war was a pretext for the elimination of the 1936 social gains. It appealed to pacifist tendencies by arguing that Russia, in its desire for peace, was right to stay out of an "imperialist" war. Moreover, it stated that the two sides were not fighting but merely watching each other, while huge profits were being made on war production and great quantities of iron ore were being sent to Germany. In this way the Communists tried to justify their support for the Nazi-Soviet pact, and to turn a harsh, tense situation to their advantage.

In May 1940 the Germans unleashed their western offensive against Belgium, Holland, Luxembourg and then France. Within a few weeks, France was defeated, and millions of people were driven from their homes. Towards the end of June, an armistice was signed, and three fifths of French territory was placed under occupation. The remainder was left under nominal French control in the form of Marshal Pétain's Vichy regime. The French Fascist elements hoped that an "efficient" state would be created, dominated by a single party, and did not hesitate to criticise Vichy from this point of view. They were useful to the occupying power as a source of internal pressure on the government, but by the time that Hitler took any of them seriously, the war was clearly lost. The dilemma of the Vichy regime, in its attempt to minimise the consequences of the defeat, was at its sharpest on the question of labour recruitment. The Nazi war machine was increasingly in need of workers, particularly skilled workers, of whom there was an abundant supply in France. Fearing that the Germans would introduce labour conscription, a scheme was promoted whereby volunteers for work in Germany were to be exchanged for prisoners of war. Although several trainloads were despatched it was not sufficient for the growing needs of the Germans, and other means were sought. In June 1942 the Nazi Plenipotentiary for Labour, Sauckel, arrived in Paris to recruit a third of a million workers. Laval was extremely co-operative,[14] but more demands followed. Then towards the end of 1942, the occupying power extended its control over the whole of France. In order to fulfill his recruitment drives, initiated in January, May and August of 1943, Sauckel resorted to the seizure of workers by police raids.[15] Well over half a million workers had been sent to Germany by mid-1943, and the German demand for 1944 was set at one million men. The numbers of the Resistance began to swell to significant proportions as workers evaded compulsory transfer and seizure.

In this situation, the employers found themselves in a very strong position regarding labour. Although their confederation was banned in 1940 along with the trade unions, its power was reasserted through the "Organisation Committees" of the Vichy government. These Committees closely integrated the trade associations with members of the higher civil service and the executive. The trade unions on the other hand, were paralysed by the Vichy legislation and were in addition decisively split into three hostile camps. The industrialists were not in favour of the government's Charter of Labour which intended to suppress industrial conflict by establishing corporations in which labour representatives would have a subordinate place. From the employers' point of view, whatever was to be feared from the labour force could be easily handled by threatened or actual deportation to Germany. One telephone call was enough. The government therefore received little co-operation in its futile efforts to implement its Charter of Labour.

The Resistance began to take shape as a movement after the German attack on the USSR in June 1941. The Jouhaux tendency, having rejected the Charter of Labour, re-established contact with the Communists, and the General Confederation of Labour was re-unified underground in April 1943. It was agreed that three of the eight members of the central executive should be Communists. Moreover, Louis Saillant, who represented the CGT on the National Council for Liberation, was not hostile to the PCF — this essentially gave the Communists parity at the top. The Communists, further, were more disciplined than the centre group and proved to be much more dynamic. Within a short time the Communists were exercising the greater influence within the CGT. Previously the Communists had agitated against Vichy, completely ignoring the presence of the Germans in France.[16] After the attack on the USSR, they fought against both Vichy and the Germans. It is to be emphasised that they fought under the slogan of a national liberation front, and did not mention the objective of social revoltuion. The *Francs Tireurs et Partisans,* commanded by Charles Tillon, led the way in organising the *maquis* both in the cities and the mountain regions. The FTP was strongly supported by the trade unions. The Paris regional federation of trade unions outlined Communist strategy in October 1943: deportations were to be resisted by every possible means; the evaders were to be organised into fighting units and trained; sabotage of production and transports was to be increased; demands were to be generalised for higher wages, adequate bomb shelters and for special compensation for bombing damages; inter-union committees at the local level were to be reconstituted.[17] Particular attention was paid to the struggle against labour conscription, which was seen as the means of organising the active core of the Resistance.[18] The further development of the Resistance movement, and an analysis of the various tendencies within it, are taken up in the next section, Chapter eleven, which discusses the foundations of post-war France.

NOTES

1. Ozouf, pp222-3.
2. Val R. Lorwin, *The French Labor Movement,* Harvard UP 1954, p67.
3. *La Droite en France* Paris, Aubier 1963, rev. ed. p225.
4. *The Right Wing in France* Philadelphia, University of Pennsylvania Press 1966, transl. from rev. ed. by James M. Laux, p298.
5. Four years later the syndicalist minority split from this to form yet another confederation, called the Revolutionary Syndicalist CGT.
6. Lucien Rioux, *Le Syndicalisme,* Buchet Chastel 1960, p43.
7. Salomon Schwarz, "Les occupation d'Usines en France de Mai et Juin 1936", *International Review for Social History* 11, 1937, pp58-66.
8. Henry Ehrmann, *French Labor: from Popular Front to Liberation,* Oxford UP 1947, pp53-4.
9. Daniel Guérin, *Front Populaire: Revolution Manquée,* Julliard 1963, pp125-6.
10. Georges Lefranc, *Les Experiences Syndicales en France de 1939 à 1950,* Aubier 1950, p241.
11. Otto Kirchheimer, "Decree Powers and Constitutional Law in France under the Third Republic," *APSR.* December 1940, p1110.
12. Lefranc, p28.
13. *Ibid.,* pp31-2; Ehrmann, p149.

14. Robert Aron, *The Vichy Regime,* Putnam 1958 transl. p381.

15. *Ibid.,* pp445, 452 and 472.

16. A. Rossi, *La Guerre des Papillons.* Iles d'Or 1954, p182.

17. Union des Syndicats de la Région Parisienne, *Bulletin,* Octobre, 1943.

18. Lefranc, pp120-3.

Chapter 9 Fascism and Modernisation

After the analysis of France as a contrasting situation in which Fascism did not develop into a predominant movement, it is useful to examine more closely the dynamics of the social process in Germany and Italy.

Kornhauser's view is that Fascism was created through a process of massification of society, in which class identities were broken down. People were then "freed to form new ties based on the commonly shared plight of mass men....."(p18) To the extent that this view emphasises the marginality characteristic of Fascist leaders, it touches on an important aspect of the problem which is documented in Lerner's study. The difficulty is that Kornhauser goes too far, interpreting the entire Fascist phenomenon in terms of marginality and the breakdown of class identities and interests. In fact a very strong class element remains which cannot be explained away. The analysis of voting behaviour in Germany showed an overwhelming middle and lower-middle-class support for the Nazis, and a persistent organised working-class rejection of it. Although Nazi ideology was bewilderingly wide in its appeal,[1] two class elements stand out boldly: it was fundamentally hostile to the free and independent organisation of labour, and it endorsed the traditional lower-middle-class anti-capitalist animosity. The latter, furthermore, created a violent basis of conflict within the Nazi movement when Hitler began to put into practice his understanding with big business. Once in power, Hitler stressed that the "revolution" was over, and that the main task was re-armament, which clearly involved a co-operative attitude towards established industrialists and bankers. The Nazi "left wing" was dismayed at this "betrayal", but was silenced in the purge of 30th June 1934, which at the same time settled the problem of the SA's relationship with the Army. In Italy, the social basis of support for Fascism was similar. An analysis of voting behaviour is not as relevant because the Fascists as a party participated only in the elections of May 1921, and were members of Giolitti's coalition of the Right, along with Liberals and Nationalists. The results did not involve a significant redistribution of seats, as against the Socialist and Popular parties, but the intransigence of the thirty-five Fascist deputies prevented Giolitti's coalition from working. The coalition had about a hundred seats out of 535. There ensued a parliamentary crisis of more than a year's duration which ended in Mussolini's *coup d'etat*. Half a year after the elections, at the Rome Congress of November 1921, the Fascist party secretariat analysed the social background of some 90,000 active members, leaders and financial supporters. The middle classes were predominant — approximately 14,000 tradesmen, 22,000 white-collar employees, 10,000 professional men, 20,000 students, 1,500 teachers and 4,000 manufacturers. There were in addition 18,000 landowners and wealthy peasants.[2] The social origin of the Fascist leadership was predominantly middle class. A later study by Lasswell and Sereno of the social composition of various agencies of Party and Fascist state revealed that one half of the Cabinet, three quarters of the provincial secretaries and higher proportions of other agencies were of that origin.[3] The class aspects of the Fascist ideology were similar to that of Nazism in Germany, but the ambiguity towards capitalism did not become a basis of conflict within the Italian movement. A facade of class collaboration was provided by the development of the corporative structure. Industrial and agrarian labour were effectively subordinated, while a far-reaching integration of business and administrative interests was facilitated. The process has been vividly described by H. Stuart Hughes:

'By the mid-thirties it was becoming apparent that Fascist Italy was acquiring a fairly homogeneous ruling class. In the institutions of the corporate state, the two chief supports of the regime, the industrialists and the higher bureaucracy, were beginning to merge in attitude and even in function: as the officers of corporate bodies, the industrialists were turning into bureaucrats, while the higher civil servants . . . . were being brought into increasingly close relation with private enterprise. Hence the Italian man in the street was not far wrong when he confused the two in his mind. His image of the typical Fascist was of a prosperous, middle-aged man, corpulent and balding, somewhat lazy and self-indulgent after the fatigues and enthusiasms of his youth, ready to relax now with his fine automobile, his villa and his title of *commendatore*.'[4]

It was not that Fascism was created by "mass society", rather that the Fascist movement in power attempted to 'massify' society. It attempted to break down established class identities, to destroy the network of intermediate social relations and to atomise the individuals by incorporating them into vast organisations manipulated by elite bureaucracies. And, as Neumann emphasised, this was done selectively. The prime objects were wage-earners, not the professional classes nor the organised industrial interest groups. Even within the Fascist-created mass-society powerful class identities and interests asserted themselves and were protected.

Furthermore, the question of marginality may be seen in the context of social class dynamics. In the case of the Nazi propagandists it concerns their alienation from the upper middle class in a situation of declining status; in the case of the Nazi administrators and police it concerns their disaffection with their *inherited* lower-middle-class career prospects in a period of severe economic and social distress. At the same time, their marginality permitted them, through the agency of the Nazi movement, to focus and express the extremely hostile reaction of the middle class in a time of acute crisis. The Italian situation was similar. Lasswell and Sereno noted that the personnel of the Fascist leadership lacked ordinary occupational skills, and owed their careers primarily to the political talents of violence, propaganda and fixing.[5] The same authors have given a graphic sketch of the conflict situation in the main region of emergent Fascism:

> 'The higher party councils give extraordinary prominence to persons from Bologna and nearby provinces: Grandi, Manaresi, Biagi, Oviglio (Bologna); Balbo, Rossoni, (Ferrara); and the *Duce* (Forlì). During the formative years of Fascism, this region was the most active scene. . . . Workers, both urban and rural, were organised, and the post-war years saw the high-water mark of union activity. The lesser bourgeoisie . . . . were alienated by the dislocation of public services through frequent strikes, and by the improving status of the manual toilers. Small tradesmen were exposed to the ever-sharpening competition of the co-operatives, which were supported by the unions.'[6]

What requires further consideration is the nature of the hostile reaction focused and expressed by the Fascist movements. An insight is provided by the concept of *anomie*. This refers to the demoralisation and disorientation which occurs when established patterns of social integration are disrupted. An anomic situation is produced, for example, by sudden economic depression. The French sociologist Emile Durkheim originally used the concept of anomie to explain why suicide rates varied according to the degree of social integration in the family, in the religious community and in other social institutions. But apart from the self-destructive effects they may have on certain individuals, anomic situations — which are situations of drastic social change — create powerful desires for political and social *stability*.

In Italy, after the First World War, there was an explosive compound of economic difficulties, social unrest, a sense of national humiliation and a breakdown of the political system. In Germany similar conditions were present and in some respects more sharply so. The sense of national humiliation was more widely spread, and the bitter political resentment against the introduction of a democratic system was not concealed by many civil servants, judges, lawyers, journalists, teachers and professors. A large part of the "establishment" saw democracy as subversive and un-German. In these conditions, the attraction of Fascism for the threatened middle strata was that it promised a spectacular solution to the problem of stability, well outside the ordinary and discredited political processes. It should be noted, however, that for the traditional conservative rulers Fascism was viewed more cynically: it was a weapon to be used against the possibility of radical change which would destroy their traditional power and influence. In both Italy and Germany, the old political leaders thought that they could bend the Fascist movement to their purposes. In both cases, they failed to understand the nature of the changes which were taking place, and the dynamic thrust of the Fascist movement. Only in countries such as Spain, Portugal, Rumania and Hungary, where the process of development and modernisation was barely felt, were the traditionalist authoritarian rulers able to harness the Fascist movements.

One aspect of the anomic situation was analysed by Talcott Parsons in his essay, "Sociological Aspects of Fascist Movements", which draws on Weber's concept of rationalisation: economic development, the growth of bureaucracy and urbanisation undermine the traditional values and modes of life; the old ways of doing things, the old expectations, the old sense of order are disrupted by a relentless process of rationalisation; the resentment against it produces an extreme "fundamentalist" reaction — there is aggression against the "subversion" of traditional values, and an exaggerated assertion of loyalty to them. The Fascist movement in both Italy and Germany, certainly drew heavily on the conservative forces in society for ideological and material support. But the fundamentalist reaction of the threatened middle classes was not simply conservative in a traditional sense; it involved a much more drastic political concept, for it radicalised reaction itself. Parsons did not see the latter side, which created totalitarian forms out of the rationalisation process. It did not merely shore up power positions which were being endangered by modernisation, rather it created new totalitarian forms by exploiting the latest techniques of communication, organisation and social control.

In this connection it is worth emphasising that the Fascist rise to power occurred in both Italy and Germany *after* the defeat and exhaustion of the labour movement; that is, after the possibility of a revolutionary reorganisation of society was totally obliterated, and after normal parliamentary democracy broke down. But it did not mean, as in the cases of Spain, Portugal and Hungary in the inter-war period, that it was possible to establish a traditionalist type autocracy. The flow and dynamic of modernisation − that is of industrialisation, urbanisation, rationalisation and social mobility − was too great. Traditional conservative positions were irreversibly undermined in the process; and the fundamentalist reaction, with its emphasis on the corporative reorgnisation of the economy, was simply an anachronism which would interfere with the superior productive power of big business and with preparations for a modern war. Once in power, Fascism had to control the entire social process in order to ride the tiger of modernisation; the "revolutionary" elements of the successful reaction were therefore beyond the control of the traditional autocrats.

Central to this type of anomic situation is the social change created by modernisation. Both the German and Japanese examples show that industrialisation, on a technological and financial level, may be carried out under authoritarian direction. But the achievement of modernisation in a social and political sense − citizenship rights, democratic practices, equality before the law, minority group rights and unrestricted educational opportunities − is not a necessary consequence of economic development. It is a possibility which may be strongly reacted against; and in the acute struggle to prevent it lies the essence of the Fascist potential. The Fascist movement did not aim at a conservative *status quo ante,* but at an ultimate solution to the threat of progressive social reform. Its totalitarianism was based on the ruthless suppression of the sources of internal conflict, and a militarisation of political culture so that aggression could be externalised.

The logic, as well as the ambiguity, of Fascism was its peculiar synthesis of conservatism and radicalism. It therefore found support both from those whose response to the anomic stiuation of the post war was a desire to establish a *status quo ante,* and from those who wanted a "spiritual", but not a social class revolution. The former were concentrated generally in strategic institutional positions − the judiciary, civil service, police and army − and the latter in the lower middle class. Organised business at first remained conservative, but in face of increasingly difficult and unstable political conditions, it eventually supported the introduction of a new order. Organised business did not create the Fascist movement with its populistic appeal, but a crucial precondition for the latter taking power was endorsement by major industrialists and financiers. A key aspect of Fascism as radicalised conservatism arises from the fact that in order to enhance its military potential the new regime had to protect industrial interests. Accelerating the trends of development, Fascism deepened the interpenetration of organised business and the State. It is often suggested that the Fascist state took the dominant male role in this particular form of coitus, but it is more accurate to describe the relationship, especially in Germany, as one of full partnership based on an appreciation of interlocking interests and shared goals. In Fascist Italy, Nazi Germany and Vichy France, organised business was brought into a more bureaucratised relationship with the State than had previously existed, but unlike other processes of regimentation, business power was protected by Party and State, not subordinate; to them. Braunthal pointed out that in Germany during the war "industry held a significant leverage in both the party and the Army" through the Institute for Business Leaders in Defence and the Defence Council.[7]

Contrasts

Although Italian Fascism and German Nazism are discussed together under the heading of Fascist phenomena, it is important to stress differences between them as well. The ideological problems facing the Italian Fascists were of a complex nature: the massive influence of the Catholic Church, the symbol of legitimacy embodied in the Monarchy and the previous experience of a liberal political structure. By contrast, in Germany the outcome of previous political and cultural developments was that the only permanent core of non-legitimation of the Nazi Regime was in the officer-corps. Even this was ambiguous, especially after the purge of SA leaders in June 1934, and Hitler's eventual victory was total. These differences are reflected in the contrasting developments of anti-Fascist Resistance movements during the war. In Northern Italy, the Resistance was mass-based, militarily active and united the various political parties in a broad programme of social and democratic change. In Germany, it was conspiratorial, isolated, fragmented and without the possibility of constructing a programme for change.

The most essential contrast is with France. In the relations between

French organised business and labour a core of anti-democratic attitudes prevailed: an unwillingness to compromise, a refusal to acknowledge the legitimacy of social demands, a basic desire to suppress and destory the organisations of the labour opponent (which was achieved in Vichy France). But the French labour movement was able to assert itself independently of the dominant power structure, particularly in the events leading to the Popular Front, and was able to retain the support of key lower-middle-class elements such as teachers and some officials and white-collar employees. This indicates that a strong democratic tendency was current in the political culture which served to link together social strata which, in the German and Italian systems, were isolated. The independent development of the labour movement, neither isolated nor rendered powerless, is a basic condition for social modernisation. In Italy the pre-Fascist liberal system isolated and alienated the labour movement so that it could not contribute positively to democratic social development. In Germany, the labour movement was partially integrated into the authoritarian structure, despite its commitment to parliamentary democracy, and was unable to sustain its independent dynamism. In France, despite the erosion of the gains of the Popular Front and the destruction of war and occupation, the labour movement was able to re-assert itself powerfully in the Resistance.

NOTES

1. See Karl Dietrich Bracher, *The German Dictatorship,* Penguin University Books 1973, pp195-204: "Toward a Middle-Class Mass Party".

2. Cited in Rossi, p163. According to Rossi there were also large numbers of involuntary members: ". . . . there were 36,847 agricultural labourers, mostly members of socialist 'leagues' forced into the *Fasci* by the offensive of the *squadristi,* and 23,418 industrial workers, taken largely from the civil service, the unemployed dock workers and the districts under Fascist military occupation. These occupations had brought the Fascists a windfall of 138 co-operatives and 614 workers' syndicates, with 64,000 members, two thirds of them from Emilia, Tuscany, and Venetia...."

3. "The Fascists", Chapter 4 of Lasswell and Lerner (eds.), *World Revolutionary Elites.* Unfortunately their phrase "lesser bourgeoisie" is somewhat confusing because it includes skilled workers (p182). The proportion of skilled workers to the other categories of the lesser bourgeoisie is not stated.

4. *The United States and Italy,* 1965 rev. ed. pp91-2.

5. *World Revolutionary Elites*, pp185-90.
6. *Ibid.*, p192.
7. *The Federation of German Industry in Politics*, p21.

Part 3 POST SECOND WORLD WAR

The following examination of the post Second World War period starts with Germany because it was the focus of international attention in two prime senses. The first was to destroy the Nazi machine militarily, and to introduce political changes through four-power occupation policies of de-Nazification, demilitarisation, and decartelisation. The second was the emergence of Cold War tensions, which eventually led to the abandonment of these policies, and resulted in the permanent division of Germany into two rival states. It is beyond the scope of this book to deal with developments in the Soviet Zone and in the DDR because this would require analysing the policies of the Soviet Union. In the Western Occupation Zones, Germans were much more involved in determining their affairs, and were given increasing scope in making basic choices. Under the powerful direction of CDU Chancellor Adenauer, alignment with the Western powers was seen as the context for efforts to achieve rehabilitation and to embark cautiously on a new democratic experience.

France is discussed in the following chapter because of its clear-cut failure to establish a viable democratic system out of the experience of Resistance and Liberation, and despite its previously established democratic traditions. The more France developed its economic and technological potential, the more its socio-political history seemed to move in reverse. The Fourth Republic, founded on the struggle and social aspirations of the Resistance, increasingly disintergrated under internal pressures and colonial wars until it was indistinguishable from the crisis-ridden, paralysed regime associated with the late Third Republic period. The Fourth was abolished in May 1958, and the Fifth Republic institutionalised the Republican monarch which the framers of the Constitution of the Third Republic wanted, but did not get. The jamboree-crisis of May to June 1968 was a brief, vivid illumination of discrepancies of French development, challenging the traditional status concepts which dominated inter-group relations in education, the professions and industrial relations.

The experience of Italy, discussed in Chapter twelve has some parallels with both West Germany and France. As in the case of the former, the Christian Democratic party emerged as the largest and most influential party in the post-Fascist period. Unlike other parties which have more well-defined social bases of support, Christian Democracy appeals to a variety of social classes and groups. The ideology combines religious affiliation and competence in pragmatic affairs of government. The religious component sets the tone, but does not determine the political programme which is left open, non-theoretical and flexible. The Christian Democrats in Italy are exclusively Catholic, and benefit from the range of organisations which are more or less directly linked to the Church. The civic Committees of Catholic Action, for example, are said to be able to deliver seven million women's votes per election. However, exact this figure may or may not be, Catholic Action has undoubtedly struck deep roots in the State bureaucracy, influencing careers patterns and the distribution of patronage. It has been able to achieve this deep penetration because the Christian Democrats are recognised as the permanent core of coalition government. Religious community criteria are not applicable to the same extent in West Germany, where Protestants as well as Catholics are involved in Christian Democracy, and where the problem of the Church (or churches) and State is not an issue. A further major area of difference is the political culture in which the Christian Democratic parties operate. Italian political culture is fragmented, with strong Communist and Catholic influences, socially isolative, and resistant to planned social change. In West Germany, there was far greater cohesiveness and stability, almost to excess in the 1950s and 1960s. The Social Democrats escaped from their near-permanent opposition role by accepting many, although not all, of the policies of their rivals.

The parallel between France and Italy is the latter's similarity to the Fourth Republic in terms of social and political immobilism, government turnover and ideological divisions in the labour movement. But a closer examination of the similarities reveals crucial differences. The democratic centre in Italy has proven to be far more tough and durable than in France, reducing the likelihood of a Fifth-Republic type transformation. Although its prolonged inability to pass urgent social reforms in the fields of education, housing and social security perpetuate uncertainties, violence and some disorder, the trade union movement's achievement of unity in action on these issues, despite deep political rifts, has shown some indications of becoming an important factor of change. This potential stands in contrast to the relative sclerosis of the French labour movement.

In Chapter 13, the post-war context of transnational relations, particularly the development of supra-national integration, is discussed.

Chapter 10 West Germany: Ambiguities

A stark simple fact dictated the immediate post-war situation: Nazi Germany was crushed from the outside by military force alone; it was not at the same time liberated by a mass political movement, as in the case of the Italian or French Resistances. There was no significant, deep-rooted struggle for liberty in Germany. There was no civil war to tear apart the Nazi state and the Nazi party, and there was no mass revolt against the Nazified Army and the Nazi police. Instead, the political and military apparatus was overwhelmed and dismantled by the pressure of its external enemies. The Germans, having fought to the end under the Nazi banner, forfeited their rights of self-determination because they failed to create a new basis on which they could reconstitute their society. Their failure, to destroy the Nazi identity themselves, was the initial and underlying problem of the post-war period. Certainly Germany was going to be occupied and governed by the Allies no matter what happened, and it had been duly agreed upon months before the war ended. But there would have been a very great difference in the relationship between victors and vanquished had there been a profound and genuine mass movement of German anti-Nazi Resistance. As it was, Germany was simply militarily defeated, and divided into four zones of occupation. The problem of creating a democratic society by artificial methods was posed.

Germany had experienced war at home for the first time since its unification. In the First World War it had not experienced devastation on its own soil, nor had it known the horror of being invaded. Now the military governments of the western Allies and of the Soviet Union assumed full responsibility for administering their zones. They initiated and supervised measures of change: denazification, demilitarisation, decartelisation and the licensing of political parties, newspapers and broadcasting. Political life was allowed to re-emerge gradually in the *Laender* and on the zonal level, and was supervised. But the initial failure of the Germans themselves to create the conditions of democratic renewal led to a complicated situation of international dimensions. The various allied military authorities had different conceptions of how their zones should be allowed to develop, and differing conceptions of their own objectives. A vicious circle of distrust and recrimination developed between them, and their relations deteriorated under the impact of the Cold-War antagonism. The result was the division of Germany into two separate states with the creation, in 1949, of the West German Federal Republic and the East German Democratic Republic.

The global antagonism between the United States and the Soviet Union indelibly marked the emergence of the new national structures. No peace settlement of the Second World War was reached. Divided Berlin and the two Germanies remained a major focal point of the Cold War. Within this perspective, the basic decisions regarding the future of central Europe were taken. In contrast with the Soviet Union's policy of extracting massive reparations from its zone, the United States poured economic aid into the Western part. Nazi Germany had systematically destroyed millions upon millions of Russian lives and uncounted economic resources. Some measure of compensation was required and it was paid by the Eastern zone alone. On the other hand, the American policy of economic aid was motivated by strategic conceptions of containing Communist expansion, and in particular of harnassing Western Germany into an anti-Soviet posture. As a result the denazification process was interrupted, War Crime trials were soft-pedalled, decartelisation was virtually given up, and the policy of demilitarisation was reversed. The consequences were generally to inhibit the necessary re-structuring of West Germany (politically and administratively) by the pressure for quick recovery. The very democratic processes which were to have been installed and cultivated were distorted by anxiety about Soviet intentions. At the same time these developments confirmed the Soviet Union in its policy of making Eastern Germany a satellite regime.

Occupied Germany

According to the Potsdam Agreement of August 1945 supreme authority over occupied Germany was to be exercised by the Allied Control Council, a four-power military body whose decisions had to be unanimous. It proved to be an impossible requirement, and by March 1946 the Control Council was virtually paralysed. Effective government existed only at the zonal level where each of the occupying powers carried out measures of denazification and reconstruction according to its own particular lights. But from 1946 there was a progressive fusion of the three Western zones, while relations with the Soviet Union deteriorated. The Western Allies came to an agreement on the reconstruction of German central agencies in March 1948, and the Russians responded by walking out of the Allied Control Council. In

June 1948 the rupture became total. It was announced that a West German federal state would be established, and shortly afterwards an important currency reform was carried out against Soviet wishes. In its turn, the Soviet Union carried out its own currency reform, carved out the separate municipality of East Berlin from Greater Berlin, and closed access to the former capital city for several months.

When the new state of Western Germany was created in 1949 it was not granted full sovereignty. Military government came to an end, replaced by an Occupation Statute which reserved to the civilian Allied High Commission substantial powers in the following areas: disarmament and demilitarisation, control of the Ruhr, foreign affairs, control over foreign trade and exchange, respect for the new constitution (called the Basic Law) and for the constitutions of the *Laender.* There were a number of other areas where power was reserved, but the Occupation Statute was gradually revised to allow greater autonomy. In March 1951, the West German Ministry of Foreign Affairs was created, and finally in May 1955 the Occupation Statute and the Allied High Commission were dissolved, thereby giving the Federal Republic its full sovereignty.[1]

The Basic Law of the Federal Republic

The Basic Law was framed with scrupulous attention to the flaws of the Weimar Constitution, and was designed to prevent a recurrence of a Nazi-type seizure of power and manipulation of legality. The role of the President was reduced in importance so that he could not act in an independent manner, as Hindenburg had done. The position of the Chancellor was strengthened so that he could impose his policies on a divided legislature, as late Weimar chancellors had no hope of doing. Correspondingly the power of the lower house to overthrow cabinets was greatly weakened. And in line with the emphasis on the principle of federalism, the importance of the upper house was increased. Moreover, elements of direct democracy, such as the initiative and referendum which the Nazis had used for demagogic purposes, were abolished. The previous electoral system of proportional representation was greatly modified to reduce the chances of small, fringe parties entering parliament. Finally, a Constitutional Court was created to act as an independent check on the political process.

The Basic Law was not imposed on the Germans by the western Allies. Rather it is a document which was drawn up by the leaders of the German parties, and represents the compromises which they were able to effect in several months of debate and discussion in the parliamentary Constituent Council. In July 1948 the western Allies informed the heads of the eleven *Laender* of their decision to create a west German state, and authorised them to convene a constituent assembly in order to draft a democratic constitution. The instructions were of a very general character: to establish a federal type government, with adequate central authority and to guarantee individual rights and freedoms. The safeguard was that before the constitution could be submitted to popular referendum, the military governors would have to approve it. The Constituent Council, therefore, had to work within the guidelines set by the western Allies, but these did not violate the constitutional traditions of Germany. The German parties themselves were able to arrive at workable compromises and solutions, and assumed full responsibility for the political framework which they produced.

The Executive

(a) President

Under the Weimar Constitution, the office of the President was a substitute for the monarchy. He was commander-in-chief of the armed forces, he had the power to appoint the Chancellor in times of crisis and to issue emergency decrees. Moreover, he was directly and popularly elected for a period of seven years, which placed him in a position above and independent of the normal political process. In con-contrast, the Basic Law has turned the office of President into a purely symbolic position. The President is indirectly elected by an electoral college, instead of by the whole electorate, for a five-year period. He may be re-elected only once. The political powers formly attached to the office have been transferred largely to the Chancellor.

(b) Federal Chancellor

The position of Chancellor was strengthened in order to prevent a recurrence of the kind of executive instability which was characteristic of the Weimar period. The underlying difficulty was the political fragmentation of the multi-party system, and the Basic Law was designed to limit its consequences. The lower house can express its lack of confidence in the Chancellor only by electing his successor by a majority vote. The idea is that in a multi-party system it is easy to find negative amjorities to remove a Chancellor, but it is much more difficult to find positive majorities to replace him. Thus executive stability in a multi-party system is reinforced. During the fourteen years of Konrad Adenauer's chancellorship there was considerable feeling that the position had been made too secure, resulting in an inflexible "Chancellor-democracy". However, it may have been due to a unique combination of circumstances. Adenauer possessed great prestige and exercised his authority in an aloof, unbending style. And given the importance of the international situation on the development of the new state, the fact that he acted as his own Foreign Minister until 1955 considerably strengthened his role as head of government. The style of governance has changed considerably since the passing of the Cologne Buergermeister. But Adenauer's "Chancellor-Democracy" should be sharply distinguished from Bismarck's rule, as well as from General de Gaulle's, because in his case the powerful executive position was based squarely on the support of a parliamentary majority.

The Legislature

Although the executive branch clearly dominates in parliament, there has been no attempt to eliminate "political intermediaries" as in the French Fifth Republic. The majority party is a government party in the British sense, being a participant in decision-making rather than a mere transmitter of decisions taken above it.[2] In the specialised parliamentary committees and in the party caucuses, the considerable legislative powers of the *Bundestag* are exercised, and the interaction between executive and parliament occurs.

Federalism

The West German Republic is federal in its structure, in accordance with the directives of the western Allies and in accordance with the desires of the German parties. After the unitary, totalitarian state of the Nazis, it is not surprising that so much emphasis was given to the notion of federalism. It is embodied in the *Bundesrat,* the second parliamentary chamber in which each *Land* is represented according to its size. The *Bundesrat* has much more legislative power than the Weimar Republic second chamber, and serves as a meeting-place for officials of the central government and the *Laender.* But it was not meant to be too much of a check on the *Bundestag,* which remains predominant in the legislative field. The upper house has no more than a suspensory veto on bills passed in the lower house, and this may be overruled by equivalent *Bundestag* majorities.

A further aspect of German federalism is the distribution of legislative powers as between the *Laender* and the Federal government. The latter has exclusive power in such key areas as foreign affairs,

currency, communications and citizenship, while it shares powers
(concurrent legislation) with the *Laender* in less vital areas — although
even here the central government possesses reserve powers in case of
difficulties. Nevertheless the powers of the *Laender* remain considerable:
the police and cultural affairs (which includes radio and television) are
exclusively their concerns. As is education; in marked contrast with
France, West Germany has no central Ministry of Education.

The Federal Constitutional Court

Under the Weimar Republic, the President was considered to be the
ultimate guardian of the constitution in times of crisis. But after the
experience of the destruction of the Weimar Republic, such a simple
approach to the problems of the constitutional practice could hardly be
repeated. The Basic Law provides measures for dealing with certain
kinds of anticipated crisis, and these have been significantly widened by
the controversial emergency laws passed in 1968. But the powers
invested in the Federal Constitutional Court *(Bundesverfassungsgericht)*
are important in normal times.

The Federal Court is the guardian of the basic rights of the
individual, as defined in the first chapter of the Basic Law. Moreover, it
has the power to outlaw political organisations of an anti-democratic
character. In 1952 it banned the neo-Nazi Socialist Reich Party which
had won more than ten per cent of the vote in some *Land* and
communal elections in the previous two years. In 1956 it banned the
Communist party, and in 1968 to 1969 the possibility was raised that
the NPD would be investigated. On a broader level, the Court reviews
legislation and administrative acts to make certain that they are in
keeping with the constitution. And where there is conflict between the
federal government and the *Land* authorities, the Court decides. For
example, in 1961 the Court decided against the Federal government on
the question of a second television network. Chancellor Adenauer
wanted to establish a television network of privately financed
programmes under the control of the central government. It would have
broken the *Laender's* control of radio and television. However, the
legality of Adenauer's efforts was contested by *Laender* where the SPD
were in power, and the court ruled against the federal government. The
Court also has the power to forestall impending acts of damage or
threatened violence. For example, in 1932 when Chancellor von Papen
abused the emergency powers to ban the Social Democrats from
government in Prussia, it was contested in the State court. But by the
time the State court found the Reich government's action partly

unconstitutional, it was too late to be meaningful. The Bonn Federal Court has been given the power to prevent a recurrence of such abuses through injunctions or temporary rulings.

The functions and powers of the Federal Constitutional Court are such that it can act as an independent check on the political process. The Court consists of twenty-four judges, half elected by the *Bundestag*, and half by the *Bundesrat*. The normal term of service is eight years. This contrasts with the Weimar practice of staffing the State court with career judges appointed for life by the Ministry of Justice. There is now a wider area of selection: from civil servants, politicians and the legal profession, as well as from career judges.

Reconstruction and Socio-Political Problems

The Basic Law was designed as the instrument of democratic renovation in a country which had previously renounced democracy. Its spirit is therefore one of caution and distrust, with an emphasis on stability, moderation and gradualness. Its object is to create the conditions of stable government which would be sheltered from the turbulence of the popular masses and totalitarian "mass democracy". A complex system of checks and balances was set up. The principle of federalism replaced that of the unitary, totalitarian state. The role of the *Bundesrat*, the federal upper house, was bolstered and the office of President was shorn of its powers. The position of the Chancellor was strengthened to insure stability against extremist pressures (negative majorities) should the electorate return too many anti-democratic deputies. The electoral laws have barriers to minor party representation. The whole structure of powers is completed with a multi-functional Constitutional Court which watches over the political process.

In the confusion and uncertainty of defeat, organised religion was the main element of continuity and protection. Preaching forgiveness, brotherhood, reconciliation, peace, trust in God's mercy and charity, it was a revulsion against the Nazi ethos. As such it played an important part in the reconstitution of West German political culture. On the most obvious level, the relevance of Christian ethics in politics was stressed in the meetings of the Christian Democratic Union and the Christian Social Union. Secondly, religious inspiration operated as a principle of unification. The division of Germany created a situation in which the former Catholic minority became, within the Federal Republic, almost half of the population. Whereas religious seperateness is maintained in educational matters, religious exclusiveness is not operative on the level of national politics. The old Catholic Centre party was broadened into the Christian Democratic party, which includes the Protestant constituency. The party has the unique advantage of benefiting from both pulpits.

De-Nazification

Another important aspect in the reconstitution of West German political culture concerns the problem of de-Nazification. It was a problem because no profound anti-Nazi resistance movement developed in Germany; consequently the task of initiating de-Nazification measures fell to the occupying forces. They were then faced with persistent German resistance which greatly hampered proceedings. It was most evident in the US zone because the Americans wanted to carry out as complete a purge as possible, and tried to survey the whole adult population of over thirteen million people. The British and the French, in contrast, concentrated mainly on the more important Nazis and did not attempt to reach the small party member. Even when the American military government changed its approach in the spring of 1946 in order to facilitate matters and to reduce the arbitrariness of the proceedings there were protests from an unexpected quarter. Not an old-boys network of the Nazi movement, but the Evangelical Church Council, which is the summit body of the Protestant Churches, unashamedly led the opposition. Carl Schorske analysed its position carefully, and concluded that by invoking the " 'natural sense of right' " against the de-Nazification law the church leaders were implicitly sanctioning "the lawless condition which the Nazis legalized".[3] Opposition on this level strengthened resistance on less high-minded levels.

As time passed German resistance to de-Nazification procedures became more vigorous. The Christian Democrats avoided responsibility for de-Nazification because, they said, that they did not wish to be involved in "arbitrary" measures which might jeopardise the legal rights of Third Reich civil servants, and were afraid of creating a body of 'second-class citizens'.[4] By contrast the Social Democrats were alive to the dangers of allowing ex-Nazis to hold important civil service jobs, but they were to some extent hampered by the fear of being branded as unpatriotic by the widespread resentment and hurt national pride. Hoping to escape from allegations of the kind made against them after the First World War the Social Democrats struck a nationalist posture. The overall effect of these various attitudes was that the political objective of de-Nazification, which was the uprooting of anti-democratic elements so that a fresh start could be made, was not achieved in depth. It may well be that the problem was too great since a whole generation was involved in the Nazi Reich. It is clear that many got away with crimes which were beyond imagination, and that at least five thousand Nazis of some consequence were able to evade de-Nazification in the western zones.[5]

The de-Nazification process was further disturbed by the development of cold war tensions. Reconstruction was accelerated, creating a shortage of administrative and professional skills. Those who could provide the required services were increasingly considered to be indispensible, and their political past was not closely investigated. A case in point is Dr Hans Globke, Adenauer's state secretary until 1963 and head of the powerful Federal Chancellor's office. His services to the Third Reich included a legal commentary on the anti-Jewish Nuremberg Race Laws. Without going so far as to look for unredeemed Nazis everywhere, it is nonetheless disturbing to consider the extent of continuity in sensitive areas such as the higher civil service, the judicial bench, teaching and the universities. Schorske pointed out that the universities were reopened so soon after the war that it was not possible to re-staff the faculties with actively democratic teachers.[6]

In the legal profession it has been estimated that a large proportion of West German judges and prosecutors were active in the Nazi system, and that over sixty per cent of the judges who passed death sentences at the time were still in office in 1964.[7] The effect on the operation of the West German legal system is noted by several leading analysts. Alfred Grosser has written:

"It was the past history of these judges which explains in great part a whole series of scandalous decisions: the suits brought by Nazi victims thrown out of court on a derisory legal quibble, former Nazi dignitaries awarded comfortable pensions, and so on."[8]

Sebastian Haffner's analysis of the consequences of the "Spiegel" Affair, discussed later in the Chapter, emphasises the continuity of the judiciary and its immunity to reconstruction.[9]

Apart from the evasions and exceptions to denazification, there was wholesale re-employment after relatively short periods of suspension. For example, 11,000 of 12,000 dismissed teachers were reinstated in Bavarian schools by 1949, as were the bulk of dismissed civil servants.[10]

Moreover, the long-term effectiveness of denazification was further reduced by one of the early acts of Adenauer's government after military occupation had ended. In May 1951 a law was passed which reinstated purged civil servants, with the exception of those actually serving prison sentences. Provisions for financial compensation for distress caused by enforced unemployment followed quickly. Terence Prittie pointed out that, in contrast, it was not until 1953 that the federal government provided compensation for the victims of Nazism. And he also emphasised that in the application of the two laws the ex-Nazis received better treatment than did their surviving victims.[11] The restoration is frequently justified on the following grounds: (a) competence, (b) political strategy and (c) the inevitability of long-term changes.[12]

What is neglected in the justification is that competence is generally a function of opportunity. Given the motivation to succeed, competence is generally acquired through the exercise of responsibility. The tragedy of post-war Germany is that in many fields, not least in higher education, too much continuity was permitted. The opportunity of allowing democratically committed people the time to acquire competence by assuming responsibility was to a considerable extent forfeited. But, runs the counter-argument, it would have had the effect of excluding thousands and tens of thousands of trained people from positions of public importance. Their hostility and resentment against the new Republic would have been such as permanently to endanger it. Therefore it was good political strategy on Adenauer's part to include them in, without looking too closely into their pasts. Their inclusion raises the hope that in the long term they will be replaced by younger men with a different political outlook. It may be replied, however, that the risks of including them were at least as great as those of excluding them. The pillars of Hohenzollern society were involved in the running of the Weimar Republic; it did not diminish their hostility nor inhibit their disloyalty. The Bonn Republic does not of course face the same problems, but the restoration has created a situation in which the quality of change has been undermined. In many areas of public life, democratic reforms and changes in attitudes and practices have been blocked or impeded. Its significance is that the re-structuring of the administrative-judicial basis of the West German state was not carried through in depth.

The Cold War and Re-armament

The Cold War had a profound impact on the remaking of German society. Two permanent national structures were created, and key policies of de-Nazification and demilitarisation were rendered inoperative or reversed. The Basic Law of the Federal Republic and the

constitution of the Democratic Republic originally forbade the creation
of armed forces. What was unexpected was not that these provisions
should be rescinded and the constitutions amended, but that it should
happen in such a short time. By the mid-1950s military forces were
established in both German states. The irony was that after 1945, West
Germany was subject to five years of Allied re-education against the
evils of German militarism, and was then called upon to arm itself
against the threat of Soviet Communism. It was by no means easy to
find a suitable context within which the West German armed forces
could be used for Western purposes and at the same time be kept under
supervision and control. The plans for a European Defence Community,
which would have created an integrated Western European army were
signed in 1952, but the French National Assembly decided against its
ratification in 1954. The alternative was to admit Western Germany
into NATO, and this occurred in May 1955. Within a few days a parallel
integration was established in the East, with the creation of the Warsaw
Pact which included the DDR.

The re-armament of Germany created a number of problems which
may be divided into two catogories. The first concerns the position of
the armed forces themselves. Would the officer corps again exert
significant political influence? Would it again acquire its traditional
social prestige? Could the armed forces be established on a new
democratic footing, uprooting the old military-nationalist traditions?
The answer to the first two questions is negative because in neither East
nor West Germany has the Army had an opportunity to claim or to
assert a "leadership" role. The conditions in both countries are such
that civilian political authority is unchallenged. The process of
dis-establishing the Prussian Junkers in the Army commenced with the
Nazification of the officer corps and was accelerated by Hitler's revenge
for the July 1944 attempt on his life. It was completed in the
destruction of the Third Reich and the military occupation. The flight
and expulsion of Germans from the eastern territories, the
establishment of Polish sovereignty as far west as the Oder-Neisse
frontier and Communist control of Eastern Germany have marked the
end of Prussian influence. In the Federal Republic, democratic reforms
of the armed services were instituted. The concept of the soldier as a
"citizen in uniform" was promulgated. There was some initial optimism
about its effectiveness, but later some doubts were raised.[13] But there
is little evidence to support the idea that the old tradition of German
soldiering has been revived.

The second category of problems concerns the effect of

remilitarisation on West German political attitudes. The key to Adenauer's policy was the integration of the Federal Republic into the Western Alliance. From this point of view re-armament was both a contribution to Western European defences and part of the process of rehabilitation. It was seen as a means of preventing the resurgence of German military ambitions, because the armed forces could not operate independently of NATO. Gradually this point of view was accepted by the majority of the Social Democratic Party. The SPD was initially a strong anti-militarist party. It had endorsed the initial Allied policy of demilitarisation, it had rejected the European Defence Community proposals and in the mid-1950s it had campaigned against the new military legislation, including the introduction of draft laws. But by 1959 the SPD changed its position in response to Russian pressure on West Berlin, and in recognition of existing alliances. It reluctantly and gradually accepted German remilitarisation in the context of NATO, and concentrated its efforts on democratising the *Bundeswehr*.

Nevertheless. a questioning of the need for a West German Army has persisted. It is seen by some, including President Gustav Heinemann, as a definite obstacle to German unification. Heinemann opposed re-armament from the beginning. He resigned as Minister of the Interior in the 1950 Adenauer government on this issue. In 1952 he left the CDU to create a new political party which would stand for a policy of neutrality. His All-German People's party was not successful, and he joined the SPD before the 1957 elections. He then made an important contribution as an SPD legal expert. His election in March 1969 as the first Social Democratic President of the Federal Republic improved the image of West German democracy.[14] A few days after the election Heinemann reiterated his basic position that German reunification could not take place as long as there were German military committments to NATO and to the Warsaw Pact. His attitude did not represent the official policy of the SPD, and there was no doubt that West Germany would continue to be militarily integrated into NATO. Its significance lay rather in the recognition that the price of remilitarisation was the continued division of Germany.

Granted that the situation is unalterable, there remained a further key problem: should the West German Army have atomic weapons? The influential leader of the CSU, Franz Josef Strauss, strongly advocated their adoption when he was Minister of Defence and later, but a strong body of opinion in West Germany was seriously opposed. The change of government in 1969 allowed the latter its expression. The Brandt government formally renounced the use of nuclear weapons

by signing the nuclear non-proliferation treaty in November, 1969.
Should a future government reverse the decision, there will be great
unease in the West and positive alarm in the East.

Economic Recovery

The resurgence of the West German economy has been frequently
described as a "miracle". But there is much evidence to suggest that the
"miracle" was more in the eyes of the beholder than in the economy
itself. The term "miracle" reflects astonishment at the rapidity with
which an apparently devastated industrial system could clear the
rubble, repair the damage, rebuild, cut through production bottlenecks
and establish high annual growth rates. It is true that destroyed
buildings and bombed-in factory roofs give the impression of ruin. It
does not necessarily follow that the heavy machinery and blast furnaces
in them have been irreparably damaged. The extent of industrial
destruction in Germany has been generally exaggerated.

The German economy proved ruggedly resistant to Allied bombing.
Its reserves of capital equipment were sufficient to replace losses. The
highest rate of bomb destruction in the machine tool industry was
about six per cent of total stock in 1944, while the industry's annual
production during the war was ten per cent of total stock.[15]
Throughout the war Germany steadily increased productive capacity by
continuous capital formation. It has been estimated that in 1946 fixed
assets in German industry were as great as in 1939 – after deducting
losses due to bomb damage and dismantling of plants for reparations.[16]

Moreover during the war Germany had reserve factory space which it
utilised to replace losses, and was able to organise colossal labour
recruitment programmes.

In the first part of the war Germany's manpower position was not
seriously strained because the succession of victories brought new
economic resources and new labour supplies to the Reich. The
seven-and-a-half million men withdrawn from the labour force for
military purposes were largely replaced by nearly four million foreign
workers and prisoners of war, and by large-scale transfers of labour
from inessential sectors of employment. As the war continued,
however, the manpower position came under increasing strain. For
ideological reasons the Nazis did not attempt to utilise German female
labour, choosing instead to recruit foreign labour by the hundred
thousand. By May 1943 over six million foreign civilians and prisoners
of war were at work in the Nazi war economy, and by the following
May there were over seven millions, representing about one fifth of the

total labour force. The numbers rose to over eight million by the end of 1944.[17] This labour was essential to the armament industries, steel, chemicals and mining. It should be noted, however, that the figures do not include the vast amount of concentration camp labour which was exploited as slave labour by the SS Economic and Administrative Office. The SS had links with many large industrial firms, one of the most notorious being the I.G. Farben synthetic gasoline plant at Auschwitz.[18] Moreover the figures of seven to eight million workers indicate only the number employed at a particular time and do not show the total number recruited. There was enormous wastage of human lives as a result of insufficient food, overwork and brutal treatment, particularly in the case of the Eastern worker. The total recruitment of foreign labour was probably over twelve million people, *not* including concentration camp slave labour.[19]

The economic benefits to the Reich of ruthlessly exploiting this great human mass have not been calculated. But there is no doubt that their sufferings contributed to the process of capital formation which steadily increased Germany's productive capacity throughout the war.

The air assault on the economy became significantly effective only in the last months of war. The destruction of transportation isolated the Ruhr area from the rest of the country, cut off coal shipments and triggered the collapse. Then came the enormous social dislocation of total defeat, multiple invasion, military occupation and streams of refugees from the East. The "thousand-year" Nazi German Reich was hammered into a pigsty. The following three years were marked by consumer shortages, black marketeering, unemployment, low production and sharply reduced standards of living. The image of ruin predominated, obscuring the underlying strength of productive capacity inherited from the Nazis. No great effort was needed to lay new railroad track, to remove blast walls, to repair damaged plant. Production could start in full again as soon as the currency was reformed to provide an adequate medium of exchange. However currency reform was more of a political problem than a financial one because it touched on the long-term aims of the occupation authorities. The Russians and the Western Allies did not agree on the future of Germany, and when the Western Allies reformed the currency in the western zones in June 1948, the Russians strongly retaliated. The result was the permanent division of Germany, but in the western zones the economy was able to begin its forward surge. The infusion of Marshall Aid as well as loans and investments from American private industry provided further thrust, as did the boom created by the Korean War.

These factors help to explain why West Germany achieved an expanding full-employment economy. Within a relatively short time it was able to provide employment for the more than nine million refugees who had fled or were expelled from Poland, Czechoslovakia and former German territories beyond the Oder-Neisse. Their smooth economic integration helped to cushion the political impact of the gigantic population transfer. The political influence of the refugee organisations has been largely of secondary importance, except that for many years their pressure reinforced the government's refusal to regard the existing map in the east as final. In the 1950s, West Germany also absorbed over a quarter of a million refugees a year from East Germany. The flow was effectively halted by the building of the Berlin Wall in August 1961. These immigrants were a substantial economic asset to West Germany because most of them were of working age and many were skilled. They represented a considerable loss to the DDR, whose total population fell from over eighteen million in 1950 to seventeen million in 1960. They were as attracted by economic opportunities in West Germany as repelled by political conditions in the DDR.

What requires further consideration is how West Germany was able to sustain its high growth rate throughout the 1960s. As Norman Macrae stressed in his comparison of British and West German economic performances, it is not a matter of attitudes to work and efficiency. The key is rather to be found in national economic policy.[20] Andrew Shonfield's study of West German economic policy shows the ways in which successive CDU-dominated governments closely guided developments, despite its official ideology of allowing market mechanisms full play.[21] In the early years it intervened to accelerate growth in basic industries, as shown by the 1952 investment programme and the creation of the Reconstruction Loan Corporation. Connected with this was the government's strong encouragement of exports, which has proved to be the major factor in West Germany's economic success. Its export drive was facilitated by an undervalued currency which gave it strongly competitive prices in foreign markets, and by the fact that there were no sizeable military and overseas commitments creating balance of payment deficits as in the case of Britain and France. The government pressed home these advantages by offering attractive tax concessions to key export industries.

Another important aspect is the relationship of government and business. As in France, big business is powerfully organised with many strong trade associations directly involved in the government machinery.[22] The relationship, which in France is the key to successful planning, was greatly facilitated in the Adenauer era by the entente which existed between the Chancellor and his advisers and BDI president Fritz Berg.[23] Moreover Germany has a tradition of close relations between the great banks and industry which re-emerged in the post-war period. Early attempts to deconcentrate economic power were given up with the onset of the Cold War and the three big banks re-asserted their influence. Their close involvement with industrial development is shown *(a)* in their control over shareholders' proxy votes and *(b)* in their representation on the supervisory boards of important firms. Furthermore the influence of the banks often ties in with the objectives of the government in promoting certain types of industrial development. Thus the Reconstruction Loan Corporation was set up as a banker's bank.

All this suggests, as Shonfield has pointed out, that West Germany possesses the mechanisms for French style planning — organised private enterprise, guided by government objectives and influenced by banking controls — except that the official CDU ideology asserted the myth of heroic private enterprise. A true West German economic "miracle" would have been the realisation of the myth. For it would have meant that the business leaders who prospered under Nazi totalitarianism, who were then restored intact and virtually immune to denazification, had transformed themselves into nineteenth-century liberal entrepreneurs! A type which the whole of German socio-economic history had previously excluded.

In the field of labour relations West Germany had the advantage of a new situation in the post-war period. The Allied authorities regarded the trade unions as a key institution in the democratisation of Germany. And among the German trade unionists there was a powerful urge to build a strong, *united* movement which would be an essential component in creating stable democratic conditions. Accordingly the trade union structure was rationalised by the creation of the German Trade Union Confederation (DGB) in 1949. Replacing the two hundred unions of the Weimar Republic, which were divided by political, religious and craft interests, is a broad structure of sixteen industrial unions. Each industrial union, such as the metal workers or the public service workers, includes all manual categories as well as salaried staffs. The DGB, whose membership approached 6.5 million in the mid-1960s, is a federation with no formal political or religious links. On the whole it is close to the SPD,[24] while including a minority Christian wing. The major trade union bodies outside the DGB are the clerical workers (DAG) and the civil servants and teachers *(Deutsche Beamtenbund)*. In the mid-1960s, DAG's membership was under half a million while some 700,000 salaried employees belonged to the DGB. The *Beamtenbund*, which conceives of itself as a professional body in a corporate sense rather than as a trade union, has a membership of two thirds of a million.

The DGB has consistently functioned in a cautious manner. It has complied with national economic policy first regarding reconstruction and then in promoting exports and industrial expansion. It has kept its demands at a very moderate level in view of the steadily increasing production. It has accepted a lower level of wages than could have been attained by militant action in order to allow high rates of capital investment. Its prime concern is with collective bargaining at national or regional level. Advised by professional economists, the union leaders negotiate wage agreements for one — or two-year periods. Since these are considered to be binding legal contracts, unofficial strikes at factory level and consequent wage drift are inhibited.

The trade union leaders wanted some measure of industrial democracy after the war. The idea of "co-determination" was to give workers' representatives the right to participate in all aspects of management. The DGB was only partially successful in achieving it after struggling hard between 1950 and 1952 against mounting opposition. Limited co-determination was instituted in the coal, iron and steel industries, but conservative opposition prevented its extension to other industries. The re-establishment of works councils *(Betriebsrate)* was a poor substitute for the changes implied in the original concept of co-determination. The works councils, which are elected by all factory employees, nevertheless have been effective aids to smooth labour/management relations. The works council has been able to deal with individual grievances and to exercise an influence over the range of issues affecting the immediate working situation. Some of its effectiveness may be attributed to the pressure of the full employment situation on the employers, who do not wish to lose labour to rival firms. Some of it too may be attributed to the docility of the German worker who accepts the paternalist outlook of the employer. The degree to which workers feel a special loyalty to their firms and are impregnated with a "company consciousness" has been frequently remarked upon. The extent to which this may be so indicates, not the embourgeoisement of the worker, but his acceptance of a comfortable, subordinate position.[25]

Concern for Political Stability

One of the outstanding phenomena of post-war Europe was the sudden rise to prominence of Christian Democratic parties in Italy, France and West Germany. These parties are distinguished by an ability to collect votes from a broad variety of socio-economic groups: white-collar employees, farmers, self-employed, workers, business and professional men. The Christian Democrats (CDU/CSU) have such a broad appeal in West Germany that their voters virtually represent a cross-section of the population; except that there are a disproportionate number of women, farmers and Catholics. The Protestant workers largely support the SPD, but Protestant white-collar employees and officials tend to favour the CDU.

A second characteristic is that although the Christian Democratic parties include a trade-union wing, it is subordinate and rarely influences policy. In the early post-war years the left-wing of the CDU was strong enough to have its ideas for a planned economy endorsed as party policy in the British zone. Within a short time, however, it was supplanted by liberal policies in the form of Erhard's "social market economy". The social basis of the CDU political orientation may be seen more clearly from the way it is financed than from its broad voting base. Instead of relying on membership dues as the SPD does, the CDU relies on funds collected from industry and business by "sponsors' associations". The funds are distributed among the non-Socialist parties. The CDU has consistently recieved a much larger share than the FDP for several reasons. Adenauer's emphasis on Franco-German friendship, European integration, and the Atlantic Alliance enjoyed broad popular support. This support was reinforced by the rapid economic recovery, which seemed to justify Erhard's policies and disarmed the SPD opposition. Between 1949 and 1969 the Christian Democrats consistently won the largest share of the total vote, and until the 1969 elections were the senior partners in the governing coalitions.

These facts provided a solid basis of political stability, which itself posed an unforeseen problem. In the long Adenauer period, the role of the executive was much stronger than had been foreseen by the framers of the Basic Law because it was not expected that one party would consistently hold the dominant position in the *Bundestag*. They were concerned to protect the position of weak coalition governments against politically fragmented legislatures. Instead a strong governmental party developed, and there was too much stability. It was

carried even further in the post-Adenauer period when the Grand
Coalition was established in the autumn of 1966. The Grand Coalition
tied both main parties to the executive, reducing opposition within the
established political system almost to vanishing point.

The Spiegel Affair

The end of the Adenauer era was marked by the *Spiegel* Affair which
involved serious abuses of power, particularly on the part of the then
Defence Minister, Franz Josef Strauss.

The CDU/CSU had won their most overwhelming election victory in
1957, with slightly over half of the total votes and enough seats to
enable them safely to dispense with the FDP as coalition partners.
Against the background of evident political stability and the satisfying
purr of rising levels of consumption, the question of Adenauer's
succession began to emerge as a key issue. In his eighties, the Chancellor
could not be expected to last for ever. In the meantime he ran the
parliamentary party in a high-handed manner, which was all the more
resented as it became clear that he wished to nominate his own
successor. He did everything he could to prevent Erhard, the party
favorite, from succeeding him, eventually deciding not to retire himself.
The consequence was that the Christian Democrats lost their electoral
majority in the 1961 elections, while the FDP, which had campaigned
strongly against Adenauer, made substantial gains. Therefore a coalition
between these two parties was necessary to form a government.
Adenauer retained his position, but by a much narrower margin, and
the opposition to his leadership within the coalition was growing. In
fact, to establish the coalition Adenauer had to sign an undertaking to
the effect that he would retire well before the 1965 elections.

If it had not been for the *Spiegel* affair, he might well have ignored
it. But at the end of October 1962 Defence Minister Strauss ordered a
police raid on the offices of the informative weekly journal *Der Spiegel.*
The charges alleged that the editors had violated official secrets by
obtaining and publishing material on the results of a NATO exercise.
However it was seen by the press and the opposition as an attempt to
silence informed criticism of Strauss' policy by police-state methods.
The situation was aggravated by Strauss' behaviour in parliament when
he tried to shift the blame onto others and then to lie his way out of
the difficulty. In the uproar the government coalition was strained to
breaking point. The FDP coupled its demand for the dismissal of
Strauss with a demand for Adenauer's definite departure in 1963.
Adenauer accepted the first, but tried to wriggle out of the second by

courting the SPD. The possibility of a Grand Coalition was sniffed at, but at the time it was too evident to the Christian Democrats that the eighty seven year old Chancellor was a political liability. Adenauer resigned as agreed in 1963, but continued to do everything he could to humiliate and discredit Erhard as his successor.

Apart from the political consequences of the *Spiegel* Affair in bringing the Adenauer era to a close, much deeper problems were exposed. Haffner analysed these brilliantly in *Encounter*. The Federal Government had done little to overcome the authoritarian ethos of the German penal system with its numerous opportunities for detention without trial and severe restrictions on legal defence. The possibilities of abuse were compounded as the system was largely run by men who had served Hitler, and who had therefore been involved in the enormous perversion of justice by the Nazi state. The man appointed Federal Attorney in 1962 had to resign because of documentary evidence that he had been involved in Nazi judicial murders. The evidence of his guilt and the pressure for his removal came from East Germany. Reflecting on these unresolved problems, Haffner pointed up the ambiguity of the Adenauer era. It was the establishment of a formal democratic framework without breaking from authoritarian traditions: "A stable democracy run as often as not by ex-Nazis, satin-smooth, impeccable, a remarkable achievement in its way, but somehow a little too good to be true: that was Adenauer's Germany, and it ended with a bang on October 26th, 1962."[26]

However the ambiguity of the Adenauer era remained. It included the caution, the fundamental desire for conservative political stability which was expressed in the Christian Democratic campaign slogan: "No experiments." Its positive side was reflected in the absorption of millions of refugees and expellees, thereby minimising the danger of an explosive nationalistic issue. Its negative side is reflected in the hostility and suspicion with which demands for long-overdue reforms in the universities were received, and in the way the two major parties resolved the post-Adenauer transitional difficulties by clinging to each other in the Grand Coalition.

The Grand Coalition

Erhard, the symbol of West Germany's economic "miracle", succeeded Adenauer as Chancellor in the autumn of 1963. However, general discontent with Erhard's leadership, exacerbated by a dispute over financial questions, prompted the Free Democrats to leave the coalition three years later. The results of the 1965 election made an FDP/SPD coalition possible, but difficult: the SPD won 202 seats and the FDP had 49, against the CDU/CSU total of 245. In reaction to the electoral disappointments in the 1950s, the SPD leaders long wanted a big coalition with the Christian Democrats. They were prepared to ride out the flood of criticism and anger within their own party to attain it. For the Social Democratic leadership, the coalition was an opportunity to taste power after many years of frustration. It was an attempt to gain enough respectability and standing in the eyes of the Protestant middle-class voter to command a durable majority. In order to arrive at this calculation, the SPD had undertaken a long retreat on all major questions of economic and foreign policy since the 1953 election. By the early 1960s, the SPD was actively trying to escape from its opposition role. It preferred a bargaining relationship with the Christian Democrats, a bureaucratic give-and-take, rather than the political confrontation involved in the government/opposition roles.

The Christian Democrats agreed in the autumn of 1966 because a coalition would allow them to remain in power while suffering from a leadership crisis. In addition they may have calculated that they could take credit for any government success, while the SPD could be blamed for difficulties. Some *Laender* election results indicate that this happened to a certain degree. But in the 1969 elections, the SPD gained twenty-two seats while the CDU/CSU lost three. It was enough to renew SPD confidence, and the leadership boldly created a new political situation by forming a coalition with the Free Democrats. The FDP lost nine seats in the election, and their share of the total vote fell to 5.8 per cent — which was barely above the five per cent minimum required to obtain parliamentary representation. Nevertheless the positive attitude of the new FDP leader, Walter Scheel, made possible the formation of a socialist-liberal coalition with a slim majority of twelve. The Christian Democrats remained the largest party with 242 seats. The Brandt government commenced its terms of office vigorously, despite its narrow majority, and by its constructive action substantially contributed to the strengthening of the democratic process. But among the many problems which had to be overcome was the legacy of the Grand Coalition itself.

The Grand Coalition had disturbing implications because it almost toally negated the notion of parliamentary opposition. For nearly three years from the autumn of 1966, the small FDP group of forty nine deputies faced a wall-to-wall government. The way was left open for the development of extremist opposition beyond the normal political processes. The neo-Nazi NPD grew considerably in those years.

Membership expanded from 7,500 in May 1965 to about 35,000 at the end of 1967. They made gains in *laender* elections, and established themselves as a national party. The 1969 election was their second federal contest, and they won 4.3 per cent of the nearly thirty three million votes. Because of the five per cent minimum requirement it was not enough to gain representation. But their electoral attraction increased at a time of high prosperity and full employment. Although failing to attain the immediate objective of entry into the *Bundestag*, it became an established political entity so that in the event of future difficulties it is not inconceivable that the NPD could replace the FDP as the third party holding the balance in an evenly divided electorate.

However this view may be too pessimistic. The NPD was formed in the autumn of 1964 from the remnants of unsuccessful or banned right-wing groups such as the German Party and the Socialist Reich party. Its initial vigour plus the political climate combined to produce unexpectedly high votes in some *Laender* elections.[27] But its capacity for expansion appears to be limited in many ways. Discontent among farmers and small business may continue to provide it with political troops. But middle-class disaffection with the Federal Republic in no way rseembles the Weimar Republic situation. Economic prosperity has continuously provided expanding opportunities, unlike the prolonged difficulties of Weimar. And the basis of the political situation is fundamentally different. West Germany cannot hope to establish an international role independent of the two great power blocs. Under these conditions it is not surprising that there is little evidence of youth being particularly attracted to the NPD. Unlike the Nazis, whose rise was based on a solid core of youth activism, the NPD cannot offer a utopia of new beginnings or total solutions.

The NPD has drawn some support from the large pool of refugees and expellees. There are, however, several limiting factors. Unemployment progressively diminished in the 1950s, and the serious housing shortage has been steadily alleviated. Laws passed under refugees' pressure contributed greatly to their relief: the Civil Service Law of 1951 and the 1952 Law for the Equalization of Burdens. There is evidence that the refugees and expellees as a whole have not fully recovered their former status[28] but the prospects for improvement have been continuous so far. Loss of status, as well as the actual displacement, breeds resentment: resentment which is loudly expressed in the network of *Landmannschaften* newspapers, periodicals and propaganda literature; resentment which is fostered in mass meetings and informal gatherings. The direct political consequences, however, have not been conspicious. The Refugee Party won twenty seven seats in the 1953 *Bundestag* elections, but were unable to win any in the next two elections and so were liquidated as a separate party. The indirect political consequences were greater, keeping alive a sense of injustice and the notion that there were lost homelands to recover. But the recovery of former territories is widely recognised to be subordinate to the problem of reunification — itself as distant a prospect as ever. On the other hand, the political drawing power of the NPD is not confined to these sources. Although relatively small, it was a broadly-based movement. It gained some urban, working-class and Catholic support, in addition to traditional middle-class, right-wing Protestant and Army backing.

Since 1970, the NPD has steadily lost ground. In various *Landtag* elections, its vote declined: in Lower Saxony from 7 per cent to 3.2 per cent in June 1970 and in both Hesse (from 7.9 per cent to 3 per cent) and Bavaria (from 7.4 per cent to 2.9 per cent) in November 1970. Its failure to maintain representation in the state parliaments occurred at a time when it might have been expected to benefit from nationalistic agitation. Chancellor Brandt's *Ostpolitik* was clearly leading to acceptance of the Oder-Neisse line as Poland's Western frontier, which meant acknowledgement of the loss of 40,000 square miles of former German territory in Silesia, Pomerania and East Prussia. However, the NPD lost votes to the CDU/CSU even in its stronghold areas of Lower Saxony and Bavaria. This may be accounted for by two factors. First, there was an entirely new political situation with the Christian Democrats being in opposition for the first time. The NPD role as a vehicle for protest was reduced. Secondly, the CDU/CSU stole NPD thunder by campaigning in an aggressive, nationalistic way. Thus, former NPD voters were given a broader choice. A front-page cartoon in *Die Zeit* (27th November 1970) showed a more-porky-than-usual Franz Josef Strauss gorging himself on NPD votes. In the accompanying article, Theo Sommer wrote that the danger was not the capture of NPD votes by the CDU/CSU, but the unpredictable and shady politics of Bavaria's Strauss. The NPD party organisation was weakened by unsavoury internal affairs and scandals, and some of its most fanatical members left to form new groups which emphasise direct action. In the federal elections of November 1972, support for the NPD declined steeply. It lost well over one million votes, so that its share fell from 4.3 per cent to 0.6 per cent of the total votes cast. Whether the NPD will be able to recover, or will fall into permanent decline, remains to be seen. The extreme right wing remains a problem. There is a core of some 40,000 "unteachables" who are member of various radical right organisations. Three main weekly papers circulate about 190,000 copies to an estimated readership of some 600,000. Compared with other Western European countries, these figures are disproportionately high.[29] The rise of the NPD was a dangerous manifestation because it was based on a deeply rooted tradition. If it is unlikely that the tradition will become dominant again, it is equally unlikely that it will disappear. Its potential development in adverse circumstances is considerable, and if misjudged it could further enfeeble the cause of democracy.

The Student Movement

The student protest movement developed most intensely at the Free University of Berlin in the 1960s. The location is symbolic, the date of some significance. The Free University was founded in 1948 by a group of teachers and students who left the Humboldt University in East Berlin because of the climate of political oppression. The new university differed from other West German universities in three respects. It was a political showpiece, glittering in the Cold War. Secondly, there was a greater degree of formal student participation in the running of the university than existed elsewhere. There were a few student representatives on faculty committees and in the Senate. Their contribution to decision-making, however, was substantially limited to student affairs, narrowly defined. Efforts to expand the area of effective participation triggered the protest movement. Despite its limitations, the Berlin system was considered to be a "model" which some students in other universities strove to realise. The third difference was a concentration of students with political interests at the Free University. They were attracted by the strategic importance of the divided city, which was much more in the centre of action and public attention than were dreary provincial university towns. And the atmosphere at the Free University was correspondingly more open and active.

   To appreciate the point a brief reference to the prevailing atmosphere in the universities after the war may be in order. The universities had never been centres of democratic and progressive ideals. The middle — and upper-class student body tended sharply to the right. Nazi student groups were the dominant political force in many places as early as 1930. By 1934 over 1,000 of 7,750 university teachers were dismissed, and Nazi control was total and unopposed. At the end of the war there was no revolt in the universities heralding a significant change. And within a very short time, far too brief to allow for restaffing and restructuring, the universities were re-opened. Returning from military service, the preponderant element in the student body wanted to take up their studies without worrying about the problems of reform. But their passivity and apparent apathy were not a-political. There were nationalist demonstrations at Munich, Heidelberg, Jena and Gottingen. Hostile acts were committed against Social Democratic and Communist student groups. The few Jewish students were hissed.[30] In the sullen atmosphere, de-Nazification was resented. The professors, who were either active Nazis or at least conventional enough to satisfy the Third Reich authorities, easily slipped back into their positions. They were not challenged by their students; on the contrary, the students virtually escorted them back. For a decade, until the end of the 1950s, the student body shut its eyes to the problem. It was left to a new generation of students, middle-class youth who grew up in the post-war period, to press for long overdue changes.

As in other countries, student unrest in West Germany in the 1960s had a dual aspect: the situation within the universities, and the impact of general political issues. The rapid increase of student enrolment strained existing facilities. The result was a drastic deterioration in the conditions of study, particularly in the humanities and social sciences. Overcrowding in some subjects transformed seminars into mass meetings of hundreds of students. Contact with teachers was rendered virtually impossible, and in some cases the decisive oral examination at the end of a long course of study was the first face-to-face meeting between student and professor.

The students at the Free University began to develop tactics of protest which could not be ignored. Finding that discussion and traditional forms of protest were not effective, the Berlin students adopted the Berkeley sit-in technique in June 1966. Under this pressure, the academic Senate did not proceed with its plan of setting a maximum period for completing studies, and renounced its prohibition of political discussions in the university. Student protest activity then intensified. Other universities began to follow the Berlin example. The notion of student representation was re-defined. Tripartite representation on all academic bodies was increasingly demanded – one third for the professors, one third for the students and one third for the non-professorial staff. Moreover the conflict was sharpened by the establishment of the Grand Coalition. Many of the liberal and left-wing students were shocked by the manoeuvre which, by its cynicism, seemed to reflect the social disaster of Germany. They felt that theirs was the only opposition left. The attitude was not confined to the left-wing

socialist students. The liberal students group (LSD) was in revolt
against the right-wing of the parent FDP, and the Humanist Students
Union was concerned to defend basic rights.

The situation was further aggravated by the unmistakably hostile
reactions of the university and political authorities, the police, the press
and the public. Tension was highest in Berlin. The public, still feeling
itself to be on the frontier of the Cold War, was hostile to the students.
The West Berlin press, which is almost entirely dominated by the
Springer corporation, was violently anti-student. The protesting
students were isolated, and treated as outcasts by the community. It
had the effect of closing student ranks, broadening mutual sympathy
and mobilising many hundreds of previously uncommitted students. A
definite stage in the escalating conflict was reached in the spring of
1967 when the rector called the police into the university to break up a
protest sit-in.

By this time the struggle for change within the university was deeply
entwined with broader political events. The connection is not
fortuitous because the pressure for change has come from politically
conscious student groups. The socialist student federation (SDS)
clashed sharply with the SPD over changes in policy which culminated
in the Godesberg Programme of 1959. The Godesberg Programme
replaced traditional Marxist formulations by an open "non-ideology".
The intention was to find electoral success through a phraseology of
appeals to the middle class and a large acceptance of Christian
Democratic policies. The SDS fought sharply against the revision, and
was formally disavowed by the SPD in 1960. While the SPD waited
patiently for the opportunity of joining the CDU/CSU in coalition
government, the SDS concentrated its efforts on university problems. It
did not disintegrate as some in the parent party had hoped it would,
but built itself into the core of the student protest movement.

Numerically the SDS was very small, having at peak periods two
thousand members. Its real strength lay in its ability to rally several
thousand students on important occasions. It established a bastion in
Frankfurt as well as in Berlin, and was influential in several other
universities. The SDS was by no means homogeneous. It consisted of
left-wing social democrats, a sprinkling of anarchists and communists
and a majority of "anti-authoritarians". Although not sharing its
ideological outlook, other student groups were influenced by the SDS
dynamic. The liberal students, struggling against right-wing tendencies
in the Free Democratic party, the humanist students, and even the
official Social-Democratic student group (SHB) were in varying degrees

involved in the protest movement.

The great rallying point after 1964 was the Vietnam War. Agitation against it pierced through the Cold War taboos of the 1950s. It was much harder to condemn American actions in Vietnam in the outpost of Berlin than in Paris where it was considered good taste. The SDS went further, linking its condemnation of "imperialism" with a rejection of the West German political system as latently Fascist. However imprecise and vague these ideas may be, the moral revulsion against the war in Vietnam was genuine.

The protest over Vietnam was reinforced by the state of domestic affairs. The formation of the Grand Coalition was a real shock which confirmed for some people the rightness of the extremist definition of the political system as tending towards Fascism. A number of circumstances were presented in support of this view: the experiences of remilitarisation; Strauss' desire for atomic weapons; the sordid *Spiegel* Affair; the moves to introduce special "Emergency Laws"; the numbers of ex-Nazis, not all of them repentant, who had found their way back to influential and sensitive positions; the activity of the NPD; the bitter anti-student press campaigns; and the weakness of the democratic political process in which opposition had almost ceased to exist. The demonstration, occasioned by the visit of the Shah of Iran to West Berlin in early June 1967, further exacerbated the feelings of isolation and menace. In the disturbances, largely initiated by aggressive police behaviour (as was confirmed by an official enquiry), many students were hurt and wounded. One student was killed by a police bullet. Widespread protests followed, and in several places Republican clubs were founded to organise an Extra-parliamentary Opposition (APO), intending to draw intellectuals, secondary-school pupils and young workers, as well as students into the movement.

One of the main targets was the Springer press, which continued violently to abuse the student and opposition movement in its illustrated tabloids. The plan was to reveal how news was being distorted and manipulated, so that its persuasive powers could be nullified. In the winter of 1968, the anti-Springer campaign lost some of its momentum. But on 11th April the student leader Rudi Dutschke was shot three times, one of the bullets penetrating into his brain, seriously endangering his life. Furious demonstrations of unexpected size took place in many large cities. They were directed against the Springer newspapers, widely held responsible for creating an atmosphere in which such an attack could occur. The demonstrations continued for a few days, involving serious clashes with the police who were defending the Springer offices. Two people were killed in the violence of the clashes. It was a foretaste of the scenes to be enacted in France in the following month. But in Germany after brief occupations of some universities, the storm diminished. There was a large demonstration in Bonn in May against the Emergency Laws, but the police did not act aggressively and there were no incidents. The German Trade Union Federation made its own arrangements for the protest, minimising common cause with the students. The protests did not succeed in impeding the passage of the Emergency Laws. In the following months the SDS virtually ceased to function as a coherent organisation. Finally in March 1970 the SDS formally dissolved itself, splitting into its component factions of extremist cells.

The SPD/FDP Coalition and 'Ostpolitik'

After the 1969 elections, the SPD changed coalition partners and opened a new chapter in its post-war history. It became the senior partner in government and vigorously pursued a foreign policy of historic significance. The CDU/CSU remained the largest party with 242 seats, a slight loss of three seats. But the SPD gained twenty two seats for a total of 224. Its gamble with the Grand Coalition paid electoral dividends because some of its leaders had gained standing before the electorate as competent ministers. The SPD boldly announced its governing coalition with the FDP — with a slim majority of twelve seats, which was soon reduced to nine by FDP defections to the opposition. The FDP had continued its downward trend at the polls, and had retained only thirty of its previous total of forty nine seats. Some of its losses were among right-wing voters who were dissaffected by the party's shift to a liberal-left orientation during the Grand Coalition. But the FDP's domestic policy remained to the right of the SPD, so that on matters of potential conflict such as the extension of co-determination in industry the SPD did not attempt to initiate reforms. A similar situation prevailed in the months following the 1972 election when the coalition was returned to power and differences on domestic issues were put aside despite the protests of the SPD left wing. However, the viability of the coalition was based on its consensus of views about establishing a new set of relations with the countries of Eastern Europe.

During the Grand Coalition, Brandt's efforts, as Foreign Minister, to improve relations with the Eastern European countries were set back by the Soviet Union's invasion of Czechoslovakia in August 1968. However, in 1970 with Brandt as Chancellor and the FDP leader Scheel

as Foreign Minister there were a series of negotiations with East
Germany, the Soviet Union and Poland. The meetings between Brandt
and Willi Stoph, DDR Head of State, acknowledged the existence of
East German statehood which former West German governments had
sought to deny. Although the meetings did not create full diplomatic
recognition, they prepared the way for further negotiations between
the two Germanies. There followed two important treaties of
reconciliation with the Soviet Union and with Poland. In August 1970
the Moscow treaty was signed — it renounced the use of force, and
established closer relations in various fields including technology and
trade. In the preceeding years, trade relations had been expanding, and
German industrialists were encouraged in their hopes of finding a larger
Soviet market for their exports. In December a treaty of friendship
with Poland was signed. Its historic significance was to accept the
divisions established at the end of the Second World War, so that the
Western frontier of Poland was acknowledged as being the Oder-Neisse
line, and claims on former German territory were implicitly
relinquished. The following September, a four-power agreement on
Berlin was signed, which together with subsequent negotiations settled
long standing disputes about the legal position of Berlin and the
problems of access and visiting rights. The *Ostpolitik* was an
international success, winning the strong approval of the Western
countries, and alleviating some of the main problems created during the
course of the Second World War and its aftermath.

The soothing of international tensions inflamed the West German
polity. The ratification of the treaties involved a serious crisis. Whereas
the role of the opposition had been reduced to a minimum during the
Grand Coalition (49 versus 447), it was out of proportion against the
Brandt government. The original majority of twelve had been reduced
to nine by FDP defections, and was then reduced, in the winter of
1971-72, to a majority of one by defections from both parties.[31] The
war of nerves became intense as the ratification debate approached. An
added dimension was a clash in the cabinet over tax reform, which
nearly resulted in the resignation of the Economics and Finance
Minister Karl Schiller. Towards the end of April 1972, the Chancellor
faced a non-confidence vote, which fell two votes short of the 249
required to remove him. The next day voting on the budget was
deadlocked. The difficulties of the government were overwhelming; but
the opposition was also in an uneasy situation. It could not lightly
reject the treaties because the Soviet Union announced that it would
not re-negotiate the terms, while Western opinion strongly favoured

ratification. Moreover, to become Chancellor through the rejection of
the treaties would have placed the Christian Democratic leader Barzel at
the mercy of his right-wing led by the energetic Bavarian Strauss and
the former foreign minister Gerhard Schroeder. The consequences
could have been dire, as an astute commentator wrote:

> 'To justify its actions it [a government headed by Barzel and
> Strauss] would have had to seek further refuge in the German
> national ideal, the authoritarian line and the appeal to chauvinistic
> emotions. On the domestic scene the conflicts would be grave. The
> left wing would make itself independent. The liberal rational centre
> . . . . would be endangered by erosion. The consolation that 'Bonn is
> not Weimar' would no longer be applicable.'[32]

In the event, the government survived both the constructive vote of no
confidence and the ratification. But there were two agonising delays
before the vote was put to the *Bundestag* in May. The opposition by
then was unable to accept or reject the treaties, and so abstained from
voting. Although it had achieved its goal, the position of the
government did not improve. The tensions and acrid atmosphere
continued. Schiller resigned; Brandt made bitter allegations of
corruption against the defectors to the opposition; and the government
had to preside over its own defeat in order to call elections a year
before schedule. The election campaign included elements of bitter
partisanship but no violence.[33] The outcome strengthened both
coalition partners,[34] and provided them with a solid working majority
of forty six. There was no doubt that their foreign policy initiatives met
the approval of the majority of the electorate, since a few days before
the elections the two German states initialled an agreement on a general
relations treaty which aimed at normalising their relationships and
furthering the process of *de facto* recognition.[35] But the mandate for
domestic reforms of taxation, social security, education and in the
industrial field was less certain. The FDP defined its position in
domestic affairs as a check on left-wing tendencies in the SPD. Since it
holds the balance of power between the two larger parties, the SPD
leadership cannot afford to lose its support.

NOTES

1. It does not apply to West Berlin which has a constitution similar
to those of the *Laender* of Hamburg and Bremen, but which is not a
Land of the Federal Republic.

2. See Chapter 11, p 174.

3. Hoyt Price and Carl E. Schorske, *The Problem of Germany* New York, Council on Foreign Relations 1947, p125.

4. John D. Montgomery, *Forced to be Free: The Artificial Revolution in Germany and Japan* University of Chicago Press 1957, p62.

5. For estimates of the extent of evasion see Montgomery, p203.

6. Price and Schorske, pp127-131.

7. Childs, *From Schumacher to Brandt* pp46-7; Richard Hiscocks, *Germany Revived* Gollancz 1966 p201.

8. *The Federal Republic of Germany*, Pall Mall, transl. by Nelson Aldrich, p111.

9. "The End of the Affair", *Encounter* March 1963, p65.

10. Montgomery, p79.

11. *Germany Divided*, Hutchinson, 1961, pp255-6 and 269-70. See also Childs, pp48-9.

12. Klaus Epstein, "The Adenauer Era in German History" in Stephen R. Graubard (ed), *A New Europe?* Oldbourne, 1964, pp129-30; Michael Balfour, *West Germany*, Benn, 1968, pp224.

13. *Die Zeit*, 18 April 1969.

14. His predecessor, Heinrich Lübke, was not able to repudiate East German reports that he had been involved in building concentration camps, and consequently resigned before completing his term of office.

15. The United States Strategic Bombing Survey, *The Effects of Strategic Bombing on the German War Economy*, 1945, p49.

16. M.M. Postan, *An Economic History of Western Europe 1945-1964*, Methuen 1967, pp23-4.

17. Edward L. Homze, *Foreign Labor in Nazi Germany*, Princeton University Press 1967, p151.

18. See *Anatomy of the SS State*, pp483-94; and Terence Prittie, *Germany Divided*, pp60-62.

19. See Homze, p153.

20. "The German Lesson", *The Economist*, 15 October 1966, pVII.

21. *Modern Capitalism: The Changing Balance of Public and Private Power*, Oxford UP 1965, Chapter XII.

22. See Braunthal, *The Federation of German Industry in Politics*, Chapters IX and X.

23. *Ibid.*, p193.

24. However it supported Adenauer's policy of West European integration, while the SPD under Schumacher's leadership and influence strongly opposed it until the latter part of the 1950s.

25. See Richard F. Hamilton, "Affluence and the Worker: the West German Case", *American Journal of Sociology*, September 1965.

26. *Encounter*, March 1963, p67.

27. 7.9 per cent in Hesse, November 1966; 7.4 per cent in Bavaria, November 1966; 7.0 per cent in Lower Saxony, June 1967; 9.8 per cent in Baden-Württemberg, April 1968.

28. See Balfour, p277.

29. For a survey of right-wing extremism in the Federal Republic,

see Bracher, *The German Dictatorship*, Chapter 9: "Breakdown and Continuity of National Socialism".

30. Price and Schorske, p130.

31. One of the defectors from the SPD was Herbert Hupka, a Silesian refugee leader, who for over two years had been in the forefront of the campaign against reconciliation. His view was that "Communism has won a victory, Germany has lost". There were frequent newspaper reports of secret offers of safe seats in the next elections for coalition deputies who were critical of the *Ostpolitik*, if they abandoned the government side to join the CDU or CSU.

32. Rolf Zundel, *Die Zeit*, 10 March 1972.

33. See William Paterson, "The West German Elections", *The World Today* December 1972 for a perceptive analysis of the campaign and the election results.

34. The final results were 230 seats for the SPD, and forty one for the FDP. CDU/CSU won 225 seats (seventeen less than previously).

35. The preamble acknowledged "the differing concepts of the Federal Republic of Germany and the German Democratic Republic on basic questions, among them the national question . . . ." but aimed at creating "conditions for co-operation" on the basis of equality, mutual respect and renunciation of the use of force.

Chapter 11 France: A Change of Intermediaries

After the Fall of France in 1940, the Vichy regime was established in the unoccupied two fifths of the country. De Gaulle initiated resistance from his London base, but months passed before much progress was made inside France. Because of the Nazi-Soviet pact, the Communists did not struggle against the occupation. Only when the Germans attacked Russia in the summer of 1941 did they undertake an active resistance role. It grew in strength as the Nazis intensified their hunt for labour, especially skilled labour. The Socialists, however, commenced their resistance much earlier. Joining together with non-Communist trade unionists, the Socialists formed a resistance movement known as *Libération*. They also had a strong influence in *Combat*, a resistance organisation without definite political complexion whose leader, Henri Frenay, was close to de Gaulle. These and smaller movements were co-ordinated on de Gaulle's instructions into a National Council of Resistance (CNR) in the spring of 1943, which the Communists joined. The CNR programme of March 1944 consisted of a plan for immediate action, measures for the establishment of a provisional government by de Gaulle, and a series of long-term economic and social reforms. Unlike the Belgian and Dutch Resistance movements, the French did not want a return to the pre-war political system. But the nature of the desired change was indicated only in the broadest terms: that a rejuvenated France, led by men who had proved themselves in the Resistance, would be truly Republican, democratic and *social*. The various Resistance groups talked the language of "revolution", "socialism", "social liberation", "workers control" and so on, reflecting profound aspirations for change, although precise limits were fixed.

The limits may be seen in the CGT slate of reforms which were incorporated into the CNR programme. It was recognised that private enterprise would continue to exist alongside an extended public sector of nationalised industries. An uncritical belief in the impartiality of the State and in the efficacy of structural reforms, as steps in the evolution towards Socialism, was perpetuated, as had been the case after the previous war. With liberation, the working class rose greatly in political importance, but there was no attempt to go beyond the framework of the CNR. Rumours of impending Communist uprisings were exaggerated. General de Gaulle established his authority in Paris smoothly. He incorporated the armed Resistance groups into the regular French army without being seriously challenged by Resistance leaders. They grumbled, but accepted his orders. And he was able to reinforce the authority of his selected delegates (as representatives of the Provisional Government) in the more recalcitrant provinces in the course of a short two-month tour.

But in the summer of 1944, it did not seem to be as easy as that. Paris was liberated towards the end of August, and within five weeks the invader was driven out of most of the country. The tasks of reconstruction could commence, but the war was still on. Moreover, the social conditions raised the fundamental question of political control of the State. No one wanted to return to the old political system; big business was gravely compromised by its collaboration with the occupying power; the Communists were at the height of their prestige and energy. As the main military leaders of the Resistance in the country, they had groups of armed men under their control. They had an important if not decisive influence in liberation committees at local, departmental and national levels. Their work in organising labour was dynamically carried out, and they dominated the CGT. The road to power seemed open to them, either through elections or by widening the area of conflict between the liberation committees and the Provisional Government.

Although there has been much speculation, no valid evidence has been produced to show that the second method was contemplated. Conflicts between the liberation committees and the Provisional Government, particularly in the south and south-west, derived mainly from the local circumstances of the liberation. In other parts of France, the delegates of the Provisional Government reported that the Communists fully supported them. Even where there was some trouble, de Gaulle's orders were eventually obeyed, especially after the return of the Communist leader Maurice Thorez from Moscow in November 1944. Thorez made his position on the legality of the Provisional Government very clear: "There is a government, and it must have one army, one only; it must have a police force, one only." Questioned by journalists he went on to say that of course the class struggle existed, but "today it is not a question of starting a debate on this issue; it is necessary to gather together the whole nation in order to win the war".[1] The Communists were concerned with what Thorez called the categorical imperative: "the unity of the Nation." In essence the situation was the same as in Northern Italy, where the Resistance recognised the Rome government as the sole legitimate authority. It placed a check on the potential revolutionary impetus of the Liberation movement, but the Italian Communists accepted it with the same alacrity as the French Communists accepted de Gaulle's transformation of the Resistance organisations, their power base, into purely consultative bodies. Communist policy was not to attempt a *coup*, but to throw themselves into a sustained campaign for mass recruitment into the party, and for participation in the elections.

At the same time, they took a very strong line in favour of wage restraint. They called upon workers to engage in "the battle for production". In the years 1945 and 1946 despite the hardships of food shortages, inflation and growing discontent in the industrial centres, they refused to endorse strike action. But in May 1946, a referendum on the constitution, which was elaborated by the Socialist-Communist majority in the Constituent Assembly, was defeated. It was a warning which the Communists heeded, and they began to campaign for wage increases. A month later general elections were held, and the Communists gained votes from the Socialists. But the biggest gains were made by the MRP, a Christian Democratic party of the centre. The Left lost is majority in the Constituent Assembly, and Communist hopes of obtaining key ministries receded.

The political situation was complicated. An elected Constituent Assembly was operating under de Gaulle's leadership until a new Constitution could be drafted and accepted by referendum. But at the beginning of 1946, de Gaulle resigned, apparently exasperated with the quarrels and demands of the parties which dominated the Assembly — the Communists, the Socialists and the MRP. When he left, these three parties formed a coalition government, known as *tripartisme*. The new constitution was finally accepted in October 1946,[2] and the third general election in thirteen months was held in November. It brought the Communists their biggest success. They gained twenty seats, bringing their total to 183. The MRP was the second largest party with 160 seats, while the Socialists held 101. The Socialists lost thirty seats, including their stronghold in the mining districts of the north. The Assembly which lasted until 1951 was therefore at first dominated by a *tripartite* coalition of the largest parties, but the partnership was an uneasy one. Thorez made a bid for the premiership, but failed. Instead the Socialist Ramadier eventually became Prime Minister. He offered five ministerial positions to the Communists, but kept them away from the key posts of the Interior, Finance and Foreign Office. In order to stay in the government, the Communists were willing to temporise on colonial questions, and even to improvise a theory that self-determination could be only justified if it benefited France as well as the colony. In the budget debate of March 1947, the PCF resorted to an awkward compromise on the question of military credits for the war in Indo-China, abstaining from the vote even though their ministers were obliged to vote in favour. The party, moreover, tried to ignore the bloody suppression of the rebellion in Madagascar, which was even more vicious than the action which the British undertook in Kenya some years later. The internal strains were growing as opposition to its role in government mounted.

In April 1947 metal workers' union leaders were shouted down when they tried to call off a strike at Renault. The workers were following an independent strike committee. It was an important event because Renault was nationalised, and it was the first time that serious discontent in nationalised industries was expressed. It was important also because Renault held a key position in the powerful Paris regional metal workers' federation. Among its members were the CGT secretary-general Frachon and the communist Minister of Labour, Croizat. The Communists decided in May that they would have to support the strike, otherwise their position in the labour movement would be too seriously threatened. The Prime Minister took the opportunity to clear them out of government. He forced the issue by calling for a vote of confidence in his policy of wage restraint, which the Communist ministers and deputies voted against. On this issue Ramadier's majority was easily assured. With the subsequent dismissal of the Communist ministers in May 1947 the *tripartite* coalition ended, and the Communists moved into serious opposition.

The reforms of the post-Liberation period — nationalisations and a form of workers' representation on the factory level called *comités d'entreprise* — were of no obvious and immediate benefit to the industrial working class. The *comités d'entreprise* were instituted in the larger firms, but were given only limited advisory functions in economic matters, and did not change the quality of industrial relations. More fundamentally the power of the unions was not directed towards raising real wages. Improved social security benefits, particularly family allowances, offered limited compensation for the stark fact that direct wages were at a low level in a period of inflation. The index of purchasing power of hourly wages in January 1946 was one third lower than in 1938 (not a particularly fat year). By 1947 the index had fallen a further twenty per cent, and continued its downward movement into the summer. With the Communists in opposition, there seemed to be nothing to hold back a gigantic strike movement. Between May and

September, however, the Communists hoped that they might be able to return to government. There were numerous strikes in the period, but they were settled quickly for nominal wage increases which were soon eroded by the inflation. The turning point came in Nobember and December when widespread unrest led to an attempt at a general strike.

De Gaulle, for his part, made a startling re-appearance in April 1947, delivering a series of speeches against what he called the regime of decadent parties. He emphatically re-affirmed his view, expressed the previous year, that a strong presidential rule was needed. He launched a "non-party" movement to reform the constitution in this direction. Unleashing a violently anti-Communist campaign, the *Rassemblement du Peuple Français (RPF)* won a sweeping victory in the municipal elections of 1947. With a large popular following created in a few months, de Gaulle appeared to the labour movement and the centre parties as a threat to parliament. A search for a "third force" as against the Gaullists and Communists, was inaugurated in parliament. Created as a left-centre grouping, the third force coalition prevented deterioration but shifted steadily to the right with each succeeding crisis. The problem was that the Socialists, Radicals, Conservatives and Christian Democrats (MRP) were divided on important issues. On colonial and economic matters Socialists and MRP were usually able to find a basis for agreement, while most Radicals and Conservatives took positions which were closer to the Gaullist opposition. But the problem of church schools cut in another direction: Radicals, Socialists and Communists were passionate secularists by tradition, whereas MRP, Gaullists and Conservatives supported Catholic aims. The first moves towards European integration brought further shifts of alignment: MRP, Socialists and Conservatives were in favour, while the Radicals split on the issue, some of them being as hostile as the opposition of RPF and the Communists.

Through these multiple lines of conflict, the Socialists found participation in the coalition an unrewarding experience because they were forced to accept compromises which alienated many of their supporters. The Communists in opposition had a freer hand, and the Socialists divided among themselves over the best tactics of competing with the PCF. By 1950 the Socialists had decided that an opposition role offered the best means of competition. The domestic situation was not insulated from the Cold War antagonisms. Following the September 1947 sessions of the Cominform in Poland, the central committee of the French Communist party decided to reject collaboration with the Socialists and to struggle against American influence in Europe, especially the Marshall Plan. Within the context of these problems, the tensions and dissensions in the working class begun to take concrete form. The Jouhaux group had created within the CGT a loose circle, around the periodical *Force Ouvrière*, as early as December 1945. By the autumn of 1947, differences with the Communist majority in the CGT had intensified, particularly over the Marshall Plan which *Force Ouvrière* welcomed. A new split in the ranks of the General Confederation of Labour was evidently building up. The strength of Jouhaux's group was concentrated at the top of the confederal hierarchy in the central office. It was supported by only nine of the forty national federations, and none of them was a major industrial trade union. When the split came, after the failure of the strikes of November and December 1947, the Communists had a much stronger trade union base than their rivals in the newly formed confederation, called CGT – *Force Ouvrière* (FO).

One of the most important trade union federations which left the CGT at the end of 1947 was the teachers' union, the Federation of National Education. They decided to become autonomous, rather than to affiliate with FO. The decision deprived the new confederation of funds, thousands of active militants and a basis of stable membership. The first congress of the FO was held in April 1948 and it was decided to struggle on two fronts: against the Communists and against de Gaulle's movement (RPF). It was not a practical policy. The defeat of the strike was not only a Communist defeat, it was the decisive turning point in the whole balance of socio-political forces. The FO leadership had been unable to offer a viable alternative to Communist leadership. Their hesitations during the strike had contributed to the defeat, which weakened them much more than it did their rivals. The result was that they had no real forces to withstand the RPF nor were they able to resist the erosion of parliamentary democracy during the next ten years. Initially handicapped by the preponderance of white-collar employees in their membership, they were never able to devise policies which would enable them to recruit workers in the basic industries. And although they claimed to be politically disinterested, they were in fact identified with the policies of the Socialist party, which was in decline. Its membership dropped steadily after 1946, and its political significance ebbed away in the swing to the right.

The other major trade-union confederation was the Catholic organisation, the CFTC. It consistently rejected offers of organisational unity with the CGT, although it was frequently ready for united action on limited issues. After the split in the CGT, the CFTC established a common programme of action with the newly formed FO. The aim was to increase real purchasing power by price controls and anti-inflationary measures. But the alliance was not effective. Rank-and-file demands, encouraged by the Communist-led CGT, for nominal wage-increases were too pressing. The trade unions were in fact caught up in the post-Liberation inflation which they were unable to break through. There were numerous strikes in the summer and autumn of 1948, culminating in a bitter, six-week mining strike. The Socialist Minister of the Interior, Jules Moch, sent troops into the mines during the third week of the strike, and a short guerrilla war ensued. The CGT tried to organise solidarity strikes. The dockers responded, but the railwaymen and the metal workers did not. The strike was defeated, and there was a large scale purge of activists. More workers left the CGT and, although there were short strikes in the autumn of 1951 and the summer of 1953 it was to be more than a decade before prolonged mass strikes occurred in the northern coalfields. With the re-establishment of collective bargaining in February 1950, a third wave of strikes occurred in key industrial sectors. The strikes did not present the unified character of the 1947 unrest, and most of them ended on the employers' terms.

Strikes in the public sector during August 1953 underlined the fact that labour discontent and impotence, not "social liberation" was the outcome of the first years of the Republic. The union-leaders, caught by surprise at the enthusiasm for strikes followed out their rank-and-file, but as no precise demands were raised, the strikes ended in confusion. By 1949 industrial production had reached its highest pre-war levels, but working-class standards of living had not improved correspondingly. Social security payments increased, basic wages did not. That is, there was a redistribution of income not from other social classes to the workers, but within the working class. Social security benefits favoured heads of large families, regardless of degree of skill. The wage hierarchy was thus somewhat flattened, but the overall level of wages was not significantly increased. The militancy of the French labour movement was not smothered by affluence, which was to be notably absent for a long time to come. Rather, the long years of apparent apathy and inactivity, which characterised the 1950s, may be explained by the defeats, disillusionments and ideological disorientation which was the legacy of the post-Liberation period. France had the lowest proportion of organised workers in the western Europe. The CGT lost about two million members, of whom only a minority joined any rival organisation. The vast majority swelled the ranks of the resentfully indifferent. The potentially explosive combination of mass pessimistic apathy and intense ideological in-biting, which characterised the atmosphere of the labour movement, are among the factors which contributed to the decline of parliamentary democracy in the Fourth Republic.

The Second Assembly, elected in June 1951, was entirely dominated by a succession of centre-right coalitions, as the Socialists had decided to retire from participation in government to avoid being saddled with compromises over policies they disliked. Ministerial instability was again a feature of the political scene, this time against a different socio-economic background. The economic problems were those of expansion rather than of reconstruction. Much remained to be done, particularly in the field of housing, but new horizons were opening with plans for European economic integration. In some quarters the plans were at first more lamented than acclaimed, chiefly because of the fear of West German competition. Negotiations were nevertheless carried forward. On the other hand, the increasing success of the economic recovery created grave problems for those sections (small farmers and small businesses) which had benefited from the lack of modernisation and the inflation. Their protests against the increasing pressure of economic rationalisation found vivid expression, particularly in the Poujadist movement. But it was ineffective against the fundamental sweep of change which had been initiated. Rural depopulation accompanied increases in the size and scope of agricultural and industrial production and commercial distribution. Urbanisation was accentuated as rapid changes occurred in the structure of employment. The agricultural sphere was shrinking, and the industrial sphere expanded moderately, while there was an enlargement of the tertiary sector in response to modern administrative and service requirements. One of the crucial factors in bringing about these changes is to be found in the relationship between organised business and the State.

Business and the State

Some writers have attempted to explain the relative slowness of France's economic growth before the 1950s by the nature of family enterprise.[3] The French entrepreneur was portrayed as lacking in competitive spirit, being more concerned to protect his established market position than to accept the risks involved in modernisation and expansion. He was not motivated by a drive for higher and higher profits; rather he was concerned with security, social standing and continuity of family control of the business.

The development of the French economic system does not fully bear out the analysis. In the first place, some of the large-scale entrepreneurial activity in key industrial branches was carried out by dynamic, family firms: for example, Renault, Citroen, Peugeot in cars and de Wendel and Schneider in steel. Secondly French economic vitality during certain periods — 1851 to 1870, 1896 to 1913 and in the 1920s — indicates that stagnation was not caused by the family firms as such. The growth of the economy in the 1950s and 1960s brought some changes in the structure of these firms, but the changes were the effect of the resurgence and not its cause.[4] In periods of expansion, it was not possible for firms (of any size or type) to act in a conservative, protectionist manner. Thirdly by seeking an explanation in terms of family enterprise a point of major significance may be overlooked: the relationship between private enterprise and the state bureaucracy. In *The Bureaucratic Phenomenon,* Crozier considered their interpenetration to be a crucial development of the post-war period. He regarded the ideology of *économie concertée* as a positive break with the past, stimulating a new managerial rationality based on the values of economic growth.

The origin of the interpenetration is to be found in the Organisation Committees set up by the Vichy regime.[5] Before the Second World War, the creation of business organisations at various levels (industrial, regional and national) had been stimulated by the growth and activity of the labour movement, and by increasing government intervention in economic affairs. At the same time industry was concerned actively to promote its interests by influencing government policies. The channels of influence were through political contacts in parliament, and with the civil service. The latter was enhanced in significance after the Second World War with the nationalisation of some major industries and the establishment of indicative planning. These changes gave the State a powerful lever in economic affairs and it took a much more active role than before. The change was prepared by the Vichy Organisation Committees. Managers and Civil Servants were brought together in the Vichy government's organisations and established procedures of co-operation which survived the great political changes of the Liberation period. The significance of the Vichy committees is that managers and industrialists learned to accept guidance from the State authorities, *and came to expect it.* It was this attitude which later enabled the Monnet plan to succeed.

The State provided the machinery for economic modernisation with successive national plans based on credit and investment incentives. Industry, commerce and agriculture were all affected by these policies

which had the objective of enabling France successfully to participate
in the wider European market. The undertaking was to overhaul
France's dated and relatively static economic system. To the extent
that it succeeded it was a triumph of national business not of private
enterprise.

The political conditions in which state-organised business
co-operation could be effective were determined in the post-Liberation
period. Big business as a whole was gravely compromised by its
collaboration with the occupying power. Therefore when the Germans
were driven out of France a peculiar situation arose: political and
economic power were dissociated. Times were hard for the businessman
whose image had lost a great deal of its "respectability". It was the
same for the conservative politician and, as was recognised by the
leaders of organised business, there were very limited possibilities for
political manoeuvring. The initiative lay with the left, which was in a
militant mood. However, a new organisation called the General
Confederation of Small and Medium Business Enterprises was created
shortly after the war and reached its peak influence by 1947. Organised
partly as an employers' association and partly as a political movement,
it presented itself as the defender of the "little man". It had some value
as a front organisation for larger interests unable to exert the political
pressures normally available to them. The small and medium business
movement (PME) led demonstrations against rationing and price
controls in 1947, campaigned against tax reforms and objected to the
introduction of a social welfare system. By the early 1950s, however,
with the recovery of confidence on the part of big business, it became
more closely integrated with the staid CNPF. At the same time, it
became more representative of the substantial medium businessman.
The small businessman who was disadvantaged by the new economic
vigour of the period turned to the vociferous Poujadist movement for
salvation. Based on the small shopkeeper and artisan from the poorer,
depopulated areas of the rural south, the Poujadist movement bitterly
accused the older PME organisation of being in league with "the fat
cats" of Paris.

Meanwhile carefully avoiding the glare of publicity and working with
"la plus grande prudence",[6] organised big business was coping with its
difficulties. Since political and economic power were dissociated, it was
necessary to create new bridges into the centre of political
decision-making. The national organisation, the CNPF, was revived
towards the end of 1945. Outwardly it was a loose, decentralised
federation. But the small executive committee of twenty eight

members, and a strong skilled president, provided an authoritative centralised leadership. Industries where small and medium-sized firms predomonated were well represented on the executive committee, to the detriment of many other important interests. But the president Georges Villiers, would often by-pass regular channels for consultations on important issues. Eventually these interests were given formal status on the executive, displacing the smaller businessmen. It was estimated that by 1956, firms belonging to the CNPF represented approximately ninety per cent of the total private invested capital.[7]

During the tripartite period, close political contact was maintained with the Radicals, who opposed further nationalisations, and with the MRP, the Christian Democrats. When de Gaulle's Rally of the French People emerged as a force of considerable importance, the CNPF leaders backed it for a time. Eventually they withdrew their support for ideological and political reasons. The Gaullist notion of reforming industrial relations through an "association" of labour and capital, publicised in 1949 (and revived in 1968), was rejected by the CNPF as had been pre-war corporatist notions. The employers' objection was that such "reforms" would alter their existing relations with labour at a time when trade unions were weak and divided. Moreover, the swing to the right was gaining momentum and there was a return to a style of parliamentary government reminiscent of the Third Republic. The alternative to parliament which General de Gaulle's movement represented did not find favour. The doctrine of the strong executive which animated the RPF was unattractive when normal conditions of parliament were possible, and when employers' influence was assured. And there was no need to accept a strong executive authority when the candidate for that position did not give much indication of appreciating the nature of the economic changes which were taking place.

The channels of contact with public authorities and administrations were established and working with increasing efficiency. The CNPF's "Service of Legislative Studies", which maintained close contact with the higher civil servants, informed parliamentary deputies of official business views on new bills. Sometimes the service went further, presenting overworked deputies with bills which were already drafted. It could be done only with the co-operation of key civil servants. In fact, links with civil service agencies were so close that leading trade associations were sometimes able to recruit their top men from the administrative offices with which they were dealing. Given the symbiotic relation which became established, it would be vastly to underestimate the cumulative influence of the trade associations affiliated with the CNPF to regard them merely as pressure groups. Ehrmann, reiterating the conclusions of a French study on the economic organisation of the State, characterised their relations with the ministries as "the core of a corporative organisation within the framework of the democratic state".[8]

This provides the key to French planning and modernisation. It is not merely that in both management and civil service positions there are men of similar socio-educational backgrounds: graduates of the *grandes écoles,* technocratically-minded and possibly with experience of both the state bureaucracy and industry. Still more important are their attitudes. The higher civil servants consider themselves to be stabilisers as well as innovators and expansionists. Their economic conceptions may be summarised as "expansion with stability" and "tradition and progress".[9] They share the same view as the business world concerning the organisation and functions of the employers' movement, and the same desire for close working arrangements. But there is an exclusivity about the relationship which affects the quality of democracy in France: it operates to a large extent outside of the public forums, and the participation of labour representatives is jealously resisted. Therefore the ideology of *économie concertée* is not simply a positive break with the past, as Crozier has suggested, but represents a strong element of continuity with the Organisation Committees of Vichy.

Breakdown of the Political System

Under the impact of the Algerian War, the breakdown of the political system and its systematic discrediting by the Gaullists, the achievements of the Fourth Republic have been almost lost from sight. The basis of economic growth was laid soon after the war with nationalisations, high levels of investment, the adoption of Monnet's indicative planning techniques, and the acceptance of European realities; that is, an understanding of the necessity of co-operating with the Federal Republic of Germany, which led France to take initiatives in negotiations for the European Coal and Steel Community and the European Common Market.

But the realistic, pragmatic orientation towards modernisation and European economic co-operation was offset by failures in two other areas which exposed the fragility of the political system. The first is that economic growth was accomplished in a manner which largely neglected or ignored the material prosperity and welfare of large sections of the working population. It was the bureaucracy which handled the problems of economic and social change, rather than the nation's representatives acting in a coherent manner through the public forum of parliament. Labour was treated as a weak special interest, if not as an enemy, and was consequently frustrated and alienated, rather than integrated into a prosperous modernising society. Since the size of the economic cake was growing, standards of living were rising in the working class in the 1950s, but as there was no attempt to redistribute national income the gap between labour's proportion and that of the consuming classes widened. Wages remained among the lowest in western Europe, although prices rose steadily, and there were considerable areas of unemployment. Housing shortages for low income families remained chronic. The resulting dissatisfactions and political apathy helped to perpetuate the divisions of the left, and inhibited the labour movement from developing its potential vitality and strength. Therefore, when military sedition threatened the "democratic and social Republic", there was almost no one to defend it, in sharp contrast with the popular rallies in defence of the Republic in past crises. Within little more than a decade after it had come into existence, the Fourth Republic had lost its legitimacy as the creation of the Resistance struggle.

The second area of failure was far more visible and spectacular. Coming after the resounding defeat in Indo-China, France's colonial policy in Algeria stirred a hornets' nest in the officer corps and brought a resurgence of aggressive nationalism at home. By 1957 a situation of virtual parliamentary paralysis had been created. Increasingly, General de Gaulle was turned to as a shield. Both those who wanted a liberal solution in Algeria, and those who wanted a French Algeria thought he was their saviour. For his part, de Gaulle did not create the crisis situation, but used it for his own purposes. He presented himself, and allowed himself to be presented, in the role of the indispensable leader who was the only alternative to civil war. His purpose was to impose his long-rejected views on political authority. He did it by allowing both sides in the conflict to feel encouraged by his views. He did not disown the conspiratorial activities of the extremists who wanted to keep Algeria French. He did not disown the hard-line views of Michel Debré, who later drafted the constitution of the Fifth Republic. And on several occasions he indicated his sympahty with the Army officers and the settlers in their struggle for "integration" with France. At the same time, he did not disavow the liberals who came to visit him at Colombey-les-Deux-Églises, his place of retirement, and who came back convinced of his desire to grant Algerian independence. He therefore allowed both sides to feel encouraged, while taking advantage of it to come to power. In fact, he left himself free to deal with the Algerian problem in his own way. It was not direct and clear, but tortuously contradictory. Self-determination was announced as the goal of Algerian policy in September 1959, but it took another three years for it to be recognised that peace could be obtained only through political negotiations with the Algerian Provisional Government. The war was prolonged without gaining any tangible benefits, and climaxed in the murderous bitterness of OAS terrorism, exacerbated nationalism, and the repatriation of roughly one million settlers.

De Gaulle's motivation may be explained on two levels. He wanted to end the war in Algeria, and saw that it could be done only by granting independence. But he wanted to retain as much French influence in the area as possible, and tried to limit concessions to a minimum. At the same time the Algerian crisis enabled him to impose his conception of political authority on France. Throughout the Fourth Republic the desire to create a strong executive state was the underlying motivation of his various political acts: his abrupt departure as head of government in January 1946; the creation of the strident Rally of the French People in April 1947, an authoritarian, Bonapartist-type political movement; his relentless attacks on the political system of the Fourth Republic and on political parties which were contemptuously dismissed as mere "intermediaries" between the Hero-Leader and the abstract People. All culminating in May 1958, after the first Algiers uprising, in his announcement: "let it be known that I hold myself ready to assume the powers of the Republic."

The New Constitution

The Fourth Republic was governed by a legislative body without a significant executive head. The reverse was true of the Fifth Republic under de Gaulle with its emphatic return to the authoritarian pattern of a powerful executive and a greatly subordinate legislature.

The Constitution of the Fifth Republic, accepted by referendum in September 1958, gives the President the right to take virtually unlimited emergency powers in face of external or internal danger (Article 16). The only limitations are that parliament cannot be dissolved, and that the Constitutional Council is to be consulted. Article 16 was invoked in April 1961, when four generals rebelled in Algeria, and it was retained in force for five months. It was used cautiously and no major changes were introduced. The background to the Article is the bitter experience of the 1940 situation when the government conceded defeat to the invading Nazis while the figurehead President had no power to cope with the crisis. For de Gaulle the lesson was clear: the nation needs strong leadership. That is, a regime in which the leadership has the mandate of the people, and can govern directly, without intermediaries such as obstructing political parties. Above all, as de Gaulle emphasised in 1947, it is a leadership which has "the means to impose the national interest, no matter what happens".

In addition to Article 16, the President has increased constitutional powers as compared with the Third and Fourth Republics. He has the right to by-pass parliament altogether and to submit certain types of legislation directly to the electorate in a referendum. He also has the power to dissolve the National Assembly, although he cannot do it more than once a year. Since the President is elected for seven years by universal suffrage, his position is not at stake if he decides to dissolve parliament — as de Gaulle did on 30th May 1968 giving him great tactical advantage in dealing with the student/worker crisis. The President is therefore in a powerful position with regard to parliament, and with regard to the lower executive since he appoints and dismisses the Prime Minister. He is able to act like the Republican Monarch which the framers of the Third Republic wanted to establish, but were not able to do. However, this was more clear from de Gaulle's rough-and-ready interpretation of the constitution, than from the constitution itself. Since the Fifth Republic has outlived its creator, the point may become important. That is, the legislative branch may be able to restrict a weaker President. In de Gaulle's interpretation, the Republican monarch assumed the role of supreme arbiter in foreign affairs, defence and European Community affairs, leaving to the Prime Minister and his cabinet an "open" sector of policy in the more routine domains of economy, administration and parliament. But he could intervene at will in the latter policy area since collective decision-making by the cabinet was non-existent. The weekly Council of Ministers meetings were formalities, approving decisions already taken.

All of this points to a drastic limitation of parliamentary democracy — the main source of policy is a President who is not responsible to parliament and who has the power to dissolve it. Thus the former emergency practices of delegating legislative powers to the executive (decree-laws in the Third Republic, framework laws in the Fourth) have become normalised, and parliament's role as a lawmaker is constitutionally limited. Moreover, the relationship between parliament and the lower executive (Prime Minister and cabinet ministers) is regulated to ensure executive advantages in censure procedure, votes of confidence, introduction of bills and priority of bills. The devices, by which the legislative branch formerly weakened the executive and gave the appearance of perpetual instability, have been taken from it.

Although subordinated, opposition was not eradicated. It survived most vigorously in the Senate, where non-Gaullists parties of the Centre-Right are strong, and where some of the Fourth Republic politicians found a home. Instead of being an ally of the government, as originally expected when its role was strengthened in the 1958 constitution, the Senate often acted as an ally of the opposition in the National Assembly. Moreover, since the bulk of legislation must pass through parliament, there is scope for exerting influence on ministers. However it is more operative behind the scenes than in open forum. Enough of the parliamentary game exists for ministers to be fairly receptive to informal pressures from their majority.[10]

The point is sometimes made that for the first time there exists in France a disciplined majority party which acts in a responsible parliamentary fashion by giving the government the necessary votes to stay in power at the end of each debate. However, the Gaullist majority party is not similar to a government party in the British sense because the structure of powers in the Fifth Republic reduced the significance of political parties. The style of authority which flourished under the Republican monarchy of de Gaulle was too contemptuous of "political intermediaries" to allow even its own party much scope. Instead, heavy reliance was placed on the higher ranks of the civil service. While vigorously attacking the role of "political intermediaries" which stand between the abstract people and the leader, the Fifth Republic has based its power on non-representative administrative intermediaries. A considerable proportion of cabinet ministers were chosen from the administrative corps during Debré's ministry. The vast personal staffs of the President and the Prime Minister, which provide so much of the information on which executive decisions are based, are dominated by career civil servants. Significantly pressure group lobbying is more than ever concentrated on the higher civil service for it is on this level that policy may be *decided* without exposure to the public forum of parliamentary debate. There is here more than a hint of the corporative practices of the Vichy Organisation Committees. It is of course true that a quasi-corporative representation of interests within the executive-administrative complex exists to some degree in other western countries. But the denial of parliament's political responsibility and the transference of semi-legislative power and influence to the bureaucracy has gone markedly further in France.

During de Gaulle's presidency the executive was assured of its independence, which meant that there was a tendency for it to absorb both legislative and judicial functions. Since the role of opposition in this structure was severely limited, the only way that it could effectively express itself was by rebellion against the whole system.

May-June 1968

On the tenth anniversary of Gaullist power, France was agog with a crisis of unprecedented dimension. Early in May the university authorities took firm action against student agitation in Paris, closing the Faculty of Nanterre and calling the police to clear the Sorbonne. The reaction of the students was not foreseen: they protested, demonstrated, fought the police and occupied various faculties in Paris and in provincial centres. Their action roused pupils in the secondary schools as well as some of the young, militant teachers. It also stirred the broad masses of the working population. By mid-May several major factories were occupied, and a colossal wave of strikes was unfurling. State power appeared to be blown aimlessly in the sky like an overinflated balloon, as a nationwide jamboree of protest, revolution, anarchy and creativity was celebrated.

There were four main aspects of the situation. First, the general political atmosphere at the end of a decade of Gaullist power in which the style of authority and its arbitrariness were deeply resented. It was reinforced by intense concern, among students in particular, about international problems: the war in Vietnam, the military regime in Greece and student unrest in Germany, Italy and the United States. Secondly, there were the daily frustrations, experienced by students and teachers, of an outmoded and overloaded educational system. Thirdly, labour discontent, long inarticulate and ignored, surfaced on a scale which dwarfed the mass actions of the Popular Front. At its height some nine or ten million people were on strike, out of a total labour force of approximately twenty million. What emerged with great force was, fourthly, a widespread questioning of traditional authority relations. In the classrooms and lecture halls, and on shop floors, the validity of formally-constituted, delegated, paternalistic authority was challenged in a spontaneous, vigorously creative manner. In medicine, the liberal professions and the creative arts, the old structures were shaken, and the all-powerful "mandarins" found themselves under the collective scrutiny of their juniors. Radio and TV journalists struggled against government censureship and distorted news coverage. Aspirations for democratic attitudes and practices in daily life were powerfully expressed.

The educational system may be taken as a starting point for an analysis of the crisis. There had been an enormous expansion in the numbers of students in higher education. In the academic year 1957-8, there were 175,500 students at sixteen universities, and in 1966-7 there were 437,600 students at twenty three universities. The University of Paris grew from under 70,000 students to 130,000 in the ten-year period, while provincial universities doubled and in some cases trebled in size. The expansion occurred partly because higher levels of qualification were required for administrative, technical and managerial occupations, and partly because of a generalisation of cultural interests and desire for learning. However, the proportion of students from working-class and peasant backgrounds has remained minimal, and most of the increased enrolment has come from the middle-class sections of the population. The establishment of new universities, the expansion of facilities, and the recruitment of new teaching staffs have been inadequate to meet the demand. The result has been great pressure on accommodation, overcrowing of lectures and libraries, inadequate laboratory facilities and extremely poor staff/student ratios in some faculties.

Similar problems exist elsewhere, but the particular feature of France is its vastly overcentralised educational administration, which negates the autonomy of the university. Although such centralisation is able to bring about very rapid changes on occasion (for example, the new experimental faculties created in the Paris area after the crisis), its normal inflexibility and lack of concern for local circumstances and problems is notorious. At Nanterre the swimming pool was completed before the library was built, and an attempt was made to prohibit fiercely activist students from holding political meetings. More generally, the movement of educational reforms on primary and secondary levels undertaken in the Fifth Republic have been characterised by high-handed bureaucratic non-consultation. The teachers' unions used to exercise an important influence in the Ministry of Education, but this has been eliminated, and their advice is unsought and unheeded.[11] Parents' associations have been no more successful. It seems evident that when consultation on planned changes in as sensitive an area as education is discouraged, then the frustrations and hostility of the people involved — teachers, parents, students and pupils — are likely to increase and intensify.

But the crisis in education was far more than a matter of numbers and facilities. It had significant socio-cultural dimensions. Essentially the problem is that both the university and the *lycée* leading to it are organised as elistist institutions in a nineteenth-century mould, wheras the type of education, and training which students require relates to a very different socio-cultural environment. In the past, although there was a great social distance between the professor and his students, there was nevertheless a certain accessibility, a certain feeling of guidance, even a sense of pride and intimacy as intimated in recollections which start with *"Mon maître, le professeur X, m'a dit ....."* But under the changed conditions in which hundreds of students attend his course, and dozens attend his advanced seminars, the social distance is unrelieved by personal touches. The climate of impersonality and anonymity is so great that there can be little feeling of guidance. The system of relationships is under severe pressure because it does not promote satisfactory learning and research achievements. The system of rewards and sanctions seems mechanical, impersonal and arbitrary. The frustration of hopes and expectations has been widespread. The involvement of the *lycées* in the May-June crisis was not simply a matter of solidarity with their elder brothers and sisters against the police and established authorities. They were questioning the examination system confronting them, they were dissatisfied with the content of their own syllabi and challenging the austere type of obedience required of them.

Similarly the relationship of the professor with his assistants is paternalistic. It is quite unlike the Anglo-American departmental system with its established hierarchy of seniority and status. The departmental system has the double advantage of offering security of status and independent responsibility to the junior staff, thereby diminishing and limiting the all-powerful position of the professor. In contrast, the European professor may act as a feudal lord because his junior staff are his assistants who depend on him personally. Authority is delegated to the assistants for teaching purposes, but they are not given independent responsibility and so do not have enough scope to develop themselves as effective teachers. They are allowed little influence on the content of the courses, and are placed in such a position of inferiority that if they want to survive they have to be subservient to their master's ideas (or lack of them). It is not surprising, then, that when the student revolt exploded some of the young teachers were ready to participate in it.

A Student Role

The National Union of French Students (UNEF) has tried to define a student role in the university and in the wider society. The student was portrayed as an intellectual worker, and a "pre-salary" was claimed in recognition of his potential value to the national economy. The amount was to be sufficient to guarantee his material independence, and allow him to live and work in satisfactory material conditions. Moreover, the student's intellectual freedom was to be protected by active participation in decision-making at various adminsitrative levels and in the teaching process. The aim was to democratise the university.

Many of the politically oriented students coupled this aim with a rejection of "technocratic society", "monopoly capitalism", "imperialism" and the Gaullist "police-state". They saw the students, fully mobilised within the context of their own problems, as capable of reaching out to form political alliances with the working class to create a dynamic revolutionary potential. From this point of view, UNEF became a remarkable organisation. Jacques Sauvageot, one of the main student leaders, pointed out that "UNEF is primarily a movement of progressive youth". That is, UNEF became a framework in which a variety of political youth groups could associate: the anarchist March 22nd Movement, the Trotskyist Revolutionary Communist Youth (JCR), the pro-Chinese Marxist-Leninist Young Communist Union (UJC-ML), the anti-war Vietnam Committee and several smaller groups. These movements were important in the explosion of May-June 1968 because of their awareness of the strategic role of the university in modern socio-economic structures and because of their desire to break down its cultural alienation. The road for them was clearly to overcome their social isolation by allying themselves with the workers. The extent to which this was accomplished during the crisis was overwhelming as compared with the drastic isolation of the German students. It should be noted that the French were able to draw upon a tradition of popular solidarity which existed in the Resistance movement, before that in the Popular Front and before that in the struggles for a secular, democratic Republic. Suspicion of the intellectual and the student exists in the working class in France as elsewhere, and the Communist party and the CGT were not slow to play on it; but admiration and respect exist too. And this aspect emerged strongly when the students refused to be beaten into submission by the police. Their courage on the barricades, and their determination to take a broad political initiative provided an opening for working-class activity. The occupation of various faculties in Paris and the provinces stimulated workers to occupy their factories and to strike. Suppressed demands and latent aspirations for industrial democracy were re-invigorated and found some expression in the colossal agitation which swept the country.

Although the scale of the strike activity was much larger than that of 1936, the outburst did not have the political thrust of the Popular Front. Then the strike wave reinforced the newly won political power of the labour movement in a critical historical period. In 1968, the meaning of the strike activity was much less clear. The Gaullist regime was badly shaken especially when the Grenelle Agreements offering higher wages and an extension of union rights were rejected in factory mass meetings. It indicated that the strikes were not primarily motivated by traditional claims. But only a few of the strike committees were organised in a potentially revolutionary manner – the Sud-Aviation factory near Nantes, Rhône-Poulenc chemicals at Vitry and the Renault plan at Flins.[12] As many of the revolutionaries pointed out, it was partly because the movement was badly hampered by the conservative attitude of the Communist party and the CGT. However, it is to be noted that the active sympathy and interest of some of the other trade unionists, particularly the CFDT, were not enough to break down the barriers to revolutionary change. There is another explanation, beyond the simple alternative that either "the revolution was betrayed" or that the movement was a chaos of unrest with no meaning.

The colossal strike was an explosion of profound discontent and frustration, a massive longing for a qualitative change of social relationships in the direction of industrial democracy, but was not a movement similar to the Popular Front. In 1968 there was little belief in the notion that social changes of this order could be attained simply through a change of political regime. At the same time the conservatism of the Communist party and the major trade-union confederation in this situation amounted to a fear of any change. De Gaulle was able to capitalise on it with surprising ease by dissolving the National Assembly on 30th May and deflecting the crisis into the familiar realm of electoral politics. As soon as the question was simplified into these terms the General could win by default. There was no other credible political force to provide an alternative. Hence the overwhelming Gaullist victory in the June elections.

Reforms were rushed through the new parliament in the autumn of 1968. But Edgar Faure's scheme for educational reforms established principles which were interpreted cautiously by his orthodox Gaullist successor in the Ministry of Education. The principles of student participation, and of financial and administrative autonomy of the universities were given limited application.[13] Months before Faure was removed, his projected reforms had come under severe pressure from those resisting change, while unrest was sporadic and bitter in many *lycées* and faculties. De Gaulle's resignation in the spring of 1969, when his referendum on regional reforms and reform of the Senate was rejected, marked the end of an era, but not of regime. With the election of Pompidou as President in June 1969, the Fifth Republic solved its problem of continuity beyond De Gaulle. He had been groomed as the General's successor. But the underlying social problems in education, industrial relations and, more profoundly, of democracy in France remained unsolved.

NOTES

1. Interview Thorez granted to a Catholic weekly paper and reported in *L'Humanité* 3 Fevrier 1945.

2. The results were 35 per cent of the electorate in favour, 34 per cent against and 31 per cent abstained.

3. David S. Landes, "French Business and the Businessman" in E.M. Earle (ed), *Modern France* Princeton UP 1951; Jesse R. Pitts, *The Bourgeois Family and French Economic Retardation* (Ph.D.diss.), Harvard University 1957.

4. See Charles P. Kindleberger, "The Postwar Resurgence of the French Economy" in *France: Change and Tradition.* Gollanz, 1963, pp129-31, and in his book *Economic Growth in France and Britain*, Harvard UP 1964, Chapter 6.

5. Henry W. Ehrmann, *Organised Business in France,* Princeton UP 1957, Chapter 2; Stanley Hoffman, "Paradoxes of the French Political Community" in *France: Change and Tradition,* p42.

6. Villiers explained his strategy to the 1950 CNPF general assembly as follows: "....because of the political atmosphere, it was always necessary to exercise the greatest caution and to be content to act for the best in difficult circumstances....it is indispensable to maintain contact with the public powers and administrations. Discussions with them have enabled us to avoid errors." *Bulletin du CNPF,* Février 1950, p3.

7. Ehrmann, pp125-6, 143 and 152.

8. *Ibid.,* 262-3.

9. See Bernard Gournay "Les Grands Functionnaires", *Revue Francaise de Science Politique,* XIV(2) Avril 1967, pp239-41.

10. Philip M. Williams views this process in a more optimistic way than presented here. See his book *French Parliament 1958-1967* Allen & Unwin 1968, p75.

11. W.D. Halls, *Society Schools and Progress in France.* Pergamon, 1965, pp11 and 162; see also, James M. Clark, *Teachers and Politics in France* Syracuse University Press 1967, pp156-7.

12. See *Esprit* Août-Septembre 1968.

13. See "Les Universités en France depuis 1968" *European University News* September-October 1972, pp5-7.

Chapter 12 Italy: The "Miracle" and Secular Crisis

Against a background of high economic performance and rapid change, the post-war Italian situation is characterised by a tangle of social and political problems. The transformation of Italy is vividly summarised in the changing distribution of the active population. Within the short space of ten years, 1954 to 1964, the proportion of the labour force engaged in agriculture fell from forty three per cent to under twenty six per cent. At the same time the proportion in industry rose strikingly from thirty one to forty one per cent. The nearest parallel with these dramatic changes was in France, where the agricultural sphere contracted by ten per cent, while the industrial sphere expanded by four per cent.

A powerful surge of industrialisation lies behind the figures. In the 1950s, the average annual rate of growth for industry was about nine per cent, and in the 1960s it was about five per cent. Since wages rose more slowly than productivity, a remarkable export drive was facilitated. For the first time, Italy became an important exporter of manufactured goods. Industrial expansion was also helped by the discovery, in 1949, of large reservoirs of natural gas. It was quickly put into use by ENI, a para-state enterprise, whose dynamic energy policy was formulated by Enrico Mattei. Italy also benefited from a gigantic tourist industry and the steady flow of emigrants' remittances. And growth was sustained by high levels of investment, made possible through the centralisation of credit controls. Unemployment fell slowly in the post-war period, and there was much pressure for using capital resources in low-productive, labour-intensive public works. The policy of investing in capital-intensive industries had to be carried out in the face of considerable job-hunger. Unemployment eased off from about two million in the early 1950s, to about one-and-a-half million in the late 1950s, and fell to less than half a million in the mid-1960s. However, underemployment continues to be widespread. It is particularly serious among agricultural day-labourers where the work is seasonal. In the mid-1950s, Italy had one of the lowest national incomes per capita in western Europe, less than half that of France or West Germany. Since then its relative position has ameliorated as far as the North is concerned.

But in the years after Fascism the very success of the national economic performance has aggravated the long-standing chasm between the North of Italy and its southern regions. As the former developed its industrial potential, becoming more tightly knit into the pattern of western European economic relations, the South remained to a large extent embedded in its desperate North African condition. Its traditional agricultural structure has not yielded much to the government's measures of reform. The vast surplus population of unpropertied, unskilled and uneducated seeks relief from its distress by migrating to the towns. But attempts to develop the South industrially have had limited results so far. New industrial plant, such as steel at Taranto and petro-chemicals at Brindisi, are able to absorb only a small fraction of the rural underemployed. Small southern towns, like Battipaglia where rioting occurred in the spring of 1969, are swamped with migrants from the countryside. The small economic progress, based on food processing industries, registered in such towns is being jeopardised by the population influx from the surrounding countryside. Meanwhile hundreds of thousands of others have migrated further afield: to Rome, Turin, Milan and all the towns of northern Italy. Tens of thousands of them have gone to Switzerland, France and West Germany in their search for work. Unprepared for mass arrivals, the Italian municipalities have not provided the necessary housing and services. The newcomers are left to squat on the outskirts in shanty towns without running water, electricity or medical and social services. The conditions of the South were brought into the North, creating large pockets of squalor and unemployment in the booming industrial areas.

The migration has done little to relieve the problem of the South. Despite the exodus of some three million people, the Malthusian population problem persists. Population increase outpaces economic growth. The death rate has been lowered by the reduction of infant mortality. But the birth rate has not dimished. To some extent it is due to an ignorance of birth-control techniques, which is positively sanctioned by the attitude of the Catholic Church, in which Italian governments acquiesce. More profoundly, however, attitudes to family size do not change in static socio-economic situations. It must be recognised that to date efforts to transform the South have largely come from the outside. The South itself has not developed a dynamic impulse for change of its own. The static quality of its mentality is reflected in the perpetuation of aristocratic status concepts and the traditional denigration of technical and commercial considerations.

Efforts to transform the South from Rome have been diluted by bureaucratic incompetence, corruption and vested interest. It is not altogether an exaggeration to say that the *Cassa per il Mezzogiorno* (the Southern Development Fund) has been treated as a hugh milch cow, a source of unending patronage, as much as a lever of development. In two decades it has invested £600 millions in the South, but much has been wasted because rational planning has been subordinated to the needs of patronage.[1]

The problem of the South was sharply posed in the immediate post-war years. The Fascists had made little effort to develop the South, so that its outmoded agriculture and high population pressure created a threatening situation. Peasant unrest and Communist penetration combined to stimulate plans for reform. In 1950 the de Gasperi government launched a ten-year land-reform programme and set up the *Cassa* as a special development fund. The aims of the land reform were to divide up the big estates and to encourage intensive cash crop farming. By the early 1960s, 430,000 hectares had been allocated to over 85,000 peasant families. The large landowners resisted strenuously and succeeded in cutting down the amount of land for redistribution by about half. Even more serious are the difficulties of transforming the mentality of the small peasant. Accustomed to working on a large estate, under the orders of a manager, he has not the attitude of initiative and self-reliance characteristic of the independent or the co-operative farmer.[2] Nevertheless some progress was registered, both in terms of increased farm production and in loosening the traditional pattern of dominance exerted by absentee landlords. But the long-term effects of reform were limited by the continuous population increase and by the fact that heavy indemnities were paid to the expropriated landlords so that the cost of the reform was very high. Aided as well by a thoroughly inefficient taxation system, the traditional landowning aristocracy comfortably survived.

Nevertheless, the actions of the development fund promise to bring more profound long-term effects. Despite the waste of money and the dispersal of effort, there is an undoubted cumulative effect. Soil erosion is being checked by afforestation, and irrigation problems have been tackled. The infrastructure of roads, bridges, power stations, sewers and ports is developing. Although private capital has been reluctant, the para-state concerns are involved in the new southern industrial triangle of Taranto, Brindisi and Bari. With continuous investments and an improvement in planning, new prospects for the South are possible. But there is a limit to what can be done *for* the South. Its future depends ultimately on what it can do for itself.

In the meantime the migration of a portion of its surplus population has not affected its underlying structure. It has merely relieved some of the pressure by spreading it northwards. At the same time the influx of labour has not solved northern Italy's shortage of skilled labour. Italy has traditionally produced superb craftsmen, but neither government authorities nor businessmen have been sufficiently alert to the problem of providing extensive training facilities for industrial skills. In face of the enormous problem of re-training migrant unskilled labour, which at best is semi-literate, the authorities have all but closed their eyes. The result, in northern towns, is the existence of a dual social structure: the urban-industrial environment and the shanty towns of the southern migrants. Isolated and deprived, they are nevertheless now part of the North and one of its major sources of discontent.

After Fascism

Rooted in the complexities of the social structure, and encompassing a diversity of ideological orientations, the Italian political system is unstable and fragmented. The tangle of conflicting interests has interrupted the flow of change required for adaptation to modern conditions, creating a log-jam of social and institutional problems. The county flounders in its political immobilism and social frustrations. Although the Christian Democratic party has remained the strongest single party throughout the post-war period, it has usually not governed alone. In seeking coalition partners, its basic strategy is to hold the centre, either centre-right or centre-left, while isolating the extreme rightists and the Communists.

However, the strategy has placed great stress on the socialists, who are sharply divided. The Social Democrats, led by Giuseppe Saragat for many years, are government-orientated and share in the "Atlantic" outlook of the Christian Democrats. They are profoundly anti-Communist, feeling that the existence of a large Communist party is a menace to Italian liberties. But they are very much the smaller of the two main socialist camps and their influence in the labour movement is limited. The Socialists, led by Pietro Nenni and Francesco de Martino, were considerably more left wing. For many years they were allied with the Communists and refused to isolate them. This derived from their historical experience. Nenni emphasised that Mussolini's rise to power was greatly facilitated by the disunity and disarray of the labour movement, while the struggle against Fascism was successfully accomplished by a united movement. The main aim of the Socialists therefore was to safeguard the unity of the labour movement. They co-operated with the Communists within the main trade-union confederation, the CGIL, without surrendering their separate identity.

The Communists, for their part, have undergone, in a general way, an experience parallel to that of their French counterparts. Emerging from the war with unprecedented prestige for their role in the resistance, the Communists secured the allegiance of many energetic and able workers and intellectuals. They were dominant in the CGIL, which for the first time was a united body, including the Catholic trade unionists. However Communist prospects were limited by the emergence of the Christian Democrats as the largest party and the persistence of the socialist tradition. Moreover with the development of Cold-War tensions the Communists played an aggressive oppositional role which was self-defeating, despite Nenni's efforts to preserve unity. Although able to sustain their position as the second largest party by drawing support from some rural areas, their political influence was curtailed.

The changes which occurred between 1945 and 1948 were of particular importance in establishing Italy's post-war orientation. The anti-Fascist solidarity which existed in the Committees of National Liberation did not last long after the war, although the Communists displayed moderation towards the other parties in the Resistance movement. Under the leadership of Palmiro Togliatti, who returned from exile in Russia in March 1944, the Communists adopted a conciliatory posture towards the monarchy and the existing government which enjoyed the protection of the Allied military authorities. It was followed in December 1944 by an agreement between the government in Rome and the CLN in North Italy. The agreement defined the latter as the delegate of the Rome government, thereby securing the position of the moderate parties in the Resistance. As in France, there is no evidence to show that the Communist leadership contemplated a revolutionary take-over.[3] They were not in a position to risk civil war and international intervention. However, the existence of a large Communist party, actively extending its influence, cast a long shadow of fear. There were reprisals against Fascists, some factory owners were temporarily dispossessed, and for a short time workers' "Management Councils" were active in some of the larger industries. Above all, Communists and Socialists participated in the national government until May 1947.

But the forces of conservatism had much greater strength. By the time the Resistance reached its height in the North, political conditions in the centre and South were returning to normal. The bulwark of the Catholic Church came out of the war with renewed vigour. And its lay arm, Catholic Action, placed its powerful organisation in the service of the Christian Democrats. The wind of change sweeping down from the North *(vento del nord)* was checked by the traditional barriers in Rome, reinforced by the watchful presence of the Allied military authorities.[4] In June 1945 Feruccio Parri became Prime Minister. A member of the leftish Action party, prominent in the Resistance Movement in the North, he held a temporary balance between the Socialists/Communists and the Christian Democrats. In Rome and in the South hostility towards the Resistance movement's policy of change created a new political current. Mobilising the fears and resentments of the lower middle class, a political movement called *Uomo Qualunque* (average man) appeared. It was symptomatic of the desire to maintain "traditional values" against the threat of left-wing changes. In November the Liberals, who are closely associated with *Confindustria,* organised big business, attacked Parri's projects for reform. The coalition government collapsed when both Liberal and Christian Democratic ministers resigned. Alcide de Gasperi, the Christian Democratic leader, became Prime Minister in December 1945. He still required the co-operation of the left-wing parties, but the impetus for change was deadened. Officials appointed by the liberation committees were replaced by career prefects, police officials and civil servants. The old bureaucracy was restored and, as time went on, was increasingly penetrated by Catholic Action interests.

In the municipal elections in the spring of 1946 and in the elections to the constituent assembly in June, the Christian Democrats aided by the civic committees of Catholic Action and the mobilisation of the female vote by the clergy, emerged as the strongest party. The Socialists and the Communists together held slightly more seats in the constituent assembly than the Christian Democrats. But the Socialists were under increasing strain.[5] Should co-operation with the Communists be maintained in order to preserve the unity of the labour movement and the impetus for change? Or should the Socialists be concerned primarily with the safeguarding of their own political autonomy and the strengthening of Italy's commitment to the West? The issue eventually split the party. In January 1947, Saragat's autonomous tendency formed a new party of its own, the Social-Democratic PSLI. The larger group, however, remained under the leadership of Nenni in the left-wing Socialist party. The gap between Nenni and Saragat was a deep ideological fissure, increasing the fragility of the political system.

A referendum, held on the same day as the constituent assembly elections, asked the electorate to decide on the future of the monarchy.

The result was a victory for the republic, although not by a great margin: 12.7 million as against 10.7 million. The involvement of the monarchy in the Fascist regime had clearly discredited it, but the monarchist tradition remained strong in the South and in Rome. It regained a certain vigour in the 1950s as a backlash against land reform.

Despite the sharpening of political divisions within the governing coalition of the constitutent assembly, the work of elaborating a new Republican constitution proceeded without major difficulties. The most delicate point was Article 7 on the relation between the Church and the State. It held that the Lateran Pacts, signed in 1929 between the Vatican and Mussolini's State, were to remain valid. The non-Communist left was strongly opposed. But the privileged position of the Catholic Church in matters of education and personal status was anchored when the Communists joined the Christian Democrats in the voting in March 1947. The gesture was clearly intended to allow the Communists to remain within the de Gasperi coalition government.

But this was becoming increasingly difficult. The Christian Democrats had been searching for ways of excluding them from office, particularly since American economic aid was tied to the strengthening of Italian democracy. The opportunity was provided when the developing tensions of the Cold War were superimposed on the inflationary domestic situation. With the cost of living rising rapidly, industrial unrest seethed in 1946 and 1947. The strikes were usually of short duration aiming to put pressure on the government and *Confindustria*.

The climate of agitation and protest enabled the Communists to reinforce their strength in the CGIL, which had expanded to well over five-and-a-half million members. At the trade-union congress of June 1947, the Communists held nearly sixty per cent of the voting strength, supplemented by the Socialists with over twenty two per cent. The opposition Social Democrats held only two per cent, as did the Republicans, while the Christian Democrats held less than fourteen per cent.[6] Shortly before the congress met, the Communists and Socialists were excluded from government positions. De Gasperi, shifting the basis of the coalition to the right, introduced a deflationary policy. It achieved its economic object, at the cost of increasing unemployment, which was already widespread. As the measures took effect the Cold War deepened with the establishment of the Cominform and its aggressive policy against the Marshall Aid Plan.

The conjuncture produced a bitter climate of agitation and industrial unrest in the autumn and winter — paralleling the situation which

existed in France. In both countries the agitation failed to attain its
political objectives and resulted instead in the splitting of the
trade-union organisation into bitterly opposed groups. The result was
more dramatic and immediate in France where the Communists tried to
lead a national general strike, which the government defeated. In Italy
more diversified and sporadic actions were undertaken, which had the
effect of accumulating tensions and disagreements among trade
unionists without providing a major incident around which a split could
occur. The situation was clearly building up in that direction, and the
events of the first months of 1948 contributed further.

National elections were scheduled for mid-April, the first under the
Republican Constitution, which had been approved by a vast majority
of the constituent assembly at the end of 1947. The Communist *coup*
in Czechoslovakia intensified the bitterness of the electoral campaign.
Taking anti-Communism as their election theme, and backed by the
clergy and Catholic Action, the Christian Democrats won decisively.
They gained nearly a hundred new seats, obtaining a clear majority in
the Chamber of Deputies. Benefiting from the high turnout at the polls,
the Christian Democrats cut deeply into the right wing parties,
particularly *Uomo Qualunque.* On the other hand, within the
"Democratic People's Front", the Communists strengthened their
position considerably with regard to the Socialists.

Although the Christian Democrats were in a position to govern
alone, de Gasperi chose to continue the alliance with the Republicans,
Liberals and Social Democrats which had been established in December.
It proved to be a durable combination which lasted for almost five
years. It strengthened the democratic centre against the Communists
and against the right wing of the Christian Democrats with its
tendencies towards intransigent Catholicism.

In the aftermath of the elections, the anti-Communist groups in the
CGIL were preparing to leave the organisation. The attempted
assassination of Togliatti by a rightist student on 14th July 1948
unleashed a stampede of events which resulted in a series of bitter
splits. The in-fighting among those leaving was as intense as the
resentments against Communist domination. The Christian Democratic
faction, headed by Giulio Pastore, was the first to go. On the day of the
attempt on Togliatti's life, there were spontaneous strikes and
demonstrations. The Christian Democratic faction threatened to break
away if the strike was allowed to continue beyond 15th July. The CGIL
executive decided it should terminate at noon on the following day. It
was enough to precipitate the split. With the full political support of

the Christian Democrats, the Catholic Unionists proceeded to organise
their own confederation. But the Social Democrats and the Republicans
did not join the new organisation. Together they were only about
one-third the size of the Christian Democrats and feared domination in
a clerically influenced organisation. Their anti-clerical traditions were at
least as strong as their dislike of Communist tactics. Eventually, in June
1949, they decided to set up their own organisation. It soon split,
however, over the question of its relations with the Christian
Democratic unions. In 1950 a new organisation was created, called the
Italian Confederation of Trade Unions (CISL), Claiming a membership
of some one-and-a-half million, its political complexion was similar to
that of the government coalition. Those Republican and Social
Democratic trade unionists who could not accept close collaboration
with Catholic unionism remained independent. Joined by other groups
which had in the meantime left the CGIL, they formed a new
confederation, the Italian Union of Labour (UIL) in March 1950. These
have remained the major trade-union organisations. In the following
two decades, the CSIL gained considerable ground on the CGIL, which
nevertheless remains the largest and most influential group.

Conservatism

The de Gasperi government presided over a period of relative political
stability and social peace in which the groundwork for future economic
advantage was prepared. Major plans for reform were adopted,
particularly land reform, the southern development fund (Cassa), and
tax reform. However opposition to these plans revealed a deeply rooted
conservatism which was dangerous in its inflexibility. The Christian
Democratic right wing, with its close clerical connections and vested
economic interests, were obstructive. They were reinforced in their
opposition by the Liberals, who became, more openly than before the
spokesmen of Confindustria. Moreover landlord opposition to the land
reforms revived the Monarchist cause, and the Neo-Fascist Italian Social
Movement (MSI) made considerable headway. MSI was even able to
create a small trade-union organisation of its own, called the Italian
Confederation of National Unions (CISNAL).

In the meantime the old state apparatus had been restored and was
increasingly penetrated by political interests. One of the most potent is
that of the Catholic Church, whose influence is maintained directly by
the higher clergy in contact with government officials, by the secular
organisations of Catholic Action and by the powerful grip which the
Christian Democratic party as the permanent core of government, holds

on the state apparatus. The cumulative weight of Catholic influence is far greater than at any time since Italian unification. It is especially strong in sensitive ministries such as Education, the Interior and Foreign Affairs, as well as in the prefectures and the development agencies. It complements and overlaps, rather than competes with, the influence of *Confindustria*. The powerful influence of the latter was consolidated during the Fascist period, and has forcefully retained its position in the Republic. Along with the Catholic Church, it represents a major force of continuity in the Italian social structure. Its weight is especially concentrated in the Ministry of Industry and Commerce and in the Treasury, as well as extending to other reaches of the high bureaucracy.

The naked exposure of the civil service to direct political influence goes far in accounting for its Byzantine qualities. The political influences are sources of favouritism, privilege, patronage; in short, the whole realm of *il sottogoverno* with its implications of corruption and arbitrariness. In this connection it is of considerable significance that roughly eighty per cent of the national civil service is composed of southerners. For titled but impoverished southern families, the civil service is a central agency of security and upward mobility, to which traditional legal education provides access. Patronage leads to tremendous over-staffing. Under Fascism the bureaucracy expanded greatly with such innovations as the Ministry of Corporations and the Ministry of Italian Africa. Although these government departments ceased to exist in the post-war period, very few employees were actually discharged. The difficulties of finding alternative employment were recognised to be very great. Even in the improved employment situation of the 1960s, applications for civil service vacancies were astronomical. On one occasion, there were 30,000 bids for seventy posts.

Over-staffing creates depressing work conditions: there is often very little to do, advancement is for the lucky few, rates of pay are extremely low, morale is low and inefficiency and corruption are rife. Many officials try to find a second job, or other means of augmenting their tiny salaries. It has long been thought that the means of reforming the over-inflated and over-centralised bureaucracy would be the development of regional administrations. Though the 1948 constitution provided for nineteen regions, only four came into existence. The realisation of the others was held back for years because of the fear of Communist domination in the central regions of Emilia, Tuscany and Umbria. But since 1970 there has been little evidence to suggest that the new regional governments are contributing to the resolution of the problem of bureaucracy.

The 1953 election results reflected the situation of political flux raised by the reform projects. All the government parties lost ground. The Christian Democrats lost eighty eight seats to right-wing opponents. The Monarchist party trebled its votes to gain forty seats, and MSI won over a million more votes to increase its representation from six to twenty nine seats. The governing centre shrunk and the extremes gained. Frustration over the delays and ineffectiveness of proposed change strengthened both Communist and Nenni Socialist representation. The electorate was more deeply divided than ever, and it was apparent that the search for a cohesive coalition would be a delicate operation. It was inescapable that major problems would be neglected in such vital areas as education, distribution of income and housing and social needs. De Gasperi was unable to constitute a coalition and had to resign. A long period of immobility ensued, extending into the next decade. The political complications intensified the bureaucratic morass, which in turn intensified the sense of corruption, vested interest, arbitrariness and estrangement. The steadily improving national economic performance absorbed some of the distress, but eventually heightened expectations for wide-ranging changes which were consistently blocked.

This was not fully apparent in the results of the May 1958 elections. Under the influence of the French crisis which brought General de Gaulle to power, moderate opinion rallied to the Christian Democrats, while the Monarchists and MSI lost some ground. The democratic centre was also strengthened by the growth of European co-operation, culminating in the inauguration of the Common Market in January 1958. Among the Christian Democrats the left-wing tendency was strengthened, reviving hopes that a fresh start could be made on modernising the social and institutional framework of the country. Yet the "opening to the left", bringing the Nenni Socialists to support the government did not occur until March 1962, near the end of the legislative period. It was in fact preceded by a brief experiment in which a Christian Democratic administration, under Tambroni, depended upon neo-Fascist support. However the temper of the country was decidedly hostile, and a vigilant anti-Fascist spirit manifested itself. The Communists seized the opportunity to display their militancy and to try to emerge from their growing isolation. The opposition to Tambroni within his own party was also strong, and the brief, stormy period of his premiership was brought to an end in July

1960. The massive demonstrations and strikes had made it clear that a government of the right would not be acceptable, and that it was necessary to find some formula which would enable a centre-left coalition to come into being.

The evolution of the Nenni Socialists was beginning to make it possible. Partly in response to Russian intervention in Hungary in 1956, and partly in response to the changing domestic situation. Nenni was moving away from association with the PCI, and was considering a closer association, even reunification, with the Social Democrats. The Socialist conditions for supporting the 1962 coalition government were fairly moderate. They included nationalisation of electricity, regional autonomy, educational reforms and rural improvements. Their acceptance was a major step in the direction of centre-left government and socialist unification.

The results of the April 1963 elections did not significantly alter Italian political arithmetic. The Communists gained a number of seats to reach a new high of 166 deputies. Some of the increase came from migratory workers crowding into the industrial triangle of Genoa, Turin and Milan. Some of it may have also come from the Socialist electorate dissatisfied with the prospect of government participation. Although the Socialists were virtually stationary, the Social-Democrats gained some ground. The Christian Democrats lost thirteen seats, mostly to the Liberals. But as the price of switching to the left, it was not too much to pay. That it was much smaller than might have been expected was due to the long term effects of the changes wrought by Pope John XXIII. His attitude of conciliation contrasted sharply with the intransigence of Pius XII towards Communism and left-wing Socialism. The left wing of the Christian Democratic party was strengthened, and their flexibility was enhanced in the search for political solutions. The conservative current in the Christian Democratic party was no longer being recharged so strongly from the Vatican. There was no longer a danger that contact and dialogue with the left would be obstructed.

Thus changes in the Catholic Church and in the Socialist camp combined to strengthen and stabilise the political system. In October 1966, after nineteen years of separation, the Socialist and Social Democratic parties reunited. Nenni was elected chairman and de Martino secretary of the former Socialist party and Mario Tanassi secretary of the former Social Democratic Party, as joint-secretaries. Saragat's approval came from the non-political heights of the Presidency of the Republic where he had been stationed since 1964. But political unity was not complete. The Nenni group remained within the Communist-dominated CGIL, with no intention of leaving it to join the non-Communist unions. And earlier a breakaway group of twenty-five deputies formed a "unity" party of their own when the Nenni Socialists joined the centre-left coalition in 1963. It meant that the new Socialist formation had only ninety five seats in the Chamber of Deputies as compared with the Communist 166.

Nevertheless the governing coalition was strongly based and raised hopes that a measure of change would be realised. The frustration was therefore heightened when it was found that the coalition could not pass urgent legislation. There was no reform of the civil service, although after the disastrous floods of November 1966 this was seen to be especially urgent. The long-awaited tax reform to create a more just distribution of income was not forthcoming. The re-structuring of the social security system, of hospital administration, of judicial procedures and of the outmoded penal code were all forfeited.[7] It was not until almost the very end of the legislative period that a law on old-age pensions was passed, but no time was found to change the legal status of illegitimate children. The catalogue of neglect included the inegalitarian educational system and the condition of the universities. A bill to reform the universities had been in committee stage for over two years when the student revolt commenced in the autumn of 1967. What tax payers, pensioners, prisoners, patients, illegitimate children and others could not do to relieve their situation of neglect, students and secondary-school pupils attempted to do by direct action. The coalition claimed credit for Italy's rapid recovery from the 1963 and 1964 economic crisis. But it was not enough as the pressure for reform began to emerge at several levels. The atmosphere of impending crisis was intensified by fears of an army take-over or an increased Communist potential. The sense of failure and frustration surrounding the centre-left coalition boded ill for the future of Italian democracy.

The results of the May 1968 elections increased the difficulties of centre-left government, but did not repudiate it. The new Socialist formation was deeply disappointed in its failure to gain seats. They had clearly suffered from being forced to compromise, and their brittle internal unity was jeopardised. After the elections they decided against going into the coalition again, and it was not until the following November that the decision was reversed. De Martino was the leader of a group putting up severe conditions for re-entry. Nenni urged a more moderate approach but was unable to prevail for some months. And only eight months later, in the summer of 1969, the socialist formation split apart, and brought the government crashing down.

The 1968 election results once again strengthened the Communist position as the second largest party, increasing their representation by eleven seats to a total of 177 deputies. Part of the explanation for their continuous electoral strength is their ability to attract the immigrant workers from the south and to appeal to a proportion of the new young voters disenchanted with the centre-left formula. The Christian Democrats, on the other hand, consolidated their position by drawing from the right-wing parties. The Liberals, Monarchists and MSI all lost some ground to them. The most serious long term question posed by the election results was whether the PCI would not have to be taken into government at some point. The Social Democrats were firmly opposed, but the left wing of the Christian Democratic Party was not. There was much talk and consideration of a *Repubblica Conciliare*, although no real efforts were made in that direction.

The Long Crisis

In 1969 the Italian paradox became dramatic and frenzied. Economically the country was sound: its currency, reserves and exports showed no brittleness despite the political uncertainties and mounting unrest. But 1969 was the year of agitation on an unprecedented scale. Students, workers, peasants and civil servants, already mobilised by the breakdown of the centre-left formula tried to batter their way forward by direct action. It was a prolonged, if diluted, Italian version of the events in France during May and June 1968. But in Italy the nature of the political regime was not directly placed in question; the problem was rather to find a way of stimulating change and of meeting urgent needs.

The centre-left coalition government was not able to re-establish itself after the May 1968 elections until the following December. Then Mariano Rumor's caretaker government was broadened to include the Republicans and the Socialists, whose unity was thinly preserved. The programme of reforms it was able to announce looked impressive, although the credibility gap was large. The state apparatus was to be reformed and updated. Autonomous regional administration was to be set up. National and regional planning was to be established. Full employment was to be assured. The social security system was to be revised and pensions improved. Tax reform would institute a greater measure of social equality. The secondary-school system and the universities would be restructured.

The pressure was such that part of the programme was enacted. A section of the university reform law was passed, coming into effect in the autumn of 1969. The need for university reform had been long recognised, and a bill had been introduced into parliament in May 1965. But the slowness of its passage inflamed student opinion. Its failure to get through by the spring of 1968 renewed student protest which raged through the election campaign in the form of university occupations and clashes with the police. The basic problems are essentially the same as in France and Germany: expanding student enrolment, which more than doubled since the mid-1950s, deteriorating staff/student ratios; outdated teaching methods; old fashined curricula; and rigid professorial control. As in France, the problems are intensified by overcentralisation and lack of autonomy.[8] The precarious situation of the assistant, poorly paid, and competing with his peers for the favours of an all-powerful professor, is itself sufficient to create a disturbed teaching environment. And it is aggravated by the absentee-landlord mentality of many professors who maintain their academic position while being fully engaged elsewhere, frequently in politics.

Once the revolt commenced, the demands of the student protest movement escalated sharply. At first the aim was to achieve effective participation in decision-making. But in face of professorial stonewalling it was raised to full control of the university. That this was taken seriously by the activists is a sign of the exasperation they were experiencing in face of academic inflexibility and parliamentary delays. But students of the revolutionary left went further, aiming to challenge the whole structure of "neo-capitalist" society. To do this they tried to form active links with the industrial working class. By persistent effort some connections were established in the main industrial areas. While its significance should not be exaggerated, it undoubtedly had an impact on the development of unrest in 1969. There is little basis for a stable, permanent link, but in an atmosphere of unrest the agitational role of such groups as the "League of Workers and Students" may have a considerable effect. They succeeded in creating a greater degree of communication with workers than had their French or German counterparts.

In the latter part of 1968 and the first half of 1969 there was a great increase in strike activity. Unrest and sporadic stoppages affected the public services, agriculture and a wide industrial front. All the major companies experienced difficulties, Pirelli, Olivetti and even Fiat, which had remained tranquil for years. Student activists were influential in the development of the Fiat situation after a series of unofficial stoppages had taken place in the late spring. Their constant activity at the factory gates enabled them to establish contact with the many southern workers employed at Fiat. They supported the main demands of slower work rhythms, a lessening of pay differentials and lower rents.

Most of the strikes were short, one-day stoppages, though some were much more prolonged. Since 1967 there had been a noticeable increase in the "wild-cat" spontaneous element, outside trade-union control, and clashes with the police were more frequent and serious. At Avola, in Sicily, in December 1968 police fired at farm labourers after an eleven-day strike, killing two people. A few months later in Battipaglia two people were shot dead during riots after a tobacco factory closed. Demands were raised for the disarming of police during labour disputes, but these were rejected by the government. The Battipaglia affair was followed by an unexpected form of protest. Prison riots occurred in several places in North Italy in protest against overcrowded and insanitary conditions. In Turin and Milan the prisons were wrecked. Prisoners were transferred to Sardinia and Sicily, where there were fresh prison riots in August.

In the meantime, on the government level, a serious crisis was developing. The storm centre was concentrated in the Socialist party. The Social Democratic tendency, led by Ferri and Tanassi, dominated the party directorate, but was weak on the local and trade-union levels. The dissatisfaction of the provincial federations was accumulating because the government orientation brought no results, while it interfered with co-operation with the Communists in local government. These tensions led to a re-alignment within the party leadership. De Martino and Giacomo Mancini combined to take control from the Social Democratic tendency. Their aim was to end the compromising attitude on the government's reform programme, and to enact legislation speedily. Nenni's efforts to reach a compromise between the two tendencies within the party failed, and in July the split occurred. The Social Democrats formed a new party, ironically called the Unitarian Socialist Party (PSU). Their three ministers resigned, bringing the government down. Rumor then headed a caretaker government, and began the agonising search for a new political combination. But the breakaway group was less successful than it had hoped. Only twenty nine deputies and twelve senators joined it, while PSI retained sixty one deputies and thirty four senators. Moreover the breakaway party's refusal to join any government which did not automatically veto Communist participation failed to impress either the PSI or the left wing of the Christian Democrats. Against a background of increased fears of a right-wing *putsch*, Greek style, Rumor formed a minority

cabinet consisting entirely of Christian Democrats. The thirtieth
government since the fall of Fascism some twenty six years earlier, it
was intended only as a stop-gap until the centre-left coalition could be
reformed. But it was forced to preside over the "hot autumn" of
unprecedented social unrest.

The autumn strikes centred on the renewal of contracts affecting
over five million workers, chiefly in the building, chemical and metal
industries. Lasting over three months, it was the biggest and most
prolonged wage struggle in Europe since 1947. In strictly economic
terms it is difficult to see why the disputes were not settled more
quickly. Many authorities considered that the wage demands were
not unreasonable. The EEC's commission said that industry
could well afford the bill, and urged the employers to be more
accommodating. Both the Minister of Finance, Emilio Colombo and the
Minister of Labour, Carlo Donat-Cattin stated that the employment
situation would benefit by it and that it would help maintain the
buoyancy of the economy. *The Economist* (27th December 1969)
reported, after the disputes were settled, that the wage increases would
not affect the expected level of investment, nor would the increase in
imports adversely affect Italy's trade balance and reserves.

Beyond the wage problems were issues of wider industrial and
political importance. The sharp divisions within the trade-union
movement had facilitated the persistence of archaic industrial relations.
The employers' federation, *Confindustria,* was virtually the same
organisation as it had been under Fascism. Its corporative orientation
and hostility to trade unionism had not lessened. As in the case of the
French and German employers, Italian paternalism aims to reduce to a
minimum the role of worker influence in the running of the factories.
But in 1969 a combination of circumstances produced a prolonged
workers' assault on this attitude. The increase in spontaneous, wild-cat
striking in 1967 and 1968 produced a more active and militant trade
union approach. Ignoring their political affiliations, the three main
trade-union organisations began to co-operate on concrete issues. Early
in 1969 their unity in action resulted in two notable successes
concerning pension increases and the abolition of regional wage
differentials. It raised the level of confidence with regard to impending
wage negotiations at a time when the political stalemate endangered the
functioning of government. As worker militancy increased, the
agitation of the far left stepped up, and the trade unions became more
united and bold in their approach. Against this, major employers like
Agnelli of Fiat and Pirelli tried to hold the line by tough actions. Fiat

was locked out in September, and then the Pirelli works in Milan, which had been restless for months, became the centre of struggle. Among the workers' demands was the right to assemble within the factory. But management was in no mood to give way, and when an atmosphere of violence developed, the works were closed down. *Confindustria* strongly backed these actions; the left-wing Christian Democratic Minister of Labour, Donat-Cattin, condemned them.

The most impressive manifestation of the evolution of the trade-union movement was its entry into the field of social policy. In the face of employer resistance, the unity in action of the three federations was re-affirmed. Representing about thirty per cent of the active population of over twenty millions, the confederations were able to ignore their deep differences and sharply to focus the rise in militancy. The Social Democratic UIL, under Viglianesi, had endorsed the left tendency in the Socialist party split and therefore was in a position to find common ground with the Socialist-Communist CGIL. The CISL, forming the core of the active lift-wing Christian Democrats, had long shed their fear of co-operation with CGIL. Deliberately isolating the neo-Fascist CISNAL, the small trade union group based mainly on agriculture and small commerce, their co-operation greatly enhanced trade-union power. Declaring their independence of political affiliations, and the incompatibility between union and political offices, they pressed for action on the most urgent social problems while carrying out full-scale industrial action.

A general strike was called for 19th November on the housing problem. The aim was to combat property speculation which has produced a situation in which many people have to spend as much as half or more of their income on inadequate housing. The drastic shortage of low-priced accommodation was to be overcome by government control of building areas and the adoption of comprehensive urban development plans. Attention was drawn to the fact that, since 1957, one third of the population (some seventeen million people) have moved into urban areas. Combined with pre-existing housing deficiences, it resulted in the most serious housing crisis in western Europe. The estimated dwelling shortage per thousand inhabitants is 13.1 for Britain, 17.8 for West Germany, 23.9 for France and 40.8 for Italy![9]

The response to the call for the one-day general strike was all that its organisers could ask, and the demonstrations were the high point of the autumn events. In the following weeks the situation gradually quietened as one set of collective agreements after the other was signed.

The building workers were followed by the chemical workers and, before Christmas, by the metal workers. However, as industrial peace was returning the nation was jarred by a bomb explosion in a Milan bank in which sixteen people were killed. The emotion it aroused tended to obscure the fact that Italy had passed through three and a half months of unrest in which millions of people had participated in strikes and demonstrations with a minimum of serious incidents. For a short period the shock gave a sense of urgency to the political brokers in their long search for a viable basis on which to recreate the centre-left coalition. But it was soon dissipated by the hard facts of political life.

The Rumor minority government carried on until early February 1970. Arrangements for a return to the centre-left coalition appeared promising after the PSI agreed to explore the possibility of renewing the partnership. However serious stumbling blocks emerged, creating a long forty eight day crisis which was one of the most severe since the war. After three weeks of negotiations, Rumor gave up trying to form the coalition, and was followed unsuccessfully by two other Christian Democrats, Aldo Moro and Amintore Fanfani. Then Rumor, though pessimistic about his chances, made a final attempt which proved successful towards the end of March. A major difficulty was the attitude of the Church. One of the few reforms of the previous centre-left coalition was a limited and cautious divorce bill, which awaited the Senate's approval. The Vatican set itself uncompromisingly against the introduction of divorce, making it clear that final approval would be regarded as a violation of the concordat. The divorce issue threatened to set the three lay parties against the Christian Democrats. However, there was general agreement that a compromise should be sought, and the issue was quietened down when the parties reached agreement on methods of contact with the Vatican.

Another problem which hampered the formation of government concerned the Communist party. The Social Democrats and the Christian Democrats were unhappy with the prospect of the PSI abandoning the centre-left formula on local and provincial levels in order to maintain or to form alliances with the Communists. There was also the issue of amnesty on charges brought against workers during the autumn strikes. The trade unions produced a document substantiating their claims that workers were being victimised. Between October and January some 14,000 charges were brought against them. Rumor's programme for the new government included promises for a general amnesty and for penal code reform. The key to his programme for tackling the log jam of urgent problems was the introduction of regional reform, with the first regional elections scheduled for June 1970. The establishment of regional government was seen as a starting point for a broad reform initiative which would include decentralising and overhauling State administration, the educational system and the State radio and television monopoly. These measures were seen as long term changes, but after a hundred days in office, Rumor resigned.

He was succeeded in August by Colombo, who maintained the four-party coalition formula with few ministerial changes. The basic centre-left orientation in the country was strengthened by the regional election results, which paradoxically made the coalition less workable for a time. While a centre-left majority was elected in the local parliaments of most regions, the question of alliances with the Communists in Emilia, Tuscany and Umbria was posed. The ensuing frictions, particularly over Socialist willingness to work with the Communists in these administrations and Social Democratic abhorrence of it, precipitated Rumor's resignation. Colombo's mediation efforts restored unity among the quarrelsome coalition partners, and he formed a new government. But there was still no opening for the broad reform initiative which the establishment of regional government had heralded. Apart from final approval of the limited divorce bill, which had been disputed in parliament for five years, Colombo's efforts to obtain moderate social reforms were unrewarded.

In the meantime, the atmosphere became increasingly tense, with street violence, bombing incidents and clashes between neo-Fascist gangs and left groups. The neo-Fascist MSI party benefited from these disturbances. Its gains in the local elections of June 1971 were considerable, and in the national elections of the following May it established itself as the fourth largest of the twenty one parties. Its share of the total vote in the national elections increased from approximately five per cent to nearly nine per cent. The national elections had been called one year earlier than scheduled in an attempt to resolve the political stalemate. The centre-left coalition collapsed early in 1972, and an entirely Christian Democratic caretaker government was established. When it failed to obtain a vote of confidence from the Senate, elections were called for May. The caretaker government managed affairs skilfully in the pre-election period, and staved off a decline in Christian Democratic electoral fortunes. However the longstanding political difficulties have affected Italy's economic situation. After 1969 the "miracle" was overtaken by stagnation with decreasing levels of industrial production and employment.[10]

The difficulties invite comparison with the French Fourth Republic. The same sense of prolonged crisis, and accumulated frustration is evident, arising from the deep ideological divisions of the electorate. But an element of contrast was the purposefulness and dynamism which the Italian trade-union movement developed in 1969. Communist, Socialist and Catholic trade unions alike have subordinated their political differences to join together in vigorous campaigns on the social issues of housing, tax reforms and improvements in social and health services. Furthermore, despite the recent neo-Fascist gains, an important measure of stability exists in the core of the Christian Democratic Party and in both Socialist parties. The democratic centre has proven to be far more durable than that in France. It would require a profound transformation for the style of the Christian Democrats to approach that of Gaullist authoritarianism. But after nearly a decade, the centre-left coalition failed to provide a more secure basis of democracy in Italy.

NOTES

1. *The Economist* 19 April 1969, p27.
2. Muriel Grindrod, "Developing Southern Italy", *The World Today* October 1965, p443.
3. Delzell, pp476 and 563.
4. Chabod, p118.
5. *Ibid.,* pp130-31.
6. Horowitz, *The Italian Labor Movement.* p209.
7. The 1931 text was still in operation at the time of writing as were many police regulations enacted by the Fascists.
8. See "L'Université en Italie", *European University News* March 1972, for a summary of problems and of projected reforms.
9. United Nations Economic Commission for Europe, cited in *The Economist* 22 November 1969.
10. The OECD 1972 annual survey of the Italian economy forecast renewed growth and a considerable balance of payments surplus. It also warned of the need to "improve the efficiency of the public administration". Quoted in *The Times* 27 November 1972.

Chapter 13 European Co-operation and Integration

The preceding chapters were concerned with trends within each country, and little attention was given to the international context. But the growth of inter-dependence among the nations of Western Europe merits special consideration. The framework for European integration was established in the 1950s, and subsequently proved its durability in the face of considerable difficulties in the 1960s. It became acknowledged as the key to prosperity in Western Europe. Its influence on the social, cultural and political structures of member countries was less determinant, but its capacity to generate change in the future is not negligible. This chapter discusses the transnational context of the post-war period, and considers the prospects for democratic change created by the enlargement of the European community at the beginning of 1973. The following chapter reviews the background to that perspective: a concluding survey of continuities between the inter-war and the post-war periods.

Aspirations for European unity were widespread by the end of the Second World War. There was deep revulsion against aggressive nationalism, and a new awareness of the limitations of the nation-state as an ultimate frame of reference. The view gained ground that political and economic problems could be resolved only at the higher level of transnational European co-operation.[1] Unity was seen as a means of supporting and reinforcing internal democratic and social renewal, and safeguarding against the possibility of a future war. Such views were circulated in the clandestine papers of the national Resistance movements and proclaimed in manifestos issued by international Resistance gatherings. Leading statesmen, notably Churchill, resonantly endorsed these ideals. The new constitutions of France, Italy and West Germany included statements indicating willingness to accept limitations of national sovereignty for the goal of an international order of peace and justice.[2]

However, ideas about the nature and scope of unity varied. The federalists sought to create a European nation on the model of the United States of America. They exercised considerable influence in the non-Communist Resistance, and after the war attracted some support among Christian Democrats, Liberals and Socialists. But at government level, a less ambitious approach to European unity prevailed for some time. The major institutions of the first post-war years — the Organisation for European Economic Co-operation (OEEC), the Brussels Treaty Organisation, NATO and the Council of Europe — were all associations of states without limitations on national sovereignty. Their uniqueness lay in the fact that they provided permanent machinery for multi-lateral co-operation and consultation on vital economic and military issues. But they were strictly inter-governmental in character, and offered no possibility for the development of supra-national integration.[3]

The ultimate aim of the supra-national approach was federalism, but its advocates saw it as a process of development which could be initiated by piecemeal measures. The main inspiration was provided by Jean Monnet, the architect of French economic planning. His tenacious commitment to the creation of a new set of inter-relationships was readily accepted in Belgium, Holland and Luxembourg, and became increasingly influential in the larger countries. In Italy, the Foreign Minister, Court Sforza, was a convinced European and was able to influence Prime Minister de Gasperi in this direction. In Western Germany, Monnet's views found a sympathetic response among Christian Democrats, and at a later stage, among the post-Schumacher Social Democratic leaders. In France, Monnet's approach became official policy at the beginning of the 1950s, a decisive breakthrough which led to the establishment of three supra-national communities: the European Coal and Steel Community (ECSC), the European Atomic Energy Community (Euratom) and the European Economic Community (EEC or the Common Market).

In the background to these developments was the super-power rivalry between the USA and the USSR. By the spring of 1947 the breakdown of the wartime alliance was in its final stages. Within two years new alliances and organisations were established. In June 1947 USA Secretary of State General Marshall offered American economic aid for the recovery of Europe. In July a conference was held in Paris to discuss ways and means of distributing the aid. The Soviet Union attended, but failed to make its argument prevail against the establishment of a general programme for European recovery. It withdrew from the conference, and in September re-established the Communist International which had been abolished during the war, as the Cominform (Communist Information Bureau). The Western powers similarly mobilised to pool their resources and formalise their commitments. The Brussel Treaty of March 1948, signed by Britain,

France and the Benelux Countries, was concerned primarily with collective defence. President Truman was emphatic in his endorsement of this step, and the American government soon proposed the creation of a more broadly based military alliance. Within a year, the North Atlantic Treaty (NATO) was ready for signing.

The problem of Germany was the most extreme focus of Cold War tensions at the time. The Soviet blockade of West Berlin commenced in June 1948, and was countered by a massive Allied air-lift which lasted until the following May. The blockade was in response to the currency reform which the Western powers carried out as a decisive step towards the creation of the West German Republic. Thus, by 1949, the polarisation of international relations had defined the contours of the post-war world. Within each country, world divisions were mirrored. The Communist parties were more influenced by the Soviet Union than by practical requirements of their own countries. Among other things, their intense campaign against Marshall aid (the arch-symbol of American Imperialist intentions) ignored the extent to which recovery and future prosperity depended upon American economic support.

If the Communist parties of France and Italy were almost by definition determined by Cold-War postures, the position of the various Socialist parties was more open. For the SPD in particular, opposition to Adenauer's policy of West German integration into the Western bloc was guided by the goal of German re-unification in a wider European setting of neutrality. In addition, there was opposition to the reversal of policies, such as decartelisation and demilitarisation which were accepted by the SPD as the basis of democratic renewal. In Italy, the Nenni Socialists were reluctant to lose contact with the Communist movement because of their strongly held view that disunity of the left had opened the way for Fascism. However, the non-Communist left was eventually influenced by the strength and effectiveness of the Western bloc structures, as well as by the intransigence and ruthlessness of Soviet actions, notably the Prague *coup* of February 1948 and the invasion of Hungary in 1956.

Although the political concept of Western Europe was established by the super-power rivalry, there remained important obstacles to unity. By virtue of its war record and democratic stability, Britain was in a position to provide leadership for European integration. But under both Labour and Conservative administrations, Britain indicated that it was not interested in anything beyond multi-lateral, loosely structured co-operation. The Scandinavian countries were influenced by Britain's approach, and did not seek integration with the continental countries.

The smaller countries, Holland, Belgium and Luxembourg, were greatly dissappointed. They had committed themselves to a customs union (Benelux) and were anxious to proceed with further measures of integration. Moreover, the problem of Germany remained crucial: by what means should the economic and military potential of the emergent West German state be absorbed? France was directly concerned, and its efforts to solve the problems were of significance.

French policy towards Germany was at first primarily concerned with obtaining reparations, controlling its industrial resources and economic activities, and securing guarantees against possible German revival (for example, the Dunkirk Treaty signed with Great Britain in 1947). But the trend of events undermined French policy. Although interested in maintaining its traditional alliance with the Soviet Union against Germany, changes in the international situation made this untenable. French demands for reparations were opposed by the United States which was concerned to facilitate West German economic recovery and to integrate the Federal Republic into the Western bloc. This enabled West Germany to press for relaxation of allied controls on production. The Americans and British agreed, but the French resisted. A compromise was worked out in the form of an International Ruhr Authority, established April 1949, but neither France nor the Federal Republic were satisfied. Moreover, there were tensions over the Saar, a German-speaking territory with extensive coal resources which France wished to control. In face of the difficulties, French policy-makers decided upon a new approach. Influenced by the views of Monnet, the Foreign Minister Robert Schuman proposed to change the context of Franco-German relations from that of rivalry to co-operation. His proposal was to create a Coal and Steel Community which would place the resources of the member countries under a collective supra-national authority. The aims were far-reaching: coal and steel, the very sinews of war, would be the first sector of integration into a Common Market, leading in the direction of full economic integration and eventual political union.

The Schuman plan was proposed in May 1950. In June, the Korean War broke out, and to offset its military activities in Asia, the USA called for the re-armament of West Germany. What had seemed unthinkable only a few years before, became an apparently urgent priority. In October, the French proposed the formation of a European Defence Community (EDC), which would integrate the military resources of the member countries under the control of a supra-national authority. Both French proposals were framed with the idea of including Great Britain and West Germany, as well as Italy and the Benelux countries. The key to both was in the voluntary limitation of national sovereignty in relation to collective decisions. The Netherlands, Belgium and Luxembourg were in favour. They had early realised that their prosperity and security lay in close co-operation and had succeeded in establishing a customs union by 1948. Italy was more hesitant about moves toward economic integration, because of industrialists' fears of French and German competition. But Italy was assured of special tariff considerations in return for acceptance of the ECSC.

In Western Germany Adenauer's leadership was exercised consistently towards the consolidation of the Federal Republic in the context of Western Europe and the Atlantic alliance. He therefore viewed projects for European integration not as a contraint upon national sovereignty but as a means for its development and expression. The ECSC proposal, for example, gave West Germany the opportunity to participate on equal terms with the other members, as opposed to being subject to the controls of the International Ruhr Authority. Great Britain's position, until the beginning of the 1960s, was in direct contrast. It had a number of commitments and options outside Europe, and did not wish to limit its sovereign independence in any way. The British attitude had considerable impact on the French position. In economic affairs, France was willing to proceed without Great Britain. The treaty of the ECSC was duly ratified in 1952 and the first supra-national European authority was able to develop its work with increasingly evident success. But in the military field, France was reluctant to proceed with the supra-national EDC project which it had proposed itself. Britain's refusal to participate left France with the prospect of being alone in the ring with the Germans. Since there was strong resistance to an abrupt up-grading of West Germany to equality of military status and since the French army was fully engaged in an intractable struggle in Indo-China (Vietnam), there were long delays in submitting the EDC project to the National Assembly.

There was a further problem. The schedule for the development of transnational co-operation envisaged by the Schuman proposal emphasised a price-meal integration of economic sectors. Political integration was a distant goal. But if EDC was to be workable it would require political control over the integrated military command. This necessitated a European Political Community. The EPC project was developed by an enlarged *ad hoc* assembly of the ECSC Assembly and was agreed to by the member governments pending ratification of the

EDC by the French. But, when the latter was finally brought forward in the National Assembly in August 1954, there was a decisive majority against it. Gaullists, Communists and most Socialist delegates were decidedly opposed. Their rejection of EDC also negated the ambitious EPC proposal of 1953. A similar configuration of opposition built up in Italy, but the ratification debate was postponed until the results in France were known. In the military and political fields, France, as Britain, refused to limit its sovereign independence for the sake of European collectivity.

The solution to the military problem was the extension of the Brussels Treaty into the Western European Union (WEU) in 1955. West Germany and Italy were included in membership.[4] The WEU is an inter-governmental body, functioning as a regional organisation of the wider NATO system, to which West Germany was admitted in 1955. The protocols of the WEU agreement included specific undertakings by Britain and West Germany which were aimed at maintaining the existing balance of power within the organisation.[5] This was far more acceptable to the French than EDC without Britain.

It appeared at the time that the outcome of the issue of West German re-armament was a setback for the concept of European supra-national integration. But in the economic field, the possibility of furthering inter-dependence remained. Some of France's industrial leaders were hesitant. The president of the metal industries was concerned about competition from modernised German industries, but accepted the necessity for further steps towards economic integration.[6] Other business leaders were more enthusiastic. The French section of the European League for Economic Co-operation was led by Giscard d'Estaing, who had wide experience in financial and industrial activities as well as in the upper reaches of the civil service. The League was particularly influential among export-minded industrialists who saw the value of a European framework. Of importance also were the attitudes of French agricultural leaders. Having experienced the benefits of plans for economic modernisation, they were willing to seek the advantages of an enlarged market and the protection it might provide for them. The architects of French planning, Monnet and his leading associates such as Pierre Uri, Robert Marjolin and Etienne Hirsch, were outstanding advocates of European integration; and the confidence they had earned in the national capacity served to strengthen the credibility of their activities supra-nationally. During the negotiations for the Common Market the agricultural leaders were in close touch with the proceedings through their government contacts, and their satisfaction was reflected in the National Assembly where most of the farm votes favoured ratification of the treaties in July 1957.[7]

Opposition to the treaty included Communists, Gaullists, Poujadists and some Radicals led by Mendès-France, but they were considerably outvoted by a majority consisting of Socialists, MRP, conservatives and most of the Radical Deputies.

The French Socialists had split over EDC, but were unanimously in favour of Euratom and EEC. Once the problem of German re-armament was settled, several factors contributed towards a European outlook in the SFIO, which was the dominant party of the Assembly elected in January 1956. The quickening pace of French modernisation, together with the growing crisis in Algeria, raised the issue of dependence on Middle East oil supplies. The issue was aggravated by Egyptian nationalisation of the Suez canal. After a few months of fruitless attempts at negotiations, France and Britain decided to reverse Nasser's action by force. However, American opposition to the invasion, October 1956, necessitated a humiliating withdrawal. In combination with the Soviet Union's invasion of Hungary the same month, its effect was to reinforce general awareness of the decline of the old European powers, and to stimulate the view that the only way of becoming more effective on the international level was to pool resources.

An important step in that direction had already been decided: to develop the potential of nuclear energy on a European basis. Mollet had obtained a formal mandate from the National Assembly in the summer of 1956 for participation in the negotiations towards Euratom. About six months later, after Suez, he obtained a similar mandate for EEC negotiations. These steps necessarily involved close contact with West Germany. Adenauer did not allow any possible feeling of rancour over EDC to interfere with his basic goal of Franco-German reconciliation and co-operation. This was being facilitated by the successful operation of ECSC, the settlement of the re-armament question, and the growing intensity of the Algerian problem which pushed older conflicts and fears into the background. While the Mollet government became emmeshed in the claim that Algeria was a French possession, it quietly relinquished claims to the Saar. Thus a major Franco-German understanding was concluded between the Socialist Mollet and the Christian Democrat Adenauer.

These developments, in turn, were of consequence in the Federal Republic. They formed part of the climate in which the post-Schumacher leadership of the SPD found it increasingly imperative to devise new policies. The SPD had voted against ECSC, but once it was established Ollenhauer and Wehner kept in touch with developments at Strasbourg and Luxembourg, and were influenced by their contacts with Monnet and his associates. Ollenhauer's participation in Monnet's Action Committee for the United States of Europe, formed in October 1955, symbolised the new commitment of the SPD to West European integration. Most German trade-union leaders favoured this orientation. In the Schumacher/Adenauer confrontation over the issues of reunification and neutrality versus integration into the Western bloc, they were sympathetic to Adenauer's approach. During the 1950s they were in touch with Monnet, who had already established good relations with French trade-union leaders and who was anxious to involve all the major interests in the work of creating the European community.[8]

But the stormy issue of German re-armament pushed these relationships into the background for some time. The SPD passionately opposed the EDC proposal, and when it failed to prevent ratification in the *Bundestag,* it brought the issue to the Federal Constitutional Court as a violation of the Basic Law. But a year later, from 1955 onwards, the re-orientation of the SPD policy was well under way. Another important section of SPD leadership were the mayors of the large towns, who tended to be Euro-Atlantic in orientation, rather than neutralist. The first generation of SPD mayors did not succeed in influencing Schumacher. But their younger proteges, Brandt, Schiller and Schmidt became more prominent in the SPD leadership after the defeat in the September 1957 elections. By that time, the SPD was part of the widening European current.

Within a year of the French rejection of EDC, the foreign ministers of the Six met at Messina in June 1955 to discuss the proposals of the Benelux countries for further measures of economic integration. An inter-governmental working committee was set up under the direction of Spaak. This committee concluded its work in March 1956 and its recommendations became the Euratom and EEC treaties which were signed in Rome the following March, and came into effect at the beginning of 1958.

In May of that year, the French political system was transformed into the Fifth Republic. The Gaullist forces had consistently opposed European projects. But President de Gaulle made no move against the communities. Devaluation of the franc and support to exporters strengthened French industrial performance as the wider market context became established. French opinion, however bitterly divided over Algeria, was increasingly favourable to European integration.

Within a few years, even the opposition of the Communist party was muted — not because of a change of heart about international capitalism — but because of the evident popularity of the European idea.[9] If the communities were a fact which de Gaulle was obliged to accept as an inheritance from the Fourth Republic, there remained much room for manoeuvre on the pending issues: *(a)* relations with Great Britain; *(b)* France's role in Europe and the World; and *(c)* the extent of supra-national integration and the nature of future political association.

De Gaulle consistently blocked all of Great Britain's moves. In December 1958, he broke off negotiations on the British proposals for a free trade area in Europe which would encompass the EEC. Since this happened not long after his meeting with Adenauer, it is probable that the latter was informed and possible that he may have approved. In the event, the West German government and others followed suit. The advocates of European integration shed few tears because the British proposals could have had a disruptive effect on the newly emergent common market, by neutralising its supra-national impetus. But de Gaulle's rejection, four years later, of the British Conservative government's application for membership in the EEC was a serious blow to federalist hopes, and the subsequent veto in December 1967 of the Labour government bid even more so. These were decisions damaging to the principles of the community because they were made without consideration of the opinions of the other members. It is probable that de Gaulle's motivation, at least in part, was to prevent the enlargement of the community so that it would not dilute the existing opportunities for French leadership. Since West Germany remained a "political dwarf" still bearing a legacy of distrust and revulsion from its Nazi past and since Adenauer was predominantly interested in Franco-German reconciliation, the opening was there.

A few days after the first rejection of British application, the Franco-German Treaty of Friendship was signed. The timing suggested that Adenauer may have concurred in the veto. He may have seen the British application in the Gaullist light — as the entering wedge for American economic dominance. The Kennedy administration was strongly advocating the lowering of trade barriers in the Atlantic world, and such a loose structure of inter-dependence had previously been the hallmark of the British approach. De Gaulle was perhaps less concerned than Adenauer that such a free trade area would be detrimental to the cause of European integration; but both were undoubtedly concerned about the risk of exposing their economies to the full blast of American competition.

Nevertheless the Franco-German treaty did not serve all the purposes which de Gaulle may have attached to it. German opinion was predominantly in favour of strong political links with America and with the NATO alliance, and was concerned that the treaty might be used by Gaullists to weaken them. When the treaty was ratified in the *Bundestag,* a preamble was inserted which specified that it was not to conflict with other commitments undertaken by the Federal Republic. Another feature of the timing of the treaty was that it was signed a few months after the *Spiegel* Affair of October 1962 which inaugurated the closing phase of Adenauer's long Chancellorship. The consequent change in CDU leadership brought forth Erhard who, with his foreign minister Gerhard Schroeder, gave priority to Atlantic commitments. In the next few years, while France sought closer relations with the Soviet Union and was increasingly critical of NATO, the Germans were most resistant to the loosening of the ties between West Europe and America. A survey of German elite opinion in 1965 showed that eighty six per cent rated German-American relations as "very important" compared to thirty four per cent for German-French relations.[10]

Whereas for the Germans under Adenauer's leadership, European integration and the broader Atlantic community were inseperably connected, the Gaullists were as anxious as the British had been to avoid restrictions on France's political sovereignty. Unlike Britain, they could not entertain hopes of a special relationship with one of the super-powers; but France's key position in Europe encouraged other visions. For de Gaulle, Europe was not to be considered merely as a piece of the jigsaw to be slotted into the Western power bloc — it was a force and a concept in its own right. Europe did not have to be a close-knit federated body to achieve this. A general loosening of solidified positions in the division of the world would provide openings for a third power such as France, the dominant political force of the Six, unhampered and unrestricted by British involvement. Thus France withdrew from the military side of the NATO alliance in the spring of 1966, and renewed its contacts with the countries of Eastern Europe. The other EEC governments did not follow France's lead, so de Gaulle could not speak in the name of a Franco-European bloc. But his initiatives did help to break through inhibitions on contact with Communist dominated countries, and so contributed to a thawing of the international climate in which the German Social Democrats and Free Democrats later developed their historic *Ostpolitik.*

Franco-German relations were at the centre of the process of

European integration, but the extent of integration and the nature of its political forms were still open questions when de Gaulle came to power. He had to decide to what extent France's limitations dictated acceptance of the supra-national context and to what extent it could act independently. The probing was many-sided and not always gentle. One aspect was to deflate the role of Euratom. This was conveyed towards the end of 1961 when Monnet's associate Etienne Hirsch was not allowed to continue as head of Euratom because of his European ideology. Later in the decade Euratom came to a virtual standstill because of differences over budgetory methods and research programmes. France and Italy wanted a national approach, whereas West Germany and Holland favoured community sharing. Financial arrangements were not agreed until the European Summit of December 1969, by which time Pompidou was installed as the second president of the Fifth Republic.

On the question of political integration, de Gaulle's views were clearly stated as the "Europe of the States" in opposition to the federalist approach of the United States of Europe. In the early 1960s it was formulated less bluntly as a plan for inter-governmental consultations – involving regular meetings, a permanent secretariat and permanent committees on defence, foreign policy, economics and cultural affairs. But the Benelux countries were vigourously opposed *(a)* to concluding negotiations prior to British membership; *(b)* to the possibility that it would cut across WEU and NATO commitments; and *(c)* that the proposed institutions would reduce the authority of the Commission and would effectively block further supra-national integration.[11]

The failure of the plan did little to enhance de Gaulle's pleasure in the community. His unilateralist approach in the following years was unreserved. After the first veto in 1963 relations within the Common Market were strained, and eighteen months later there was a serious crisis. The issues concerned *(a)* proposals to strengthen the Commission by providing it with a source of revenue independent of the national governments and to increase the effectiveness of the European Parliament by giving it more budgetary controls; and *(b)* financial regulations for a common agricultural policy. France was hostile to *(a)*, but strongly in favour of *(b)*. The West Germans were particularly reluctant about the proposed system of agricultural financing and no agreement was reached by the end of the negotiating timetable. The Commission tried to bargain the agricultural policy for French acceptance of the greater degree of integration implied in the other proposals. But the Gaullists were adamantly opposed to granting a larger role to the Commission, and therefore boycotted the community from July 1965 until January 1966.

The seven-month boycott ended in a compromise which conceded much to France. The supra-national proposals were set aside, and the power of the national governments relative to the Commission was strenghened. It was further agreed not to follow the timetable of the Treaty of Rome whereby voting on the basis of a qualified majority in the Council of Ministers would take place on a greater range of topics. The new agreement was that the Council of Ministers would seek unanimity and avoid majority decisions. The compromise was clearly to hold supra-national authority at a minimum and to maximise the scope of national sovereignty. It remained in force over the next years; but several important developments contributed to the formation of a new atmosphere.

The upheavals of May and June 1968 undermined de Gaulle's personal authority, and after his retirement in 1969, a more prudent Gaullist leadership emerged. This cleared the way for the third British application, which seemed assured of success by May 1971 when Prime Minister Heath and President Pompidou met in Paris. Pompidou had previously initiated an EEC Summit meeting at The Hague in December 1969, at which it was agreed to open negotiations for the inclusion of Britain, Ireland, Denmark and Norway. Among the other matters agreed were agricultural financing regulations, new initiatives for research in Euratom, the development of plans for economic and monetary union by 1980 and the institution of regular consultations at foregin minister level. While progress towards the more ambitious goals has been slow and beset with difficulties, there can be no doubt that the interlocking of economies was not only irreversible, but was itself a dynamic process which contained further possibilities for integration. Foremost among these were the development of regional policy and the strengthening of the role of the European Parliament.

The main conclusion to be drawn is that the supra-national idea has survived many obstacles to remain a dynamic force within the European community. It has brought about a new relatedness among the member nations, going beyond inter-governmental co-operation. Some elements of economic integration have been achieved and others are planned, but integration on political, social and cultural levels remain a distant prospect. How far it is possible, or desirable, to proceed in the direction of federalism is unclear.

Article 2 of the Treaty of Rome defined the goals of the EEC as follows:

> 'It shall be the task of the Community, by establishing a Common Market and progressively approximating the economic policies of member states, to promote throughout the Community a harmonious development of economic activities, a continuous and balanced expansion, an increased stability, an accelerated raising of the standard of living and closer relations between its member states.'

The term "closer relations" is open-ended. The Luxembourg compromise of January 1966 defined it close to the minimum, in line with de Gaulle's "Europe of the States". In the communique of the European summit conference in Paris in October 1972, the phrase "European Union" was given no more specific meaning than in Article 2 of the Treaty itself. Federalism was clearly not on the agenda, although it is a possible future objective. Raymond Aron, the French sociologist and political observer, reflected on its desirability in these terms:

> 'The old nations still live in the hearts of men, and love of the European nation is not yet born — assuming that it ever will be. But the federation of the Old Continent is held in check less by the survival of nationalism, large or small, than by another cause, simpler and often unrecognized: the present mixture of cooperation and integration in Europe and within the Atlantic Alliance is sufficient to assure the achievement of prosperity and security. It is not sufficient to create a European state. Rather, one might ask: What would be the object of a European state? To have a sense of vocation, Europe would have to discover a goal. What could this common goal be? A will to push Soviet Communism out of eastern Europe? But if this Soviet retreat is to be peaceful, is a European bloc something to be hoped for or something to be feared? A will to become a great power? But, in the nuclear world, do we want one more superpower?[1,2]

Whatever forms of association may be ultimately created, the problem of democracy within the EEC has become increasingly acute. The European Parliament was conceived as a consultative body and is devoid of effective powers. It cannot appoint members of the supra-national Commission; it cannot influence the Council of Ministers which is not responsible to it; its financial powers are limited to the fraction of the Community's budget concerned with administration and information; and its members are seconded from national legislatures rather than being directly elected. The weakness of Parliament also reduces the authority of the Commission because the latter has no basis of democratic legitimacy. This further undermines its position in relation to the Council of Ministers and its powerful offshoot, the Committee of Permanent Representatives.

But the Commission is nevertheless exposed to accusations of being an elitist body of technocrats because of its remoteness from national parliaments, the European parliament and ordinary citizens. A re-definition of the role of the European Parliament is imperative if European integration is to bear any meaningful relation to a minimal concept of democracy. When the EEC was created, and during its first decade, the overriding question was the relationship betwen national sovereignty and supra-national authority. The problem remains to the fore in the second decade, but it can no longer be isolated from a vigorous effort to democratise the Community.

The entry of Great Britain, effected on 1st January 1973, provided a new opportunity for strengthening European institutions. Direct contact with British traditions had been seen as one of the main pillars of the new Europe after Fascism. But the long delay has reduced its potential impact. The impoverished and ravaged Europe which looked to Great Britain for a lead, and was disappointed, has since found its own prosperity and self-confidence. The British role can no longer be conceived as primary. This may perpetuate fears in Britain that its traditions will be neutralised in the larger context. A possible consequence is that British governments may be content to place prime emphasis on inter-governmental action, and discourage efforts for change in the workings of the EEC. On the other hand, the enlargement of the Community took place during a period of transition in France and substantial change in the West German polity. The second Brandt Government, elected in November 1972, has repeatedly emphasised its concern to strengthen democracy at home and within the Community. Such resolve may be strengthened by the link with Britain, and in combination may provide the necessary impetus for instituting reforms in the EEC structure. But to be effective institutional reform in the EEC depends ultimately on the vitality of democracy within all member countries. If in Italy reforms are endlessly delayed or if the role of parliament in the government of France is not enhanced, then the resulting social and political discrepancies among the Western European nations will create further barriers to common understanding and to the integrative tendencies that have been set in motion.

NOTES

1. For a perceptive discussion see Max Kohnstamm, "The European Tide", in Graubard, *A New Europe?* esp. pp142-3.

2. The preamble to the Constitution of the Fourth Republic of France includes the sentence: "On condition of reciprocity, France will accept the limitations of sovereignty necessary to the organisation and defence of peace." The preamble of the Gaullist Fifth Republic reaffirms this, at least by implication. The Italian Constitution states: "Italy consents, on condition of parity with other states, to limitations of sovereignty necessary to an order for assuring peace and justice among nations; it promotes and favours international organisation toward that end." The Basic Law of the Federal Republic of Germany states: "The Federation may, by legislation, transfer sovereign powers to international institutions."

3. The lack of progress towards the creation of a European parliament led to the resignation of Paul-Henri Spaak, Belgian Socialist Foreign Minister, from the presidency of the Assembly of the Council of Europe, at the end of 1951. He continued to play a major role in the search for European integration, and later presided over the negotiations leading to the establishment of the EEC and Euratom.

4. The Anglo-French Dunkirk Treaty of 1947 was directed against a possible revival of German aggression. But when it was extended in the following year to include the Benelux countries (the Brussels Treaty) its focus was shifted to defence against the Soviet Union.

5. PEP, *European Organization,* Allen and Unwin 1959, pp211-3.

6. A.R. Métral, "La Méchanique Française en Face des Problemes Nationaux et Européens", supplement to the bulletin *Les Industries Mécaniques* Mars-Avril 1953, pp11-12.

7. Kohnstamm, pp160-61.

8. *Ibid.,* pp153-5.

9. Raymond Aron, "Old Nations, New Europe" in *A New Europe?* p43. During the 1960s the European Communist parties were increasingly concerned to influence the EEC institutions from within rather than to boycott them. See *The Times* 12 December 1972, "British Communists' lonely stand against co-operation with the EEC."

10. Lerner and Gordon, p232. Panelists were not limited to one choice of "very important" relations.

11. Achille Albonetti, "The New Europe and the West" in *A New Europe?* pp110-11. Roger Morgan, *West European Politics since 1945,* Batsford 1972, pp200-01.

12. *A New Europe?* p61.

Chapter 14 Conclusion

The immediate post-war period opened a perspective of change: actively in France and Italy under the stimulus of the Resistance movements; passively in Germany under four-power military government. The political settings were transformed, but with the defeat of the common enemy neither the Resistance movements nor the occupation authorities were able to maintain their unity of action. The divisions were gradually polarised into the deep conflicts of the Cold War, which facilitated the restoration of economic and administrative elites and preserved an underlying social continuity. Since the relationship between political change and elite persistence was particularly ambiguous in the case of West Germany, it is convenient first to consider the situation in Italy and France.

The Resistance programmes aimed at a renewal of democracy, enhanced by a genuine social morality. But the compromises established among the various parties and movements of the Resistance in the situation of war dissolved into sharp oppositions once reconstruction commenced. There was no longer a formula, such as a common struggle for liberation, which was capable of aligning the policies of the Communist party, representing the largest sections of organised labour, with other parties. The Communists followed policies (opposition to American aid; support for the actions of the Soviet Union in Eastern Eurpe) which created deep divisions on the left, and made it as difficult as in the pre-Fascist period to overcome isolation of the labour movement and constructively to influence social and political developments. After 1947, the labour movement declined steadily in political influence, whether Socialists like Nenni in Italy attempted to co-operate with the Communists, or like Mollet in France opposed them.

In Italy, the pattern of the war itself placed some checks on the potential for change. While the Resistance was engaged in a long military struggle in the North, the Centre and the South were returning to normal. The restoration of the governmental apparatus in Rome, with the support of the Allied military authorities, checked the impetus for change which swept down from the North. In the following years, the Catholic church played an increasingly important role. Direct

218

participation in the political system was no longer in question as it had
been after the First World War. Unlike the Popular Party, the Christian
Democratic Party did not attempt to be an autonomous organisation,
independent of the hierarchy. There was a much greater and more
explicit degree of mutual commitment. The clergy left no doubt that it
was a Christian duty to support the political representative of
Catholicism. Catholic Action, a lay organisation with a vast
membership, close contacts with the major interest groups and deep
cultural influence in the civil service, was fully mobilised to this end.
The predominance of the Christian Democratic Party established a
broadly cohesive force at the core of the post-war polity.

There have been two major consequences: on the one hand, it has
provided more stability and coherence than was achieved in the French
Fourth Republic, where the democratic centre failed to survive; but on
the other hand, the Christian Democratic ideology was not sufficiently
flexible to adapt to the changing social circumstances created by the
tempo of economic modernisation.[1] The need for reform was widely
acknowledged — the transformation of the economic and social
structures of the South; a solution to the increasingly urgent housing
and urban problems of the North; the creation of new patterns of
industrial relations; updating the educational system, the legal system
and the civil service. But either the reforms were not carried through
with sufficient vigour or they were blocked and delayed in the
legislature. Traditional conservatism was not confined to one party —
but more important than Liberals, Monarchists and neo-Fascists
combined, was the powerful right wing of the Christian Democrats.
During the papacy of Pius XII, 1938 to 1958, its predominance ruled
out centre-left alliance. The reasons were not dissimilar to those of
the early 1920s, when the clerico-Fascist tendencies in the hierarchy
and in the Popular Party vehemently rejected the possibility of an
alliance with the Socialists as a means of strengthening the democratic
system. Then, as later, there was an uncompromising refusal to allow
greater scope to organisations which were regarded as hostile to the
influence of the Church. However, the advent of Pope John XXIII
helped to create a more relaxed and liberal atmosphere, which
stimulated an "opening to the left".[2]

As it gathered momentum in the early 1960s, there was a
considerable shift within the leadership of the Christian Democratic
party. The influence of the left wing became more pronounced, and the
expectation grew that a vigorous programme of reforms would be
carried out. If the centre-left coalition had been able to accomplish this,

it would have contributed to the breakdown of patterns of social isolation and alienation, and established a more secure and effective political system. But the coalition did not fulfill its promise; it led to more than a decade of frustration over the blockage of reforms. This magnified existing social cleavages and reinforced the polarisation of ideologies. Tendencies on the extreme right and the extreme left have strenghened, and politically motivated violence has notably increased. The division between left and right within the Christian Democratic party has become pronounced, the gap between Social Democrats and Socialists has widened, and the large Communist party has remained in a *cul-de-sac*. The centre-right coalition which emerged after the May 1972 elections was unable to alter these trends.

Yet there are elements in the situation which could lead to greater flexibility and to qualitative changes. Liberalising tendencies within political Catholicism may be able to strengthen their organisational bases and to develop methods of more independent action. Catholic trade unions, for example, have joined forces with other unions in pressing for basic reforms in housing, welfare and education. Their non-Catholic partners have displayed an equal flexibility in acting outside of the framework of political-party affiliations. Within the on-going duality of Church and State, there may be found a potential solution, promised in the "opening to the left": the relative modernisation of the Church which could create the basis for greater degrees of co-operation and social trust, leading to genuine compromises over the problems and pace of reforms. The effects of such change could be far-reaching, encouraging groups to aggregate their mutual interests and to transform them into coherent policies.

Optimism, however, must be guarded. The catalogue of outstanding problems could create havoc not because they are intrinsically intractable, but because of the historic and continuing weakness of the central political framework. The liberal secular state created a national framework, stimulated economic development, and brought Italy to the threshold of the modern world. It did so, however, by imposing its structures on the South, and more generally on an indifferent if not hostile rural population. In its relative social isolation, it did not gain the support or the loyalty of the mass of its citizens — in sharp contrast with developments in the early years of the Third Republic in France, where the loyalty of the mass of the rural population was a solid pillar of Republican strength. Moreover, the secular state in Italy had to impose its authority in direct confrontation with the Roman Catholic Church, which regarded the former as a negation of divinely-convenient social order. Therefore, neither the social nor the ideological foundations of the State were sufficiently comprehensive to enable it to meet the demands and to absorb the changes emerging from the process of economic and political modernisation.

The decade of relative stability at the beginning of the twentieth century ended with increasing industrial and urban strife, and culminated in "Red Week" of June 1914. Further militancy was blocked by Italian intervention in the Great War, but this itself created a tide of difficulties which flooded the post-war period. Intervention in the war was decided neither by parliament nor by public pressure, but by secret diplomacy and arbitrary executive action. The ensuing hardships and sacrifices were therefore experienced as purposeless and meaningless, giving rise to implacable demands on the State in the war's aftermath. While the urgency and the depth of crisis intensified the pre-existing social cleavages, the moderateness of government actions — in face of land hunger and peasant land seizures, unemployment and industrial unrest — made it appear weak and vacillating to both those who were struggling for change and those who were strenuously resisting it.

The crisis was resolved in Fascism, which claimed to anchor the authority of the state and to enhance national identity and pride. It is undoubtedly true that Fascism created a greater national awareness, but its long-term effect did not strengthen the central political framework. Its repressive stance towards demands for participation and its arbitrary actions perpetuated a situation in which major system parts remained unintegrated, without opportunity of establishing patterns of inter-communication and reciprocity. Therefore demands, if they could be articulated at all, were raised in isolation, not as policies but as ultimata. The mechanisms for aggregation of interests and for transforming them into viable policies were absent, as were attitudes of subject loyalty necessary for the administrative application of policies. Since decisions were arbitrary, rather than arrived at through processes considered to be legitimate, the application of decisions did not bring forth the subject's commitment. He may have been forced to submit, but that did not create a sense of loyalty. Fascism inherited these attitudes, and bequeathed them in a state of exasperation.

The subsequent experiences of anti-Fascist Resistance and creation of the Republic did not resolve either the structural faults of the system-parts interaction nor the alienative quality of the political culture. The anti-Fascist movement, itself a political amalgamation, was fragmented by the exigencies and alternatives of the immediate post-war situation. The Resistance heightened participation potential, which Fascism had sought to control and suppress, but it did not enhance social cohesion. The intractable problem of the South, the isolation of the labour movement, the weight of traditional conservative tendencies in the Church hierarchy and in the right wing of the Christian Democrats, the long periods of political sterility have left unresolved the core social problems of modernisation. By the late 1960s and early 1970s, this began to raise serious doubts about the future of Italian democracy.

In France, the underlying instabilities were differently organised. The Third Republic, born of military defeat and punctuated by sharply divisive crises, nevertheless achieved an increasing legitimacy. The burden and sacrifices of the First World War enhanced it further. But within the Republican form, a structural imbalance — alternating between concentrated executive authority and the undisciplined play of parties in the legislative arena — was both cause and consequence of blocked processes of decision-making. Hence the chaos of authority when France fell to the Nazi invaders in 1940, the difficult birth pangs of the Fourth Republic, and the subsequent series of crises which led to the breakdown over the Algerian problem.

The first years of the post-war period were marked by successive crises which shifted government coalitions steadily to the right. After the Communists were dislodged from government participation in the spring of 1947, there were a series of coalitions involving Socialists, MRP, Radicals and Conservatives. There were sharp disagreements on financial and economic issues, as well as the question of support for Catholic schools. The coalitions were held together more by fear of Communist and Gaullist extremism, than by willingness to work out common policies. The Socialists were caught between the demands of their rank-and-file and competition from the Communist party on the one hand, and the concessions demanded by their non-Socialist coalition partners on the other. In the 1951 elections, the Socialist vote declined considerably, and this reinforced their decision to adopt an opposition role. The formula for a stable governing coalition remained elusive. Although the dangers of extremist opposition on domestic issues receded, the problems of foreign and colonial policies became more vexed. The leftward swing in the final elections of the Fourth Republic, in 1956, gave the Socialists a dominant position in the coalition game. But the successful negotiations for the establishment of Euratom and the EEC were overshadowed by the Algerian conflict. Throughout the Fourth Republic, the relative ineffectiveness of the parties in the legislature enhanced the role of the civil service elite in decision-making. This was also connected with the enlargement of the economic role of the state through nationalisations and the adoption of indicative planning techniques. While the politicians grappled unsuccessfully with the issues of colonial war and frequently shed their political principles in the process, the highly-skilled administrative elites in liaison with organised business were modernising the economic structures of the country.

With the advent of the Fifth Republic, the role of the executive was powerfully reinforced at the expense of the political parties. But the exercise of presidential functions was not a simple expression of charismatic authority. The executive apparatus was expanded by the establishment of new channels of administrative competence. By-passing the open forum of debate in the National Assembly, policies were formulated and executed from "above".[3] As in Bismarck's Germany, this contributed to the reinforcement of elitist concepts of social order, in spite of rapid economic and technical change. The contradiction between the two created a profound sense of social frustration which was vehemently expressed in the events of May and June 1968. The unique executive role had been accepted as authoritative in a situation of paralysis, but it had to be imposed on a recalcitrant reality. Reliance on large-scale police activity, aggressively-toned propaganda, media censureship, executive decree and frequent personalised appeals concretely revealed the limitations and doubts underlying the symbolic legitimacy evoked by the Gaullist Republic.

The events of May and June 1968 staged a colossal panorama of dissent, dramatising the issues of educational reform, censureship of the mass media, and aspirations for more equitable social, professional and industrial relations. Even the surge of the Popular Front in 1936 was dwarfed in comparison. But in the aftermath of both these crises of revelation, the fundamental dichotomy of French political culture remained. In 1968, it was less the strength of conservative reaction than the lack of appropriate means for transforming aspirations into viable programmes of change which brought the movement to its close. Thus the regime was able to preside over the return to "normal" despite the puncture of de Gaulle's credibility and the irrevocable undermining of his personal prestige.

In Germany, the post-war period was marked by tensions between political change and social continuity. The Weimar experience of democracy had demonstrated the vulnerability of a Republic which was not accepted as legitimate by the surviving elites. After 1918, the key military, economic, administrative and judicial positions remained firmly in the control of traditional elites. After 1945, measures were taken to prevent a possible recurrence of this situation. But the relative failure of the de-Nazification programme created opportunities for a large-scale restoration. There was more continuity of administrative and economic elites between the Third Reich and the Federal Republic than there had been between the Third Reich and the Weimar Republic.[4] The resulting anomalies have been underlined by many observers. Rudolf Augstein, editor of *Der Spiegel,* was particularly critical of the role of Chancellor Adenauer:

"The Germany to whose Government he acceded in 1949 was hardly in a mood for repentance and self-examination. No Chancellor who based his thoughts and actions on the horrors of the immediate past could have prevailed. But Adenauer so conducted himself as if he regarded oblivion of the past as the citizens' first duty . . . . We may make so bold as to ask whether the Federal Republic gained lasting prestige or solid strength when it was lightly decided, for remilitarisation's sake, to pardon useful but compromised individuals and to give them official appointments. (Those from the Security Services and the Gestapo went, most aptly, straight into the Office for the Protection of the Democratic Constitution, where they could continue uninterrupted with the monitoring of telephone conversations). For all the praise heaped on it, the Adenauer era cannot escape the stigma of having preferred, more than did the Reich of Bismarck, solutions 'somewhat outside legality'. The last Adenauer Cabinet contained three State Secretaries who, during the Third Reich, had been officially employed in activities contrary to international law and human rights."[5]

The veteran political writer Sebastian Haffner, in contrasting the "secret authoritarian and the public democratic Germany", has been particularly critical of the judicial system. Reference was made in a previous chapter to his comments on the role of the Office of the Federal Attorney in the police raids on the offices of *Der Spiegel* in October 1962. His remarks on the judicial system merit quotation:

"The public has been reminded with a shock that the German penal system is still deeply authoritarian in spirit, rooted as it is in the most reactionary period of mid-nineteenth-century Prussia (when the overriding object of legal policy had been the suppression of the democratic tendencies revealed in the revoltuion of 1848.) The Prussian penal system of the 1850s had been taken over with hardly any alteration by the German *Reich* after 1871, and then by the Federal Republic after 1949. And this system is still, after all, handled very largely by the same men as under Weimar (when the crisis of confidence in German justice arose) and under Hitler."[6]

The problem of West German elites is discussed in Dahrendorf's book, *Society and Democracy in Germany*. One strand of his analysis, in a chapter entitled "Lawyers of the Monopoly", stressed the importance of the law faculties as a training ground of the elite. The traditional authoritarian concept of the law and of the State, as an abstract higher community, has been perpetuated in legal studies. According to Dahrendorf, its influence is widespread — in the civil service, judiciary and in organised interest groups where lawyers are prominent. About one half of the two thousand incumbents of top positions in the higher civil service and elsewhere are graduates in law. There is a notable pattern of social continuity and self-recruitment as sons tend to follow their fathers' career patterns. He also noted the restoration of industrial and financial leaders, and the re-establishment of the pre-1933 pattern of social recruitment in the military sphere, after the period of disarmament.

However, Dahrendorf's theory of elites, as developed in other Chapters of his book, raises a number of issues. He suggested that there has been a long-term change from the "monopolistic" power elite which governed Imperial Germany to the pluralistic structure of the Federal Republic elite. His reference to pluralism is to diversity of social origin, rather than to the existence of a competitive spirit. That is, the elite does not compete internally in a liberal democratic fashion, but has created a cartel for the administration of public affairs. He called it a "cartel of anxiety", because it is said to lack the self-confidence of a socially established elite. It is characterised by a profound absence of a desire to govern, an unwillingness to assert political leadership. In his view, there is a kind of "headless authoritarian" mechanism through which West Germany is governed. The first point of criticism of this theory is that his notion of the diversity of social origin is not consistent with his own description of its social and cultural cohesion. Moreover, his characterisation of the elite as a "cartel" suggests a significant degree of common purpose. But it is explained as "anxiety" due to a lack of self-confidence. No evidence is presented in support of this assertion. Secondly, the characterisation of the elite as a "cartel" is flatly contradicted by its description as a "plurality without unity". The latter is particularly open to question because it does not consider the relationships which exist between the major interest groups and the spheres of government.

Braunthal's study of *The Federation of German Industry in Politics* documents the full scope of involvement of a powerful interest group. The study concentrates on the period of Adenauer's chancellorship, when the BDI was able to develop particularly close and direct relations with the executive. It is unlikely that such close contact could have been maintained with later chancellors, particularly Brandt, but it would require a detailed study to ascertain the degrees of conflict and the modes of compromise on various domestic and foreign issues. An example from Braunthal's study may suffice to illustrate the problem. In 1951 Adenauer negotiated a reparations agreement with Israel. The BDI expressed its strong opposition; fearing, among other things, the loss of potential Arab markets. But Adenauer was not dissuaded. It was then suggested by the president of the BDI that the government should take steps to promote economic and cultural relations with Egypt and other Arab countries. The government acted upon this suggestion.[7] In this case political policy and economic interest did not seem to coincide at first, but measures were devised to overcome possible discrepancies. Therefore Dahrendorf's assertion of a simple lack of relationship ("plurality without unity", "headless" authoritarianism) ignores significant aspects of policy formation.

There are further difficulties in his analysis. He contrasted the behaviour of the West German elite with that of a liberal elite which is not afraid of internal conflict and has the self-confidence to rule in a democratic fashion. If this is so, it stands in contradiction to his evaluation of the long-term effects of Nazism:

> 'While the social revolution of National Socialism was an instrument in the establishment of totalitarian forms, by the same token it had to create the basis of liberal modernity.... (p412)
> ....it was Hitler who effected those transformations of German society that made the constitution of liberty possible. (p413)
> ....the earthquake of National Socialism was to push German society to the point of its social development that made modernity and liberalism a real possiblity.' (p64)

The suggestion is that the conservative tradition was abolished in the experience of the Third Reich and World War. But the totalitarian forms were innovations whose purpsoe was to control and manipulate the social process in order to prevent radical change by destroying its potential sources in the labour movement and in liberal-democratic sections of society. The term "social revolution" does not seem to be a fitting reference to such a process.[8] It does not take into consideration the extent to which the traditional conservative elements participated in the destruction of the Weimar "constitution of liberty". And by implication it overstates the degree of incompatibility between authoritarian and totalitarian principles. The transition from a regime which organised the systematic slaughter of millions of human beings to a society in which liberal social development is possible requires more than a negative condition of change. The transition from Nazism was not marked by a surge of democratically-inspired Resistance, nor was there (in Dahrendorf's own analysis) a break from the older authoritarian traditions of political culture, nor did the illiberal "cartel of anxiety" forfeit its elite positions.

The inconsistencies of Dahrendorf's approach arise from the fundamental ambiguities of the post-war situation. These have been lucidly summarised by Bracher:

'The Adenauer era offered little more than a transitional solution. By combining democratic and authoritarian elements, Adenauer's chancellor-democracy bridged the gap between the vacuum of defeat and a stable system of government; for the first time, Germans were shown that parliamentary democracy can bring security and economic progress. But the rapidly growing identification with the system of the chancellor-democracy was made possible also because basic political problems (reunification, the eastern border, social reforms) were shelved, and because Adenauer's style perpetuated an unpolitical, bureaucratic-authoritarian tradition which many critics felt was reminiscent of the Wilhelminian era. Political participation and a voice in government were limited to elections; political education was relegated to formal courses in governmental institutions or diverted to the black-and-white categories of the Cold War. What was lacking was a testing by example, the experience of governmental crisis, which when mastered prove the superiority of a mature democracy over authoritarian ideas of order; what was lacking was the preparation for a time of normalization in which political acceptance is no longer won via the simplified alignments of the Cold War, when democratic consensus can no longer base itself on an overriding anti-Communism.'[9]

The post-war period may be characterized, therefore, by the compromise effected between efforts for rehabilitation and democratic renewal, and efforts to minimise the social and cultural consequences of defeat. What Darhrendorf overlooked was that the introduction of liberal modernity requires profound changes of socio-cultural attitudes, which were compromised in the Federal Republic. The transitions of the post-Adenauer period showed many signs of a retreat from democratic procedures. The major parties formed a Grand Coalition in 1966, which all but obliterated the role of opposition in the *Bundestag* and stimulated the growth of political extremism. The NPD was able to establish itself as a fourth party, represented in many *Landtage,* and in the 1969 federal elections approached the minimum five per cent needed for parliamentary representation. The Extra-parliamentary Opposition of the New Left won fewer converts, but did capture some liberal sympathies until its emphasis on "total" democracy and its uncritical support for all forms of student protest became more apparent.

However, the establishment of a new coalition after the 1969 elections marked an important change. The SPD had made use of its period in office with the Christian Democrats to initiate a new policy towards East Germany and the Soviet bloc. In collaboration with the FDP, it was followed through with vigour and determination in the next three years. Although the thin government majority was eroded by unprecedented defections to the opposition, the challenge was successfully met in the November 1972 elections. The results demonstrated that the coalition's *Ostpolitik,* which had won world-wide approval, was also supported by a majority of the West German electorate. The SPD victory created the possibility for a programme of domestic reform as well, although the FDP campaign was based on the promise to hold the SPD in check in this respect. Nevertheless the changes since 1969 have contributed significantly towards an alleviation of the burden of the past, and towards the strengthening of democracy in West Germany.

In the major countries of Western Europe, the post-war situation afforded unique opportunities and challenges. Within the first decade, 1945 to 1955, the development of multi-lateral co-operation among European governments provided a framework for unprecedented economic prosperity and military security. Moreover, significant efforts were made to overcome the dangerous rivalries of the past by the creation of supra-national integration. In the following decade, the

European Communities became the basis for continuing economic growth and modernisation. But the assertion of national sovereignty, particularly on the part of France, limited the scope of supra-national authority. The question of the enlargement of the Community was posed, but not answered in the affirmative until well into the third decade. The relative success of the EEC, and its expansion, does not alter the fact that it was grafted onto older national structures, which are characterised by deep-lying tensions between authoritarian and democratic tendencies. The farther the process of integration goes, the more these ambiguities will affect the workings of the European Community.

NOTES

1. There is some evidence to suggest that political dogmatism is more pronounced among Christian Democrats than among Socialists and Communists. See La Palombara in Pye and Verba, p295.
2. See Giorgio Galli and Alfonso Grandi, "The Catholic Hierarchy and Christian Democracy in Italy", in *European Politics*, ed. by Dogan and Rose, Boston, Little Brown & Co 1971, pp353-9.
3. See Chapter 11, p174.
4. Data collected by W. Zapf, reported in Dahrendorf, "Recent Changes in European Class Structure", in *A New Europe?* p308.
5. Augstein, *Konrad Adenauer*, Secker and Warburg 1964, trans., pp110 - 111.
6. "The end of the Affair", *Encounter* March 1963, p66.
7. Braunthal, p305.
8. The term has nevertheless gained some currency. Dahrendorf's Chapter 25 is entitled "National Socialist Germany and the Social Revolution", and Schoenbaum's social history of the 1933-9 period is entitled, *Hitler's Social Revolution*. In contrast, Bracher's view is that of an alliance between "social groups threatened by crisis" and a dictatorship manipulating popular resentments. "It considered itself revolutionary even though for the most part it served to cement the existing order." *The German Dictatorship*, p604.
9. *The German Dictatorship*, p616.

Suggested Reading

Bendix, Reinhard. *Nation-Building and Citizenship.* Wiley 1964.

Landes, David S. *The Unbound Prometheus.* Cambridge UP 1969. Reprinted in expanded form from *The Cambridge Economic History of Europe*, Vol. VI, part I, 1965.

Stearns, Peter N. *European Society in Upheaval: Social History since 1800.* Macmillan 1967.

Weber, Eugen. *Varieties of Fascism.* Van Nostrand-Reinhold 1964.

Weiss, John. *The Fascist Tradition.* Harper and Row 1967.

Woolf, S.J. (ed.) *The Nature of Fascism.* Weidenfeld and Nicholson 1968.

Bottomore, T.B. "Class Structure in Western Europe", in *Contemporary Europe: Class, Status and Power*, ed. by Margaret Scotford Archer and Salvador Giner. Weidenfeld and Nicholson 1971.

Dogan, Mattei and Rose, Richard (eds.) *European Politics: A Reader.* Little, Brown and Company, Boston 1971.

Graubard, Stephen R. (ed.) *A New Europe?* Oldbourne 1964.

Lerner, Daniel and Gorden, Morton. *Euratlantica: Changing Perspectives of the European Elites.* MIT Press 1969.

Lipset, S.M. and Rokkan, Stein (eds.) *Party Systems and Voter Alignments: Cross-National Perspectives.* The Free Press 1967.

P.E.P. *European Political Parties.* Allen and Unwin 1969.

Postan, M.M. *An Economic History of Western Europe 1945-1964.* Methuen 1967.

Schonfield, Andrew. *Modern Capitalism: The Changing Balance of Public and Private Power.* Oxford UP 1965.

Smith Gordon. *Politics in Western Europe.* Heinemann 1972.

Barber, James and Reed, Bruce (eds.) *European Community: Vision and Reality.* Croom Helm 1973.

Camps, Miriam. *Britain and the European Community 1955-1963.* Oxford UP 1964.

Hodges, Michael (ed.) *European Integration.* Penguin Books 1972.

Ionescu, Ghita (ed.) *The New Politics of European Integration.* Macmillan 1972.

Newhouse, John. *Collision in Brussels.* Faber and Faber 1967.

P.E.P. *European Unity: A Survey of the European Organisations.* Allen and Unwin 1968.

Pryce, Roy. *The Politics of the European Community.* Butterworth 1973.

ITALY

Chabod, Federico. *A History of Italian Fascism.* Weidenfeld and Nicholson transl., 1963.

Clough, Shepard B. *The Economic History of Modern Italy.* Columbia UP 1964.

Croce, Benedetto. *A History of Italy 1871-1915.* Oxford UP transl., 1929.

Delzell, Charles. F. Mussolini's Enemies: *The Italian Anti-Fascist Resistance.* Princeton UP 1961.

Felice, Renzo De. *Le Interpretazioni del Fascismo.* Bari, Editori Laterza 4th ed. 1972.

Finer, Herman. *Mussolini's Italy.* Gollancz 1935.

Gramsci, Antonio. *The Modern Prince, and other writings.* New York, International Publishers transl. 1968.

Halperin, S. William. *Mussolini and Italian Fascism.* Van Nostrand 1964.

Helmreich, Ernst (ed.) *A Free Church in a Free State?* Heath 1964.

Horowitz, Daniel L. *The Italian Labor Movement.* Harvard UP 1963.

Hughes, H. Stuart. *The United States and Italy.* Harvard rev. ed. 1965.

Grindrod, Muriel. *Italy.* Benn 1968.

La Palombara, Joseph. *Interest Groups in Italian Politics.* Princeton UP 1964.

La Palombara, Joseph. "Italy: Fragmentation, Isolation, Alienation", in *Political Culture and Political Development* ed. by Lucian W. Pye and Sidney Verba. Princeton 1965.

Mack Smith, Denis. *Italy, A Modern History.* University of Michigan Press 1959.

Poggi, Gianfranco. *Catholic Action in Italy.* Stanford UP 1967.

Rossi, A. *The Rise of Italian Fascism, 1918-1922.* Methuen transl. 1938.

Salomone, A William (ed.) *Italy from the Risorgimento to Fascism.* Doubleday 1970.

Tempi Moderni, "Nuova Classe Dirigente e Partecipazione", 24,25, 1966.

Webster, Richard A. *Christian Democracy in Italy, 1860-1960* Hollis and Carter 1961.

FRANCE

Aron, Robert. *The Vichy Regime 1940-1944.* Putnam transl., 1958.

Blondel, Jean and Godfrey, E. Drexel. *The Government of France.* Methuen 1968.

Crozier, Michel. *The Bureaucratic Phenomenon.* Tavistock Publications transl. 1964.

Ehrmann, Henry W. *French Labor: from Popular Front to Liberation.* Oxford UP 1947.

Ehrmann, Henry W. *Organized Business in France.* Princeton UP 1957.

Hoffmann, Stanley, et al. *France: Change and Tradition.* Gollancz 1963.

Lorwin, Val R. *The French Labor Movement.* Harvard 1954.

Ozouf, Mona. *L'École, L'Église et la République, 1871-1914.* Paris, Armand Colin 1963.

Posner, Charles (ed.) *Reflections of the Revolution in France: 1968.* Penguin Books 1970.

Rémond, René. *The Right Wing in France: from 1815 to de Gaulle.* University of Pennsylvania Press transl. 1966.

Rieber, Alfred J. *Stalin and the French Communist Party, 1941-1947.* Colombia UP 1962.

Seale, Patrick and McConville, Maureen. *French Revolution 1968.* Penguin Books 1968.

Thomson, David *Democracy in France since 1870.* Oxford UP fifth ed. 1969.

Vaughan, Michalina and Archer, Margaret S. *Social Conflict and Educational Change in England and France, 1789-1848.* Cambridge UP 1971.

Wahl, Nicholas. "The French Political System" in *Patterns of Government* ed. by Samuel H. Beer and Adam B. Ulam. Random House third ed. 1972.

Williams, Philip M. *Crisis and Compromise: Politics in the Fourth Republic,* Longman third ed. 1964.

William, Philip M. and Harrison, Martin. *Politics and Society in De Gaulle's Republic.* Longman 1971.

Wright, Gordon. *Rural Revolution in France.* Stanford UP 1964.

GERMANY

Bracher, Karl Dietrich. *The German Dictatorship.* Penguin Books transl. 1973.

Braunthal, Gerard. *The Federation of German Industry in Politics.* Cornell UP 1965.

Craig, Gordon A. *The Politics of the Prussian Army: 1640-1945.* Claredon Press new ed. 1964.

Edinger, Lewis J. *Politics in Germany.* Little, Brown and Company 1968.

Feldman, Gerald D. *Army, Industry, and Labor in Germany 1914-1918.* Princeton 1966.

Grebing, Helga. *The History of The German Labour Movement.* Wolff transl. 1969.

Grosser, Alfred. *The Federal Republic of Germany.* Pall Mall transl. 1964.

Grosser, Alfred. *Germany in Our Time.* Pall Mall transl. 1971.

Grunberger, Richard. *A Social History of the Third Reich.* Weidenfeld and Nicholson 1971.

Hannover, H. and E. *Politische Justiz 1918-1933.* Frankfurt-am-Main, Fischer 1966.

Hughes, Everett C. "Good People and Dirty Work", in *The Other Side* ed. by Howard Becker. Free Press 1964.

Irving, R.E.M. and Paterson, W.E. "The West German Parliamentary Election of November 1972", *Parliamentary Affairs* Spring 1973.

Joll, James. "The 1914 Debate Continues", *Past and Present* July 1966.

Kirchheimer, Otto. "Germany: The Vanishing Opposition", in *Political Oppositions in Western Democracies* ed. by Robert A. Dahl. Yale UP 1966.

Kolinsky, Martin and Eva. "The Treatment of the Holocaust in West German Textbooks", *Yad Vashem Studies,* Jerusalem, Vol. X 1974.

Kraunsnick, Helmut, *et al. Anatomy of the SS State.* Collins, transl. 1968.

Lerner, Daniel, *et al.* "The Nazi Elite", in *World Revolutionary Elites* ed. by Harold D. Lasswell and Daniel Lerner. MIT Press 1966.

Merkl, Peter H. *Germany: Yesterday and Tomorrow.* Oxford UP 1965.

Mosse, George L. *The Crisis of German Ideology.* Grosset and Dunlap 1964.

Neumann, Franz. *Behemoth: The Structure and Practice of National Socialism 1933-1944.* Harper & Row reprinted 1966.

Paterson, W.E. "Foreign Policy and Stability in West Germany", *International Affairs* July 1973.

Rosenberg, Hans. *Bureaucracy, Aristocracy and Autocracy.* Harvard UP 1958.

Schorske, Carl E. *German Social Democracy 1905-1917*. Wiley 1955.
Waite, Robert G.L. *Vanguard of Nazism*. Norton 1969.
Wheeler-Bennett, John W. *The Nemesis of Power*. Macmillan second ed.
    1967.
Yad Vashem. *Jewish Resistance during the Holocaust*. Jerusalem 1971.

Index